DRAMATIZING THEOLOGIES

Cross Cultural Theologies

Series Editors: Jione Havea and Clive Pearson, United Theological College, Sydney and Charles Sturt University, New South Wales, Australia

This series focuses on how the "cultural turn" in interdisciplinary studies has informed theology and biblical studies. It takes its leave from the experience of the flow of people from one part of the world to another.

It moves beyond the crossing of cultures in a narrow diasporic sense. It will entertain perspectives that arise out of generational criticism, gender, sexual orientation, and the relationship of art and film to theology. It will explore the sometimes competing rhetoric of multiculturalism and cross-culturalism and will demonstrate a concern for the intersection of globalization and how those global flows of peoples and ideas are received and interpreted in localized settings. The series will seek to make use of a range of disciplines including the study of cross-cultural liturgy, travel, the practice of ministry and worship in multi-ethnic locations and how theologies that have arisen in one part of the world have migrated to a new location. It will look at the public nature of faith in complex, multicultural, multireligious societies and compares how diverse faiths and their theologies have responded to the same issues.

The series welcomes contributions by scholars from around the world. It will include both single-authored and multi-authored volumes.

Published
Global Civilization
Challenges to Society and to Christianity
Leonardo Boff

Forthcoming
Bibles and Baedekers:
Tourism, Travel, Exile and God
Michael Grimshaw

Art as Theology:
The Religious Transformation of Art from the Postmodern to the Medieval
Andreas Andreopoulos

Black Theology in Britain: A Reader
Edited by: Michael N. Jagessar and Anthony G. Reddie

DRAMATIZING THEOLOGIES

A PARTICIPATIVE APPROACH TO BLACK GOD-TALK

Anthony G. Reddie

LONDON   OAKVILLE

Published by

UK: Equinox Publishing Ltd
Unit 6, The Village
101 Amies St.
London, SW11 2JW

US: DBBC
28 Main Street
Oakville, CT 06779

www.equinoxpub.com

British Library Cataloguing-in-Publication Data
A catalogue record for this book is available from the British Library.

Library of Congress Cataloging-in-Publication Data
Reddie, Anthony.
  Dramatizing theologies : a participative approach to Black God-talk /
Anthony G. Reddie.
      p. cm. -- (Cross cultural theologies)
  Includes bibliographical references and index.
  ISBN 1-84553-077-2 (hb) -- ISBN 1-84553-078-0 (pb)
  1. Black theology. I. Title. II. Series.
  BT82.7.R44 2006
  230.089'96--dc22
                                2005032071

ISBN   1 8455 3077 2   (hardback)
ISBN   1 8455 3078 0   (paperback)

Typeset by CA Typesetting, www.sheffieldtypesetting.com
Printed and bound in Great Britain by Lightning Source UK Ltd., Milton Keynes and
Lightning Source Inc., La Vergne, TN

Contents

Introduction

Form, as they say, has much to contribute to content and its viability. A desirable (theological) content presented in an uninteresting form will not appeal, except to ones who have patience to decipher; but a (theologically) dreadful, painful or destructive ideology that is presented in a powerful form would draw a following. Indeed, the more dynamic the form the more intoxicating the experience of the content becomes; and the more powerful the experience the freer from the constraints of time and space the participants could become. When form and content bond, the energies of the event attract and captivate, and at once release the participants, even if momentarily, whether the event in question happens at a worship space or in a theological hall, as it often does at sporting arenas and nightclubs. When form and content gel, in other words, a high is attained.

Eventually, one hopes, form and content would meet at the realms of practicality. It is at that crossing point that *Dramatizing Theologies: A Participative Approach to Black God-Talk* stands, setting a space for the crossing of Black experiences and identities—with alertness to the subjectivity of the voiceless and the concerns of Womanists—with the scars of modern diaspora and displacement, theories and practices of Black Theology and Christian Education, and much more. The contact zone, if you may, is on the stage of drama and play.[1]

Throughout *Dramatizing Theologies*, Anthony G. Reddie unpacks the theological teachings contained in some of the scripts he has written, some of which are still confrontational, such as the characterization of God as a Black woman, and in the process illustrates that drama is simple and entertaining in form but it is an effective medium for disseminating complex theological ideas. Drama is still an open door for contemporary theological and biblical pedagogues,[2] as it was for philosophers and literati in the past.

The disposition of the scripts that Reddie shares and interprets is interactive and interdisciplinary with a "bottoms-up" orientation, in the sense that he tunes in to the burdens of ordinary people in addition to the findings of privileged experts, and the mixture of languages and nuances used is edifying. *Dramatizing Theologies* is thus crosscultural in many regards.

Reddie's drive to make theological principles and teachings accessible to voiceless and theologically-untrained subjects locates *Dramatizing Theologies* in a long tradition of contextualizing works. This tradition includes the translators of scripture, then and now, who transform ancient texts into understandable languages, and even to storytellers and gurus in oral cultures, ancient and current. One may add here that this tradition goes back to the recorders of memories and ideologies, ancient and modern, who preserve those for later generations and other contexts. Contextualizing, one may argue, is at the heart of all language forms. When a language, verbal or otherwise, does not contextualize, failing to make sense in a particular context, then the proverbial tree has indeed fallen in the forest but no one from the context in question knows that it has fallen. In this regard, *Dramatizing Theologies* is an attempt to empower especially the voiceless and non-subjects to tell the falling of the trees in the theological forest. And to tell it with characters!

In form, *Dramatizing Theologies* is engaging; in content, *Dramatizing Theologies* is empowering and transforming. These, form and content, will gel differently for different people in different contexts, testifying to the energies of Reddie's imagination and writing.

Jione Havea and Clive Pearson

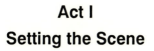

Act I
Setting the Scene

1 A Voice for the Voiceless: Setting the Context and Background for this Work

Introduction

The basis of this work first emerged in the summer of 1986. I was a member of the "Birmingham University Methodist Society" (B.U. Meth. Soc.). The group was guided by the Revd Dr. Stuart Burgess who was the Methodist chaplain assigned to look after the material and spiritual welfare of we Methodist students. The goodly folk of B.U. Meth. Soc. engaged in a variety of activities and explorations that were to shape the religious consciousness of a whole generation. It was a life-changing process for me and for others.

It was during this formative process in my religious and social development that I began to write in earnest. Prior to attending university, I had secretly penned the odd sentence of poetic doggerel or some hopelessly politically and theological incorrect piece of rhetoric. It was while at University, in a wonderfully eclectic and self-consciously clever Meth. Soc. that I discovered my talent for writing, particularly within a dramatic idiom. For someone who had suffered from a debilitating stutter for most of his teenage years, the discovery of another language of communication that did not depend upon oral fluency was, without wishing to sound overly grandiose, most definitely a "God-send."

I still remember the first "dramatic" comedic piece I wrote. It was a short comedy skit entitled *The Calling*.[1] It was written for an evening service in a local Methodist church led by the Meth. Soc. The theme for the service was "being called," and in an act of reckless bravery, quite unlike me at the time, I rather rashly volunteered to write a skit for the service. This was the autumn of 1985.

Come the summer of 1986 and I was ready to attempt something much more ambitious. It was the time of the annual summer term retreat. On occasions such as this one, the group of students belonging to the Meth. Soc. would decamp from our usual surroundings of Selly Oak Methodist Church, in Birmingham, and descend upon a Methodist Church in the surrounding area. We would sleep in sleeping bags on church floors and spend time in reflection and worship. It was on one such occasion that I discovered through heated debate that the whole world did not share my formative conservative evangelical theology. In fact, there were numerous ways in which one could understand the person of Jesus, interpret the Bible, make sense of the resurrection or work out one's notion of what it meant to be saved. Names such as Schleiermacher and Tillich became a part of my vocabulary. The attempts of my peers who were studying theology at the university to help me understand the claims of these two theologians did not bear much fruit. I remained wedded to the quasi-biblical literalism that carried all the answers to every perceived question one could imagine.

I do not remember the theme of the retreat. In fact, I remember very little of that weekend, save for one artefact that has stood the test of time and that is the short piece of drama I wrote for that event. The skit I penned for that weekend serves as the central piece of reflection for this work. It is a piece to which I have returned on numerous occasions, often stunned, if you forgive my immodesty, at the simplistic and yet profound way in which it deals with a number of major theological issues in the space of five or so pages. I was a callow twenty-one year old when I penned *My God!?*

The journey from being a tortured, ambitious and spectacularly unsuccessful commercial dramatist, to becoming a Black Christian educator and Black theologian, is not one that need detain us at this juncture. There is enough of my subjective narrative in this work already, without me burdening you with yet more. Part of the process of that slow metamorphosis emerged during my time with the *Birmingham Initiative* when I undertook doctoral research amongst multi-ethnic churches in that city. I have commented on the importance of that project in a previous book.[2]

It was during this period of research that I began to develop an ongoing method for trying to teach Black people of all ages the central tenets of the Christian faith, which are informed by the ideas and theories of Black theology. In more recent times I have sought to use a variety of methods and materials to assist predominantly inner-city people to reflect upon the nature of God, in Christ, through the lens of the experience of the marginalized and oppressed.[3]

In that time, I have used drama, particularly comedic skits, plus participatory exercises, games and stories in order to create a bridge between the experience of the learner and the various emancipatory themes and concepts of Black and Liberation theologies.[4] In terms of trying to create a model for introducing one of the central concerns and contentions of Black theology to predominantly lay people, I have often used my old skit, *My God!?*

Central to the development of Black theology has been the most existential of questions, namely who is God? Whose God is God? Writers such as James Cone[5] and more latterly Dwight Hopkins,[6] plus within the British context, Robert Beckford,[7] have all addressed the central concern of Black human existence—where is God and where does God stand in the midst of all our trials and tribulations?

In many of the slave narratives from the Americas and the Caribbean, Black slaves often contended that their White slave masters could not be worshipping the same God as themselves.[8] Both the slave and the slave master could not be correct in believing that God was on their side. *My God!?* served as a dramatic introduction to this most basic of questions. The use of these materials was not always a carefully thought-out approach to the education and nurture of Black and other marginalized lay people in inner-city churches. For the most part, I had an intuitive sense that this material would create an affirming learning environment for such individuals which, in turn, would lead to greater opportunities for genuine dialogue and participation from what are often passive and disempowered people. My motto has often been "If it works, then leave it well alone." As a scholar with a passion for trying to find out more and know more, such complacency could not go unchallenged for very long. As I am often telling my students, "ignorance is not bliss, it is simply a bad position to be in." I needed to know why these particular forms of educational material strike a chord with marginalized and oppressed people, and to what extent do they enable such individuals to tease out and hold on to theological concepts and themes that speak genuinely to their experience?

In order to make some sense of these materials I have created over the past few years I needed to locate a number of helpful models or varying types of framework that would assist me in structuring my thought and this work. In the first instance, I returned to the world of educational theory.[9] As I have detailed in my previous book, the development of this text arose as a kind of precursor to *Acting in Solidarity*.[10] In writing *Dramatizing Theologies* it was my intention to build upon the more creative practical materials of *Acting in Solidarity* by producing a more theoretical book that would analyse the relationship between Black theology and dramatic, dialogical sketch material as a means of producing a more accessible and democratic approach to undertaking Black theological conversation.

In the previous book, I began from the premise that the significant developments in the Black liberation theological movement has been by means of creating new liberating forms of practice. Given the importance attached to reflective action (often termed within the academy as "praxis"),[11] within liberationist approaches to theology, I have sought, therefore, in my own work to commence with an analysis of action as my initial point of departure. In effect, my starting point has often been "what is needed in this situation," which, in turn, is followed by the next question, usually, "what can make this situation better?"

Having discovered drama and dialogue as an important means of enabling Black and other marginalized people to reflect upon matters of faith, *Acting in Solidarity* was an attempt to catalogue some of the more successful and effective pieces of dramatic Christian writing I had created over the past few years. The aim was to present these pieces in a form that would assist in enabling these individuals to reflect critically upon their experiences and faith, in order to become more autonomous believers, less inclined to be swayed by the blandishment of those considered their social betters.

My aim, initially, was not to create an abstract theory that did not relate to the concrete needs of marginalized and oppressed peoples. Rather than by beginning with theory, I wanted to develop a more reciprocal relationship between practice and theory, in order to develop practical resources for critical, radical thinking in order that Black theology might come to life and speak authentically to the experiences of those whose inalienable, God-given right to be free is always under threat from oppressive forces. This method for undertaking Black theology, by means of interactive dramatic Christian sketches, which involves a reflection and action paradigm, will be analysed in greater detail in the following chapters.

My intention in this work is to outline an approach to Black theology (in terms of articulation and pedagogy) by means of drama and dialogue, with a view to developing a more accessible method for engaging in God-talk that is reflective of Black experience and their accompanying expressions of faith.

The Shape and Scope of the Work—"Acts" and Chapters

In attempting to create an interactive and participative method for undertaking and articulating Black theology I have sought to incorporate a range of methodologies and concepts for the development of this work. The first chapter seeks to outline the background and substantive content for this work. While I believe the efficacy of this work transcends the immediate context from which it has emerged, I am nonetheless, as a contextual theologian, obliged to detail the nature of the situation in which I reflect and write. This work has been approached through the framework provided by drama theory and participative, experiential learning. In that respect, the major themes and narrative developments in work fall within a context of a "dramatic act." Each act (and there are three of them in this work) represents a major development in the construction of the work. The major discursive shifts in thinking and action are detailed in each dramatic act. Act I, entitled *Setting the Scene*, represents the first major tranche in the evolution of this project—namely, to identify the context and the basic existential nature of the problem—seeking to work in solidarity with those who I have termed the "voiceless." Within this act is the first chapter. This chapter is an attempt to conceptualize, by way of an opening piece of drama, the nature of disenfranchisement of the poor, marginalized and oppressed, the majority of whom are Black people of African descent.

By introducing and analysing this drama, I am outlining the central point of departure for a process I am terming "dramatizing theologies" (a participative approach to Black God-talk).

Act II, *Outlining the Drama*, incorporates two chapters and details both the historic developments of drama within Christian practices and also my initial and more worked attempts to do theology by means of a dramatic format. Chapter 2 attempts to place the development of "dramatizing theologies" into a cultural and historic context and seeks to compare this new process for articulating and doing theology with other, long established means for engaging in creative and constructive God-talk.

Chapter 3 is in effect my exploration of the dramatic pieces that constitute the heart of this creative and participative process of "dramatizing theologies." Within Chapter 3 I introduce *My God!?*, the central sketch that serves as the basic paradigm for detailing the process of dramatizing theologies. The central importance of this sketch will be explained in Chapter 3, but at this point it is important to assert that *My God!?* offers a creative example for how substantive theological concerns can be undertaken by means of Christian drama.

Act III, *Detailing the Denouement*, is comprised of three chapters and details what I have termed the denouement to this participatory process of theological exploration. I have used the term *denouement* in order to reflect their dramatic outcome and resolution to this interactive process. The three chapters in this, the final act, are an attempt to detail the methodological and procedural issues and concerns that arise in the construction and development of the process of dramatizing theologies.

Chapter 4 looks at the development of an underlying method for bringing drama and Black theology into dialogue. This section aims to open out the process of dramatizing theologies in order that its efficacy and utility can extend beyond the idiosyncratic interests of the author. How can other people be enabled to engage in the process of dramatizing theologies in order that voiceless people can be given a voice in the development of theological discourse?

Chapter 5 outlines the creative emergence of an interactive, action-reflection model of engagement that builds on the insights of the previous chapter in order to enable marginalized and oppressed peoples to become central players in the development of theological thinking. I have termed this form of engagement "theology from the bottom up."

The final chapter attempts to outline some of the practical applications for dramatizing theologies. The principal arena that might benefit from this participatory model for undertaking theological inquiry is the developing arena of church-sponsored racial justice initiatives. By attempting to link the central themes and concepts of dramatizing theologies with the development of training materials and other concomitant programmes in racial justice training I want to demonstrate how this participatory model for talking about God can enable people from disparate backgrounds to engage with one another.

Establishing the Identity of the Voiceless

This work outlines a new participatory approach for undertaking Black theological discourse with marginalized and oppressed peoples. My dialogue partners in this work are disenfranchised Black people of mainly Caribbean descent living in the UK.

The impetus for the work first arose a number of years ago when I first began to work alongside local church congregations in the West Midlands area of the UK. The majority of these church communities were Black majority, comprised mainly of African Caribbean migrants, many of whom had travelled from the Caribbean to the UK in the 1950s and 60s. They and their descendants now constitute the majority of the membership of these faith groupings, located primarily in inner-city, urban priority areas of large metropolitan cities.

On my travels with the various groups I noticed that an ongoing feature of these churches was the almost complete silence of the mainly older Black members.[12] In matters of theological reflection, worship, mission and pastoral care, particular groups of people (often a remnant of White middle-class persons living in suburbia and communing into the church) often dominated the discourse within the church. The articulation of spiritual and theological matters by Black people was largely absent within the church.

What was also significant within these settings was the sense that what these Black people had to say was largely ignored or not considered to be of any import. It was not so much that they were ignored (which in many respects was the case), as their voice was not considered of sufficient importance to affect the discussion to any great extent. It is instructive to note that these individuals in these churches were the recipients of a pernicious phenomenon which sociologists and anthropologists have termed a "hierarchy of credibility."

In a previous piece of work I have identified this hierarchy of credibility as

> [a] social ranking that confers a greater degree of credibility and reliability upon some people often at the expense of others. The latter are perceived to have less status than the former.[13]

The social ranking within a hierarchy of credibility is linked explicitly to our notions of epistemology and what we assert as being truth. Black theologians have long argued that the alternate truths of Black experience (which often stand in stark contradistinction to White hegemony) are often disparaged or denigrated by those who possess the power to nullify the voice of the other.[14] As many Black people of Caribbean origin can testify, what is recognized as truth is linked directly to "who you know and who knows you."[15]

As I have stated elsewhere, the truths of the Black experience within a Diasporan context have always existed within a contested framework, which has demanded a range of socio-political and theological tools in order that it can be explicated and expressed with confidence and alacrity.[16]

What has became patently clear in the years when I was engaged in face-to-face work with predominantly Black Christian communities was the dual struggle under which many of these often marginalized and poor communities labour. That struggle was a dialectical tension between the more obvious forms of marginalization and estrangement from White authority on the one hand and the less obvious distance from and paternalism of Black professionalism.

In terms of the former, one can see this evident in the all-pervasive construction of White hegemony, which is documented in greater detail within this book. In terms of the more disguised features of the latter, Black professionalism has become no more adept at engaging with and conferring dignity upon poor, marginalized and detached Black people than their patrician thinking White counterparts.

In short, poor Black people have traditionally suffered from a form of "double jeopardy."[17] On the one hand, they are denied a voice by the claims of White hegemony, which has overlooked, disparaged and denigrated them; while on the other hand, Black professionals have ignored their voice, on the grounds that it lacks the eloquence and the "niceties" of their own particular type of discourse.

In terms of the latter, one can legitimately claim that there is at least a sense of solidarity and empathy for poor Black people, which is rarely found within the collective and corporate ranks of White power.

This sense of empathy and solidarity should not, however, disguise us from recognizing that this is still a perspective that is steeped in paternalism and pity. Black professionals often look down on and exhibit a form of embarrassment at their lowlier compatriots, recognizing in them, aspects of their own journey from such relatively unpromising beginnings towards respectability and seeming acceptance.[18]

I have lost count of the number of occasions I have been on committees and consultative meetings when both White and Black middle-class professionals (one has to be middle class to be admitted to these particular arenas and engaged in the ensuing discourse) who have taken delight in talking about poor and marginalized people (especially Black people) and rarely with them. The occasions when Black "Community leaders" speak for their people (having rarely sought any mandate on which to make any pronouncements) are much too replete to detail at this point. Suffice it to say that on such occasions when such lofty, sententious rhetoric is uttered, poor, voiceless Black people are just that—voiceless people who are not present and not always consulted when their "betters" are talking about them. I have addressed aspects of this phenomenon in a previous piece of work.[19]

The development of this attempt to create a more democratic and participatory approach to undertaking Black theological work with and alongside voiceless people arose from a particular incident a number of years ago. In the early 1990s I first became an active member of a Black caucus support group within the Methodist Church in Britain. The Black Methodist Group (BMG)[20] as it was then named was founded in the mid 1980s by a group of Black Methodist ministers (initially called the Black Methodist Ministers' Group—BMMG) in order to challenge the endemic racism within the church. In the early 1990s at the time of my initial involvement, the group became embroiled in a relatively short, but intensely angry debate with members of the White hierarchy of the church. A number of influential people within the BMG mounted a spirited and ultimately futile campaign to challenge the church hierarchy to change their minds over a particularly controversial decision that had been taken, which, it was felt, militated against the work of the BMG and Black people in general within the Methodist Church in Britain.

Neither the details of the dispute nor particulars of the final decision need detain us at this point. What was quite instructive at the time was the seeming self-righteous rhetoric of both sides of the dispute. On the one side, members of the White hierarchy felt sufficiently emboldened to take a major decision without any seeming regard for the Black constituency that would be affected by their decision. On the other side, my peers and I were equally confident in our claims to speak for the many others who would be adversely affected, so we believed, by this erroneous decision.

I say "so we believed" because, in truth, no attempt was made to consult with those who were not the leaders of this campaign. The campaign assumed that others were in agreement with our stance. We simply decided our course of action and implemented it without recourse to those for whom we claimed to speak.

Looking back, one might even cynically state that part of our reasoning, albeit in a sub-conscious vein, was the desire not to be encumbered by the innate conservatism and moderation of ordinary voiceless Black people.

As I will demonstrate at a later point in this text, it is not uncommon for ordinary Black people to exhibit attitudes and theological beliefs that are markedly more moderate and conservative than their so-called intellectual betters.[21] Aspects of this tension are expressed by the Black practical/ pastoral theologian Dale Andrews in his book *Practical Theology for Black Churches*.[22] I suspect that had we, the leaders of this campaign, sought out ordinary poor, voiceless Black people, we might have found such individuals most inhibited, diffident and, perhaps, antagonistic to our desire to "rock the boat." Our refusal to consult with the group, for whatever the motives, meant that we were no less complicit in the hierarchical and damaging process of ignoring the claims of the "least of these"[23] than were our White adversaries.

The opening sketch which forms a part of the dramatic material that seeks to provide the substantive content for the process of "dramatizing theologies" was written during the heightened months of that campaign. I have returned to it because within the few pages of highly charged polemic (the writing in this piece mirrored the blaze of anger that is detailed by James Cone in his first writings[24]) I sought to give voice to the leaders on both sides of the dispute. What is missing in this dramatic scenario is the voice of the voiceless.

In writing the sketch I quickly discounted the voice of those who are the most marginalized and oppressed. The setting of this piece and the fictional characters that populated it are both equally oblivious of the presence, and therefore the voice, of those who are the most vulnerable and least able to stake their claim in the world.

For sure, I remain clear that either side of the debate are not equally culpable. I remain convinced that both the decision itself and the process by which it was taken by the White people with power were wrong. I am equally clear that it is the White people who hold the power in the sketch; just as I am clear that it is White people who hold all the "aces" in the world. So I am not saying that the actions of the Black people in the sketch are wrong, or those of Black Liberation theologians for that matter. Neither am I saying that we (both then and now) hold equal responsibilities for the voiceless, marginalized and oppressed condition of Black people in the world today.

The blame for such matters (if blame is the correct recourse—I feel that blame is not a particularly helpful construct with which to work, however) lies with White hegemony, not with Black Liberation theologians trying to engage in anti-hegemonic struggle.

And yet, despite these very necessary caveats, I remain struck by the alacrity of both groups, particularly the Black protagonists, to ignore the voices of those who are and remain the voiceless. It is often the case that many Black Liberation theologians are no more comfortable engaging in face-to-face discourse with voiceless Black people than are the White experts, who the former so easily criticize and critique.

Often, Black Liberation theologians are no less armchair activists than the classical White theologians they denounce. I stand condemned on such grounds as do many others. This work is an attempt to create a participatory approach to Black God-talk, in which the voice of the voiceless is a crucial component in both the process and the substantive content of any theologizing.

So, as a way of introducing the central ideas in the process of dramatizing theologies, I offer you the script of *We Know Best*, my attempt to provide a fictional account of the dispute that raised my awareness of the voiceless nature of poor Black people in Britain and the world.

WE KNOW BEST

Inside a committee room, somewhere in central London. Behind a table, there sits three white middle-aged men. After a very short interval, there is a knock at the door.

WHITE MAN NO. 1: [*Calling out*] Come in.

[*The door opens and two black people enter the room. One is a man, the other a woman.*]

WHITE MAN NO. 1: Please take a seat.

[*The two black people do so.*]

WHITE MAN NO. 1: I'm glad you could make it. Now I am perfectly aware of the deep sensitivity of this matter and I would like to make it clear from the outset, that we, the central steering committee, fully understand your situation.

BLACK WOMAN: You do?

WHITE MAN NO. 2: Of course we do... We feel your anguish.

WHITE MAN NO. 3: We have your best interests at heart.

BLACK MAN: Well that's alright then, I feel better already.

WHITE MAN NO. 1: The facts of the matter are as follows. Due to a number of personnel and budgetary difficulties, the central committee has to regretfully inform you that the Affirmative Action Development Scheme will have to close at the end of this month.

BLACK MAN: But you do have our best interests at heart?

WHITE MAN NO. 1: Am I right in assuming that I sense a little hostility here?

BLACK WOMAN: I'd re-tune my radar if I were you. There's more than a little hostility in here.

BLACK MAN: Four hundred years of hostility to be precise.

WHITE MAN NO. 2: We understand your feelings, but you do have to see things from our perspective.

BLACK WOMAN: And that is?

WHITE MAN NO. 2: [*Looking at his two colleagues*] Shall I explain our position?

WHITE MAN NO. 3: Go ahead, Roger.

WHITE MAN NO. 2: Obviously, it goes without saying that we are upset and saddened that such a decision regarding the Affirmative Action Development Unit has had to be taken.

BLACK WOMAN: Obviously.

WHITE MAN NO. 2: [*Slightly thrown, but continues*] But I feel you should be aware that there did exist a number of quite intractable difficulties that plagued the working of the unit, and it was felt from our point of view that the best means of ironing out these troubles would be to discontinue funding; thereby giving all sides the opportunity to look again at the structure and workings of such an initiative.

WHITE MAN NO. 1: I would like to endorse the sentiments of my colleague by stating, quite categorically, that there exists no malicious intent whatsoever in the making of this decision. It was exercised purely upon logistical grounds. When the various teething and personnel problems have been eradicated, we shall be more than happy to look closely at re-engaging the work of the unit once more. Your input would be greatly appreciated on this matter.

BLACK MAN: Why do you want our input?

WHITE MAN NO. 3: Well… Hmmmmmm.

WHITE MAN NO. 2: Well, because it does concern yourselves.

BLACK MAN: It's a bit late to be asking us for our concerns now. You've already made your decision.

BLACK WOMAN: It's like inviting a guest to a meal, after you've already eaten all the food and cleared away the cutlery.

BLACK MAN: If you had really wanted our input, you would have invited us to a meeting before you made your decision.

WHITE MAN NO. 1: But it wasn't that simple.

BLACK WOMAN: It never is.

WHITE MAN NO. 1: You have to see things from our perspective... The Central Organization felt that the unit in question was not achieving the stated objectives it was originally set up for. It was therefore felt that some new mechanism must be found to ensure that these future goals were to be met.

BLACK WOMAN: From your perspective, of course.

WHITE MAN NO. 1: Pardon? I'm afraid I don't fully understand your last remark.

BLACK WOMAN: When you say "it was felt," what you really mean is, you lot felt the unit was not achieving its specific aims. You didn't ask us what we felt about the work of the unit and, if you had, you would have found that we the practitioners on the ground, we the recipients of the unit's activities, are more than happy with its work and the resulting achievements... But as I said, our opinion doesn't count.

WHITE MAN NO. 3: I think you're being slightly unfair.

WHITE MAN NO. 2: Not to mention unreasonable. I find your somewhat caustic attitude to be most unhelpful.

BLACK MAN: And now we get down to the crux of the matter. You find us to be unreasonable and unhelpful. Well, isn't that a shame? How dare we feel upset and suspicious at your decisions? After all, you the big chief knows best. We should be happy that you've made your executive decisions, without any recourse to our feelings, and closed down the unit. We should be grateful because, after all, doesn't the big boss man know best? We should come into your room, all full of happy Caribbean smiles, do a quick limbo dance and then lie prostrate on the floor and tell you how grateful we are that you have decided to cut our unit. And people say that paternalism no longer exists?

WHITE MAN NO. 1: I think you are dealing in the realms of hyperbole. This has nothing at all to do with paternalism. This is simply a question of effective management of resources and seeking to find the best way forward.

BLACK WOMAN: With you always holding the upper hand. You make the decisions and we have to take it and like it.

WHITE MAN NO. 1: Now that is not the case.

BLACK WOMAN: Change your decision then. We like the way the unit is being run. We have confidence in the man running it. We think it is meeting our needs. Restore the unit to its former position and leave the personnel as it is.

WHITE MAN NO. 3: You may be happy, but the organization as a whole is not, and don't forget it is the organization's money which funds the unit.

BLACK WOMAN: And that effectively explains everything... Your money... Sounds like a nasty whiff of racism here?

WHITE MAN NO. 2: Now please... Let us keep unhelpful and destructive terms like racism out of this conversation. This has nothing at all to do with racism.

BLACK WOMAN: Of course not... Of course this has nothing at all to do with racism. You, of course, have decided that the unit is not meeting its stated aims. This decision is fuelled no doubt by your basic antipathy to its work in the first place. You have a basic prejudice against the work of the unit. You are not happy. You also have the power to effectively implement your prejudice to the betterment of yourself and to the detriment of ourselves. And we are powerless to do anything about it. You decide. You hold all the power and we hold none. Now tell me that isn't racism?

WHITE MAN NO. 2: But we do have your best interests at heart.

BLACK MAN: And that is paternalism... Something you've been practising for the last four hundred years.

WHITE MAN NO. 3: I must say that this particular attitude you are adopting is not helping matters at all.

BLACK MAN: And what attitude would help? Complete subservience? We knowing our place? I doubt it... And as for you having our best interests at heart, well that's a fanciful notion if ever I heard one. The fact of the matter is, and I hate to sound so hard and uncompromising, but there does not exist one institution, organization or body which is run by or dominated by White people that has ever had Black people's interests at heart as its number one priority. Not one. All organizations run by a particular elite... in most cases... [*Looks at the three men*]... white middle-aged, middle-class men... are always run for the benefit of themselves, or people like themselves. On the rare occasions they attempt to take on board the opinions and needs of others, it is usually done so, either to placate their consciences, or is simply a PR exercise and nothing more. The powerful remain powerful and the dispossessed remain just that. No real steps are ever taken towards bringing effective equality, because that would mean the elite having to divest themselves of power and why should they want to do that? So they pretend. They say the right things, make right sounding platitudes, but in the final analyses they make sure that their ends and opinions count, to the virtual exclusion of everyone else. This organization we are all members of is no different from any other White-dominated organization. We all know where we stand. You at the top and we at the bottom.

WHITE MAN NO. 2: But don't you...

BLACK WOMAN: [*Interrupting*] Perhaps our attitude is not helping matters, but then again, nothing is going to help matters. You certainly aren't. You are incapable of doing so. As Black people, we have to look to ourselves for support and sustenance. We can no longer sit back and wait for your paternalism and goodwill to give us what we want and desire. Depending upon goodwill, where no goodwill exists, is a foolhardy tactic and we as a people have been foolhardy for long enough. We should face the facts and decide to take matters into our own hands. We have to set our own agenda and decide to do our own thing.

WHITE MAN NO. 3: That kind of talk is very, very dangerous. Once you begin to go down the road of separatism, then no one ever comes out the winner.

BLACK WOMAN: We didn't say anything about separatism. We just intend to set our own agenda and do things our way without any interference from you. We are not going anywhere. You don't get rid of us that easily.

WHITE MAN NO. 1: Militant action is not the answer.

BLACK MAN: And blind subservience and trust isn't the answer either.

WHITE MAN NO. 2: [*Upset*] But but... This kind of talk won't help anybody. We'll all get hurt.

BLACK MAN: How can we get hurt? We can't be hurt anymore than we already are. You've already closed down our unit, how can things get any worse? We have nothing to lose. We have nothing, nor should we expect anything. We can't lose.

WHITE MAN NO. 1: But this is still separatism!

BLACK WOMAN: Funny how you're worried about separatism now. When you were happily excluding us from all power, keeping us in our place and making decisions on our behalf, you didn't seem too worried about separatism then... You didn't even give it a second thought, or if you did, you certainly didn't do anything about it. Now we're thinking of going our own way, you're suddenly worried about us being separate. Well, we are not worried. We've already made our decision. We know what we have to do. The ball's in your court. You can either treat us fairly and we mean fairly, not just the cosmetic version, or else we shall pursue our own way forward without you, and we can do it. Make no mistake about that. If we want it badly enough, we can do it.

BLACK MAN: You heard the sister... The rest is up to you.

[*Both the man and the woman get out of their seats and make for the door.*]

WHITE MAN NO. 1: Don't go... There really isn't any need for this... I'm sure we can work things out amicably... After all, we really do have your best interests at heart. Trust us, we know the full facts. We know best.

BLACK WOMAN: [*Looking back momentarily*] I really believe you, when you say that! You really believe it. That's the sad thing about it. You really do believe it.

THE END

Analysing the Sketch

There are a number of things to note about the dynamic inherent within the sketch. The first point to note is the gender imbalance in the group. There is one woman in the drama, and until quite late on in the proceedings, she speaks the least of all the characters. This point is amplified to even greater effect in the central sketch in the theological schema entitled *My God!?*

On a recent re-reading of *We Know Best* I was struck by the polemical nature of the piece. The discourse is angry and combative. There is a distinct adversarial feature to the conversation between the two sets of participants. The opening and wary pleasantries between the combatants is soon exchanged for biting, sarcastic polemics from the Black participants. A feature of the sketch are the long speeches made by the characters. On a number of occasions, they engage in lengthy rhetorical polemics, where the focus of their discourse is not on dialogue or elucidation, but rather, is an exercise in didactic bombast! The White characters are unable (or should I say not permitted) to respond, as they sit on the receiving end of a deluge of withering rhetoric.

Re-reading *We Know Best* in Light of Robert Beckford's *God of the Rahtid*

Black British theologian and cultural critic, Robert Beckford, has explored the dynamics of Black rage and anger in the context of post-colonial Britain in a previous piece of work. Since the publication of *Jesus is Dread*[25] in 1998, Robert Beckford has established himself as one of the most urgent and pressing voices in contemporary theological discourse. In both *Jesus is Dread* and *Dread and Pentecostal*[26] Beckford has used a multiplicity of sources to explore Black theological and cultural ideas with reference to issues of Black empowerment and racial justice.

In his third book, *God of the Rahtid*,[27] Beckford tackles one of the most pressing issues affecting Black people in Britain—namely, that of rage. This text commences with an analysis of post-colonial Britain, particularly in the aftermath of the Brixton nail bomb in April 1999. Beckford argues that Britain is country in which the racialized oppressed permeates the very fabric of the nation.[28]

At the dawn of the twenty-first century, Black people are trying to come to terms with and exist within a context that both validates and legitimizes the institutional and casual incidences of racism against people of colour.[29] It is within this climate that Black people are struggling with a phenomenon he terms as "low level rage." Beckford defines the latter as "related to internalized rage in that it is experienced in mind and body. It is manifested in anger, depression and anxiety."[30] The high incidence of mental ill health (particularly schizophrenia) amongst African Caribbean communities in Britain adds substance to Beckford's contentions.

Having initially analysed the many contexts in which Black rage is to be located, the author outlines his own personal collision with the pernicious and debilitating nature of Black rage. In a moving section of the book, Beckford articulates the veneer of Black professional and personal mobility that encouraged him to suppress his rage at the altar of progress and advancement.[31] Personal circumstances, however, remind him of the fallacious nature of much that can be understood as Black acceptability. As a Black theologian, I have found these words to be apposite, for they remind me of sage-like utterances of the African American comedian and cultural commentator Dick Gregory. Gregory once remarked (and I am paraphrasing in the interests of polite convention) that Black professionals were only one argument away from being the subject of a racial epithet.[32]

Beckford draws upon Black theological insights concerned with the nature of the Kingdom of God, and argues that our understanding of the Kingdom provides the necessary tools and resources for a redeeming construct of Black rage.[33] Redemptive vengeance, argues Beckford, can be found within the notion of a realized eschatology, in which the agency of God, incarnated within the ministry of Jesus, provides the focus for harnessing the emotive power of Black anger.[34]

Re-reading this sketch in light of Beckford's *God of the Rahtid* has been quite instructive. When I had first composed this piece I did not possess the scholarly tools to provide a critically centred rationale for the actions and thought patterns of the Black protagonists in the drama. My attempt to detail the reality of this event was to seek recourse in drama. As I have outlined in my previous book, drama provides an opportunity to create a context and find words for a particular setting in order to unmask experiences and feelings that, hitherto, often remain unexplored.[35] Beckford's analysis of "low level rage" is highly suggestive in the development of the process of "dramatizing theologies"; for lying beneath this transformative process is a desire to provide a schema that enables marginalized and oppressed Black people to discover their voice in order to articulate their pain and frustration.

Analysing *We Know Best* in light of Beckford's work reveals the cathartic, expiated desire of the Black characters in being liberated to "speak words of truth." This sense of release is manifested in a torrent of words in which the many years of pent-up, subterranean anger is set free, within the confines of a seemingly polite ecclesial meeting. When Beckford states:

> In my working adult life I have only ever once called an individual a "racist" to their face. I have generally avoided accusatory politics, but on this occasion after four years of the subtlest racialized hostility, I erupted. My anger was full and volcanic.[36]

he is re-enacting the very dynamics of this fictional sketch written a few years prior to his real life event. The cathartic sense of release in "telling the truth and shaming the devil"[37] is reflective of Beckford's assertion that "the truth shall set you free."[38]

The Black characters in the sketch become critical subjective agents able to speak the truth in a challenging and dynamic way. Yet their truth-telling remains individualistic and disconnected from the wider concerns of other Black people. This is not to suggest that they are not concerned with the hopes, aspirations and needs of poor, marginalized and oppressed

Black people, but it is worth noting that throughout the drama we see no evidence that they have consulted with or taken counsel from others. To what extent are the two characters speaking for themselves or on behalf of others?

This question is more than a matter of simple semantics for it goes to the heart of the nature and intent of this enterprise. If the two Black characters are speaking with the cognizance of others then their discourse in this context is naturally imbued with a marked sense of mutuality and collegiality. If not (which I believe to be the case), then their discourse is a possibly presumptuous and somewhat detached form of rhetoric that reveals echoes of the kind of assumptions made by their White adversaries.

This dilemma and contextual struggle lies at the heart of this research. Can Black Liberation theologians exhibit greater levels of engagement and mutuality with poor Black marginalized and oppressed people, which go beyond notions of tokenism, paternalism and condescension?

I am not suggesting that *all* Black Liberation theologians are guilty of the sort of detachment and distance evidence by the sketch and my previous comments. Black and Womanist scholars such as Lee Butler,[39] Jeremiah Wright[40] and Linda E. Thomas[41] are but three exponents (of many) who have engaged with Black subjects in a reciprocal fashion in their exploration of Black theological and religious themes. My central concern in this work is to move from the kind of close engagement with those who are the voiceless, in which one seeks to observe, interact and document, to a position where that very interaction becomes the means by which one's theological construction is undertaken. In short, the very dynamic with voiceless people creates the content of Black theology, but not from an historic perspective;[42] but rather from within the context of contemporaneous experience. Like Lynne Westfield,[43] it is my intention to use the contemporary experiences and discourse of, hitherto, Black voiceless people to assist me, by means of drama, to create a new approach to and a dynamic for the articulation and doing of Black theology.

What Does it Mean to be Rendered Voiceless?

To belong to British society and that of the church, for a Black person, necessitates a denial of one's self. To be voiceless is to have one's experiences, history and ongoing reality ignored, disparaged and ridiculed. It is to be rendered an insignificant presence, amongst the many who are deemed one's betters and superiors.[44] Reflecting upon a Caribbean aphorism, which states that "Who feels it knows it," to be voiceless, therefore, in twenty-first century Britain and the wider world is to find that what I know or have felt is of no consequence to the nation or world as a whole.

What I know and have felt is dismissed as untrue and without any social, political, cultural or theological consequence. As Robert Hood has shown, within the development of Christian thought and tradition, the established church has drunk deeply from the well of western epistemological thought, but shown scant regard for the contribution of African cultures and traditions in the shaping of Christian doctrine.[45] As I have demonstrated in a previous piece of work, it is interesting to note the privileging of Eurocentric knowledge claims, as partial as they are, over and against the substantive oral traditions and wisdom of African peoples.[46] In short, whatever Black people know is of supreme unimportance because, in the final analysis, we do not matter.

Although many people from these disaffected and unpromising backgrounds have progressed from the enclosed confines of poverty, alienation and marginalization, it should be noted, however, that there are many who cannot point to any sense of improvement, social or otherwise. These often forgotten, faceless and voiceless figures inhabit the often unchanged world of the inner-city. Writers such as Kenneth Leech have written extensively about the marginalization of the urban poor and their estrangement from the wider society and the church.[47]

One of the central arguments of this chapter is that there are additional burdens and pressures that are placed upon people who are not White, living in this country or across the wider contours of the "new world order." Feminist and Womanist[48] theologians have long spoken about multi-dimensional oppression. That is, the diverse ways in which social, political, cultural and economic pressures are played out on poor, dispossessed and marginalized objects, coalescing around issues of "race," ethnicity, gender, sexuality, class and geographic and social location.[49] It is the uniqueness of these challenges that have stymied the voice of the urban, disaffected poor.

In making a claim to identify with the "voiceless" I want to suggest that British society and the so-called first world have found convenient ways of ignoring the claims of those who have been pushed to the margins, and whose presence the corporate whole has identified as being undesirable or subversive.[50] The noted sociologist, Paul Gilroy, has been an ardent campaigner and chronicler of the subtle and not so oblique pressures that have been exerted upon minority ethnic people in their attempts to find an accommodating space and place within this island.[51]

It is not my intention to claim a privileged role for Black people, as the recipients of the dubious honour of being the "most oppressed of the oppressed." This would be a fatuous and inane form of discourse. What I want to assert, however, is that due to a unique set of circumstances, many dating back several hundred years to the birth of slavery, Black people have been the recipients of a pernicious, psychological attack that threatened their very existence as human subjects created in the image of a Supreme being.

African American scholars, such as Asante, estimate that upwards of 20 million African people were transported between Africa, Europe and the Americas over a three hundred year period.[52] Inherent within that Black transatlantic movement of forced migration was a form of biased racialized teaching that asserted the inferiority and sub-human nature of the Black self.[53] The effects of such biased, self-serving instruction are still being felt—the continuing tendency of Black people to internalize their feelings of inferiority, coupled with an accompanying lack of self-esteem. The internalization of this demonized instruction has led to Black people directing the fire of their repressed and disparaged selves onto their own psyche and that of their peers with whom they share a common ancestry and ethnic identity.[54] This can be seen in the growing incidences of lateral violence, more popularly known as "Black on Black crime" in inner-city areas in Britain and in the United States.

The popular debate surrounding the socialization and educational attainment of Black children and young people in Britain, although a seemingly contemporaneous issue, has its roots in the prolonged attack upon the African self during the era of slavery.

One of the enduring legacies of slavery, argues Ella P. Mitchell, was the inextricable link between the role of the matriarch in Black corporate life and the development of a Black conception of Christianity, which reflected that maternal dominance. The forced removal of the Black male as part of the machinery of slavery ensured that the role of Black women continued to be all-pervasive in the socialization of the Black child.[55]

The dominant role of Black women, in comparative terms, coupled with the most pernicious effects of racism, has made the struggle of Black males, particularly in western societies, an acute one. A number of writers and educationalists have asserted that Black males exhibit disproportionately higher levels of disaffection and marginalization in White-dominated societies in the West than their female counterparts. This differentiation can be attributed to the disparity between the codified forms of behaviour displayed by Black males and the values and norms of White power.[56] In effect, there is a greater variance between the behavioural patterns of Black males and the standardized and accepted norms designed and policed by White male authority. This argument is given apparent validity by the number of studies undertaken by researchers that have placed the Black male as the central subject in the research enterprise.[57] This discussion is one that resonates with a growing number of parents of Black children who are struggling in various State school systems.[58]

The struggles of ordinary poor, disenfranchised Black people in Britain have been documented in a number of arenas, some of which are detailed in this study. The disaffection of Black youths, particularly males, has led a number of Black British theologians to search for viable models and tools by which these seeming insoluble problems can be overcome.[59]

These various approaches to affirming and empowering Black youth fall within the framework of Black Practical theology. These have been helpful in highlighting some of the significant challenges and outlining the hoped-for outcomes in the development of positive identity construction of Black youth in Britain.

What many of them have lacked, however, is a critical form of pedagogy that might turn their helpful conceptual analysis into a workable programme of Black practical theological engagement. Like many of their counterparts in the US these works have not been able to create a sustained methodology for working alongside and with marginalized and oppressed Black people, particularly those who are under the age of twenty-five.

The search for an engaged form of methodology for undertaking Black theological work with those I have identified as the voiceless took me into the area of religious education. The aforementioned Black theological studies lacked the necessary methodology for combining the insights of Black theology with the much needed tools of educational pedagogy in order to create a critical model of reflection. The model of which I speak is one that would assist Black voiceless people in their holistic development, thereby giving them a voice, and a subjective presence in the world.

Jack L. Seymour has provided a helpful overview of the relationship between education and Christian theology through the lens of the Religious Education Association from 1950 to the present day.[60] Writing of the development of the work of post-war Christian educators in the United States he says:

> These Christian educators were convinced that education by itself could not discover the grace of God, God's offer of reconciliation and redemption, and God's call to mission and engagement. It needed theology. In turn, theology needed educational processes to empower persons to encounter the story of faith in such a way as to lead to lives of faith and responsibility to God and others.[61]

The desire to find a theological form that would provide a framework in which I could locate my process of "dramatizing theologies" led me into the arena of religious education. Within this particular discipline, combining the insights of educational theory and method with theological reflection, lay the seminal figure of Paulo Freire. My engagement with Freire has provided the essential thematic and conceptual tools from which I have been able to construct the overarching basis for creating a participative approach to undertaking Black God-talk.

The Influence of Religious Education as the Framework for "Dramatizing Theologies"

Assessing the work and "ministry" of Paulo Freire

The name Paulo Freire is one that has exerted a profound hold on the imagination of educators the world over. Freire's groundbreaking work in devising appropriate pedagogies or strategies of teaching for poor, marginalized and oppressed peoples is legendary.[62] My initial engagement with Freire has been detailed in a previous piece of work.[63]

In the context of this work, I want to look briefly at some of his thinking, particularly in the context of religious education, and the empowerment and affirmation of those who are without a voice. In my previous work I have outlined Freire's influence on the development of what I have termed *A Black Christian Education of Liberation*.[64]

Let me begin by offering some brief bibliographical details on Paulo Freire. My apologies to those for whom this is more than familiar territory. Paulo Freire was born in 1921 in Recife, in North Eastern Brazil, into a situation of extreme poverty. It was this experience that led Freire to dedicate his life to the struggle against poverty and hunger, so that other children would not have to know the agony he had experienced. Freire developed a philosophy of education that challenged poor and oppressed people to reflect upon their individual and corporate experiences and begin to ask critical questions about the nature of their existence. Why were they poor? What structures or people had control over their lives?

The radical nature of this critical approach to the task of teaching and learning brought Freire to the attention of the military government in Brazil in 1964. He was subsequently imprisoned and then exiled. In exile, he began to refine further his educational philosophy and method.

He came to international attention with the publication of his first book *Pedagogy of the Oppressed*,[65] which laid the foundations for a seismic shift in the whole conception of how poor, oppressed and marginalized people might be educated. In the realms of theological thought and Christian education, Freire's ideas are credited with being an invaluable source for Gustavo Gutteriez's groundbreaking text *A Theology of Liberation*,[66] and the basis for a committed and ideologically driven theology of and for the poor. Freire's later work with the World Council of Churches throughout the 1970s and 80s as an international consultant led to his work becoming hugely significant in many parts of the world, especially amongst poor and oppressed peoples. Paulo Freire died in Rio de Janeiro on May 2, 1997, at the age of seventy-five. He has bequeathed a legacy of commitment, love and hope for oppressed peoples throughout the world.[67]

The importance of Paulo Freire cannot be overstated. In developing a rigorous and critical approach to the task of educating those who are poor and oppressed, Freire created an essential template by which religious educators might re-conceptualize their task. One of Freire's central concepts was that of "conscientization." This is a process where poor and oppressed people are enabled to become critically aware of the circumstances in which they live and the ways in which their humanity is infringed upon and blighted by the often dehumanizing contexts that surround them.[68] Allen J. Moore, commenting on this aspect of Freire's work, says:

> Conscientization in Freire's work is apparently both an individual experience and a shared experience of a people who are acting together in history. A way of life is not determined from thinking about the world but is formed from the shared praxis. In this critical approach to the world, basic attitudes, values, and beliefs are formed and a people are humanized or liberated. Conscientization, therefore, leads to a life lived with consciousness of history, a life lived that denounces and transforms this history in order to form a new way of life for those who are oppressed.[69]

Freire's approach to education has opened up new vistas for religious educators, along with pastoral and practical theologians. His work contains a profound humanizing spirit that draws extensively upon his Roman Catholic upbringing and catechesis. The religious teaching he would have received was one that emphasized not only the inherent sinful nature of humankind, but also identified God as being in an ongoing redemptive relationship with those whom God's very own self had willed into being. This perspective is expressed in powerful terms by John Westerhoff III, one of the most influential religious educators in recent times, who writes:

> God is that power within human life and history which calls, inspires and aids us, but will not take away our freedom to even destroy ourselves; however, God acts within human life and history to redeem and transform our deaths into life.[70]

For one who would not consider himself a theologian or a religious educator, Freire's work has always been marked by a firm, implicit theistic content. This became increasingly visible as his writings matured and he advanced in years. John Elias, in his assessment of Freire as a religious educator, states:

> The religious element in Freire's social philosophy has become increasingly more explicit in later writings and speeches. He sees the Christian Gospel as proclaiming the radical re-ordering of society in which men [sic] are oppressed... Christians who involve themselves in revolutionary action against oppression involve themselves in a new Passover, a new Easter.[71]

In a moving letter to a group of theological students, Freire speaks of his own Christian commitment and theological understanding.

> His words [Christ's] are not a sound that simply blows in the air: it is a whole way of knowing... I cannot know the Gospels if I take them simply as words that come to rest in me or if, seeing myself as empty, I try to fill myself with these words. This would be the way to bureaucratise the word, to empty it, to deny it, to rob it of its eternal coming to be... On the contrary, I understand the Gospels, well or badly, to the degree that, well or badly, I live them.[72]

Freire's words lead naturally into the final section of this chapter. For Freire, the liberation of the poor and the oppressed, the way that they might be enabled to discover their voice, is by means of them becoming critically aware of themselves and the situation in which they exist.[73] This process does not invite the poor and the oppressed to reflect benignly upon their situation; rather it calls for action, or praxis, in the language of Freire.[74] Freire's work is committed to the building of community in which the presence of God in Christ in the power of the Holy Spirit is at work in the midst of such Koinonia.

Freire reminds us that the transformational effect of being incorporated into Christ,[75] through the power of the Holy Spirit, leads to a whole new way of being and knowing. In effect, we are new creations in Christ. Cheryl Bridges has developed an approach to Christian religious education that is influenced by her Pentecostal background. Bridges has created an educational schema she describes as "Pentecostal formation."[76] Drawing upon the influence of the nineteenth-century Holiness movement in the United States, alongside the Pentecostal assertion in the primacy of the Holy Spirit, Bridges has created an approach that seeks to empower and affirm the poor and the oppressed, i.e., to give them a voice by which they might articulate their experiences.[77] The importance of the Holy Spirit to her educational approach can be discerned when she says:

> In sanctification, the believer learns to walk in perfect love and to exist in harmony with the will and nature of Christ... God will one day be all in all, and for the Pentecostal believer, this holy consummation can occur in believers' lives as a sign of the age to come. Therefore, issues of racism, sexism, oppression and violence are issues of sanctification.[78]

Applying Freire to the Needs of the Voiceless

I have appropriated Freire's critical pedagogy in order to create an overarching framework in which to locate my participative approach to undertaking Black God-talk. I have used Freire's work as a Black Liberation theologian. I make no apologies for seeking to use the basic concepts of Christianity and a radical interpretation of Christ's teaching and example for my work, for these have provided fertile ground for Black resistance to oppression for the past five hundred years.[79] The commitment to building radical communities for the new creation has been a central illuminating motif in Black Christianity since the epoch of slavery.

This work is one that seeks to affirm those whose voice has rarely been heard outside of a few select situations where such individuals experience a sense of being valued and feel "safe." My approach, affirmed by the critical thinking of fellow Black scholars in a number of disciplines, some of which I have detailed in this chapter, has been an attempt to harness the emotive power of the Christian faith in order that those who have traditionally been without a voice might be enabled to gain one for the purposes of their ongoing liberation.

Giving a voice to the voiceless by way of dramatizing theologies is nothing less than a process of critical advocacy. It is a way of assisting marginalized people to learn more about themselves and the world, through the framework of religion. It is a process of being nurtured and educated into such a world-view and being enabled to understand more about the kind of faith that can sustain and empower.

In the context of my own work as a Christian educator and Black theologian, I have unashamedly used the Christian faith as my vehicle for attempting to liberate those who are poor and oppressed. But just in case any of you are thinking that I am a Christian exclusivist, I acknowledge that aside from the substantive questions around relative and absolute truth claims of the various religious codes, I believe all the major religions to possess an essential ethical and moral underscoring that is efficacious for human flourishing. This commitment to human flourishing assumes even greater import when it is linked to issues of human identity and survival, particularly for minority ethnic people living in Britain. Stephen Carter writes:

> One of the understandings I share with many liberation theologians is the understanding of the tremendous importance of preserving religious communities not only as centers of difference, that is, places where one grasps the meaning of the world as different from what you find in the dominant culture, but even more so as centers of resistance.[80]

Carter has eloquently summarized the basic premise behind this chapter. Dramatizing theologies—a participative approach to Black God-talk in relation to voiceless people in Britain (and all over the world)—is to be committed to a project that seeks to enable individuals and larger corporate bodies to recognize their innate uniqueness and to build communities of resistance. The justification for using the phenomenon of religion in this process can be found in a subsequent comment from Carter who states:

Nobody ever was persuaded to go out and risk life and limb because they read a smart article on philosophy and public affairs. No one ever said they were going to organize a march and be beaten up by the police because of something they read in the *New York Times* op-ed page. It is only religion that still has the power, at its best, to encourage sacrifice and resistance.[81]

In a world that is still reeling from the cataclysmic effects of September 11th in New York and July 7th in London, it would be remiss of me if I did not acknowledge the dangers of religiously inspired action for political and social change. Clearly, the emotive and motivating force that is religion can be a force for ill. And yet, despite such necessary caveats, I still want to argue the case for a form of Black theological reflection as the most powerful force for giving a voice to the voiceless.

In asserting this position, I am aware of the potential fault lines and dangers. The threat of nationalism and fundamentalism are real concerns for all citizens living within what we might broadly term the liberal democratic tradition. Writers such as Parekh have attempted to analyse the tensions between liberal democratic traditions and the religious and cultural plurality that is a common feature in many of the countries that adhere to the philosophic conventions of the former.[82]

This work has been informed by the central tenets of the Christian faith and the emancipatory teachings of the Jesus who is Christ. The Christian faith remains, for the greater majority of Diasporan Black people, the essential lens through which our gaze into the future for a more complete and affirmed humanity has been undertaken.

In the following chapters I will outline an approach to undertaking Black theological thinking and the doing of Black theology using the methodology of dramatic sketches and dialogues. Can the use of drama and dialogue provide a creative means for marginalized and disempowered lay people to both think creatively and learn some of the central ideas of Black theology in an accessible form?

Before outlining an approach to articulating and doing Black theology by means of Christian drama, I want to outline some of the existing ways in which the church and writers and theologians have used drama as a means of expressing Christian ideas and themes. I will seek to demonstrate the significant difference in my approach, and how this method to doing theology differs from how Black theological ideas have been expressed in the past.

Act II
Outlining the Drama

2   Getting All Dramatic: The Development of Christian Drama

In this chapter I want to analyse the development of drama and assess its role within Christian education and worship. This will involve a brief discussion on the historical developments in the role of drama within the liturgical and pedagogical life of the church in the West. This will be followed by a more detailed examination of the nature of Christian drama as manifested in a plethora of published texts in hard copy and in electronic formats. What type of Christian drama is being published and used at the present time, and what kind of theology is espoused in these various texts?

By analysing the texts of these various pieces, I want to suggest that, for the most part, the plethora of material that has been produced has rarely accorded with the central tenets of Black theology. Indeed, it is more than true to report that Black people, both visually in marketing terms (front-cover photographs, for example) in addition to substantive content are painfully invisible when considering the merits or otherwise of Christian drama. Within the field of Christian drama, there is no more appreciation for the contextual needs of Black people than is the case in most mainstream generic schemes or scholarly work in Christian education and nurture. I have challenged this naïve and somewhat simplistic "colour blind" doctrine in a previous publication.[1] Then finally, I will outline the new approach to Christian drama I am proposing—one that fuses Black theological thought and its accompanying concepts within a dramatic, dialogical format, in order to create a new method for articulating and doing Black theology. A more detailed analysis of this new method will be discussed in the following chapters.

My Genesis as a Christian Dramatist

My confessional introduction to this text described the youthful exuberance and presumption that gave rise to my first ever dramatic skit, *The Calling*. Having written my first piece for that act of worship, the following eighteen months at university saw me expand my range, producing a number of additional sketches for a variety of occasions, many of which were included in worship settings.

The many occasions when drama was used as a pedagogical and evangelistic tool within worship during those student-led services were very much part of a larger movement of the appreciation of the dramatic arts within contemporary Christian practice; although I should stress at this point, however, that this development was still within a distinctly Eurocentric framework.

(Christian) Drama?

At this point, I think it is worth saying a few words about what I mean when I am using the word "drama." It is beyond the scope of this text to mount a detailed investigation into philosophical tenets of drama theory, although some of this work will be discussed in later chapters. Rather, I want to simply outline a number of issues and initial concerns that inform this work.

According to the online Yourdictionary.com, drama is often conceived as

> (a) prose or verse composition, especially one telling a serious story, that is intended for representation by actors impersonating the characters and performing the dialogue and action. (b) serious narrative work or program for television, radio, or the cinema.[2]

Additional definitions include:

1. Theatrical plays of a particular kind or period: *Elizabethan drama.*
2. The art or practice of writing or producing dramatic works.
3. A situation or succession of events in real life having the dramatic progression or emotional effect characteristic of a play: *the drama of the prisoner's escape and recapture.*
4. The quality or condition of being dramatic: *a summit meeting full of drama.*[3]

A more technical and philosophical appraisal of the term and the nature of drama will be attempted in Chapter 5, when I discuss the educational and theological method at work in this approach to using drama as a means of undertaking and teaching Black theology.

If the term drama, as defined in brief terms above, can be seen to be a generic activity that is an inherent part of human expression, then what differentiates Christian drama from her more generic compatriot? Is there such a thing as Christian drama? In many respects, in posing this question, one is obliged to make recourse to a much broader philosophical debate concerning the nature of all artistic and intellectual enterprise that carries the nomenclature of "Christian."

Within the discipline of Christian education, there has been an ongoing debate surrounding the efficacy and accuracy of using such a term as

"Christian education." Critics such as James Michael Lee and Paul H. Hirst have challenged the appropriateness of using such a term.

Lee has argued that education is a generic term that relates to the process of teaching and learning. The rules that govern this enterprise are established by a broad arena of philosophical thought that dates back to the Greeks. To speak of education being Christian or otherwise is an inappropriate term, as Christian education is governed by the same tenets or "laws" of pedagogical practice and human learning as is so-called "secular" education.[4]

Paul Hirst is even more sceptical about the relationship between theology and education and whether arising from this relationship we can speak with any integrity of an enterprise called "Christian education." Hirst believes that to speak of a distinctively Christian form of education seems to make no more sense than to argue for a Christian approach to mathematics or engineering.[5]

John Hull, writing in response to Hirst's polemic, mounts a spirited defence in favour of a reasonable and carefully nuanced relationship between education and Christian theology, which would give rise to an open, liberal and critical approach to the discipline of Christian education.[6]

Jeff Astley has written extensively on the underlying philosophy of Christian education, arguing that Christian theology provides both the rationale and the content for a Christian approach to learning.[7] David Willows argues for a more distinctively Christian approach to education, asserting that Divine revelatory knowledge is the basic essence of Christian theology and any accompanying approach to the teaching and learning process.[8]

My own perspective on the philosophy of education for Black theology will be detailed in Chapter 4. In a previous publication, I have nailed my colours to the mast that legitimates and justifies both the approach and the nomenclature of Christian education. It is my belief that there exists a Christian inspired approach to general education that is informed and influenced by a broad range of beliefs, values and assumptions concerning Divine agency and human nature, in addition to the specific intentionality of Christian learning and formation.[9]

The reason why I have taken a little time to outline some of the overarching concerns within the field of Christian education is due to the relationship between Christian education and Christian drama. Drama, when used within a generic or specifically Christian context by writers and performers who see their "art" and its accompanying expression as being influenced (and driven in some cases) by a commitment to Christ and his teachings, has often been created with an educational intent in mind. The aim of much Christian drama is to communicate the central tenets of the Christian Gospel and to proclaim the Kingdom of God.[10]

Christian drama, as I will illustrate shortly, has been a part of church tradition and practice since the early Middle Ages. Many would argue that God's revelation to humankind as it is depicted in the Bible is in its very self a document that is replete with dramatic occurrences and possibilities.[11] Michael Perry, writing in the preface to the *Dramatised Bible*, says:

> The *Dramatised Bible* creates the opportunity for a vivid presentation of Bible narrative and teaching. Generations of ministers and teachers or youth and children's leaders have done it before—turned the Bible text into drama so that worshippers or students can become actively involved in its teaching.[12]

In my previous book, *Acting in Solidarity*, I based a series of Christian sketches around biblical narratives, attempting to re-cast them in an alternative setting to the one for which they were first written.[13]

Christian drama, like its bigger sibling Christian education, is based upon the relationship between Christian theology, rooted in the revelation of God's own self as attested in scripture, experience, tradition and human reason, and the more generic enterprise of drama. While drama can be defined as a generic human activity not linked to any specific religious, moral, philosophical or ideological tradition, this discipline or activity when combined and infused with Christian content, in terms of motivation, subject matter and instructional or formational concerns, can be defined as being Christian drama.[14]

The work of the Religious Drama Society of Great Britain (RADIUS) has done much to establish a broad rationale and an underlying conception of the potential and importance of drama within church and the wider Christian influenced contexts of this country. Promoting the importance of drama that is informed by a Christian purview is one of the central aims of RADIUS. In its own words, RADIUS exists

> [t]o encourage drama which illuminates the human condition. It believes that the central point of reference for this purpose is Jesus Christ; but it recognizes that many contemporary dramatists do not share this view and welcomes all attempts to create a true dialogue between men in their social relationships, believing that this will make clearer man's relationship with God.[15]

The Development of my Own Writing

As I was beginning to develop my writing skills, I was very much influenced by the work of Paul Burbridge and Murray Watts. Burbridge and Watts' highly influential texts on Christian drama spurred me and many of my peers into our first youthful forays into creative dramatic writing. *Time to Act,*[16] *Lightning Sketches*[17] and *Red Letter Days*[18] became required reading for myself and my writing and performing peers within the Birmingham University Meth. Soc.[19]

Aside from offering a wealth of scripted material for public performances, Burbridge and Watts' books provided a much needed justification for such apparent reckless nonsense that was seen to be done in the name of Christ and Christian expression. Coming from a conservative Methodist evangelical background, I had imbibed a great deal of the implicit suspicion towards the dubious enterprise of "play acting." A non-conformist inspired holiness tradition of dutiful piety ensured that only those expressions of human activity which were perceived as being unequivocally efficacious and praiseworthy were justifiable in Christian terms. Burbridge and Watts provided a robust and stout defence for Christian drama, stating that:

> A lot of people have been brought up in a strict church tradition to regard drama as wrong. You notice that we say "Christian tradition" for the simple reason that we do not believe that genuine Christian tradition, least of all the Bible, condemns the performance of plays or sketches. But nonetheless church traditions of various kinds have opposed the theatre (justifiably in many cases, bearing in mind the corruption in theatres and acting troupes since time immemorial). This, however, is a separate issue. The nature of drama cannot be blamed for the abuses of actors, just as commerce cannot be held responsible for corrupt practices in the business world.[20]

The authors gave my peers and I much needed justification to transcend the restrictive church backgrounds from which many of us had emerged. If drama was not in itself inherently bad, then was there a positive rationale for engaging in this form of creative enterprise, save for the youthful desire to "show off" in front of our peers? Burbridge and Watts continue their case by stating that:

> Drama is a gift from God to help us explore the world, enjoy it, to be moved by suffering, to laugh at the funny side of life, to provoke ourselves and others to thought.[21]

Drama, as the authors remind us, has been an important element within the Christian tradition in Britain since the early mediaeval period.[22] They state that:

> The earliest English drama derives from the Latin mass of the middle ages. The simple refrains of the liturgy were elaborated first into dramatic dialogues between the officiating priests and then into playlets on the events in the life of Christ. Latin soon gave way to the vernacular and the result of this development was the many different cycles of mystery plays, some of which have been revived and are regularly performed today.[23]

Historical Developments

As Burbridge and Watts rightly surmise, one of the most significant developments in the role and the utility of drama within Christian liturgical and pedagogical practices arose within the context of the traditional mass during the Middle Ages. O. B. Hardison feels that the inherent embodied re-enactment of Christ's presence at the mass provided a natural setting for the development of drama within the context of the liturgical life of the church.[24] Hardison believes that a number of significant developments regarding the relationship between the role of the priest within the mass and the ecclesial dramatic intent inherent within this sacred rite arose in France around 850 CE.[25] Reflecting upon this period, and the role of mass as a repository for the development of drama within the church, Hardison writes:

> Without exception they present the mass as an elaborate drama with a definite role assigned to the participants and a plot whose ultimate significance is nothing less than a renewal of the whole plan of redemption through the re-creation of the life, death and resurrection of Christ.[26]

It is interesting to note that Hardison does not make any clear distinction between the utility of drama within the context of worship and the role of drama as a pedagogical device. In more recent times, there has been an ongoing discussion between the relationship between worship and learning. Often times, it has appeared that there is a fundamental divide between Christian educators, whose primary concerns are those associated with the process of teaching and learning, versus the liturgists who would want to detach any educational function from the role of worship in the life of the church.[27]

This dichotomy has been challenged in recent times by a number of North American scholars who have argued that we need to see worship and education as being more intimately linked. Debra Dean Murphy, for example, argues that the unhelpful dualisms between heart and head, intellect and emotions, propounded by the Greeks have led us to separate the educational function (*didache*) from the process of worship (*leitourgia*). This dichotomy often serves as one of the intellectual bases for the separation of learning from worship. It can be overcome, she argues, if we see these differing facets of the churches' life as being more intimately linked.[28] Robert K. Martin's perspective on the relationship between worship and education is, in many respects, even more radical than Murphy's, for he argues that not only should these differing aspects of the churches' mission be brought together, but we should conceive them as an inter-related and inter-penetrating dance.[29]

The mediaeval mystery play

While the role of drama within the sacred mass was often implicit and inci-
dental to the overall rationale and purpose of this liturgical re-enactment, its
primacy and educational importance becomes visible and intentional within
the mystery plays of the later Middle Ages. It is beyond the scope of his study
to mount an exhaustive investigation into the development, role and importance of the mediaeval mystery play to the role of drama in the church.

Rosemary Woolf argues that there is a complex relationship between
liturgical drama and the mediaeval mystery plays. She cautions against
the assumption that there is an axiomatic link between the former and
the latter.[30] According to Woolf, the origins of the mediaeval mystery play,
which can be dated to around the fourteenth century, were multifarious
in form and were conceived partly as an expression of liturgical embellishment and as a "propagandist concern to instruct the laity."[31]

Woolf charts the development of the mystery play from a loose set of
liturgical fragments (of the tenth century) to a more stylized and system-
atized structure whose collective elements might be described as resembling
a play.[32] Woolf describes some of the differing features of the mediaeval
mystery play, such as the difference between these models of Christian
drama and the more recognizable passion or nativity plays. The latter two
forms share a common focus upon one central, consistent narrative theme,
rather than the more disparate and eclectic structure of the mystery play.[33]
The mediaeval mystery plays address major theological themes such as the
incarnation, Christ's ministry, the passion and eschatology.[34]

Many scholars have understood the mystery play as a top-down control-
ling device to ensure doctrinal compliance and to provide harmless, non-
licentious entertainment for the hard-working and ill-educated laity. Woolf,
again, states that mystery plays offered some escape for the poor and were
viewed by religious authorities as more efficacious "than the frivolous pas-
times with which they would otherwise occupy themselves."[35]

A counter argument concerning the role and the relationship of mystery
plays and religious drama with the poor has been propounded by Claire
Sponsler.[36] Sponsler argues that through elaborate ritual of dress, role play
and covert action within the overarching framework of the religious drama,
poor people were able to often subvert the conventional quasi-authoritarian
constraints of the mediaeval church.[37]

The role of drama in Black religious experience

My brief assessment of the historical roots and development of drama
within the church has, hitherto, concentrated upon White European traditions. While there is no exhaustive literature detailing such developments

within Black majority ecclesial settings, it would be incorrect, however, to surmise that drama was absent from Black religious expression. With reference to our previous discussion on mediaeval mystery plays, it is interesting to note the adoption of this dramatic framework within the context of South African life. What has appeared to be a classical format of late mediaeval English sensibility has been contextually relocated within the South African experience by such exponents as the *Yiimimangaliso: The Mysteries*.[38] This South African version of a traditional English mystery play attempts to address contemporary socio-cultural and religious issues of that nation from within a striking traditional dramatic liturgical form.

Within the African Diaspora, the religious and theological developments within the life experiences of the disenfranchised Black working-class—who I have described as the voiceless[39]—have been accomplished by a variety of means. This study argues that dialogical drama can provide a creative and accessible means for further developments in a practical articulation of Black theology that will affirm and strengthen these people. While I am arguing for a self-conscious, deliberate structuring of dramatic material for the affirmation and empowering of the Black self, I would argue that drama has been one of the primary means by which Black people constructed a creative strategy of resistance to the de-humanizing tendencies of White supremacy over the past five hundred years.

Carnival and Masquerade

The dramatic impulse within Black Diasporan life can be seen within the historic and contemporary practice of carnival. The annual Notting Hill carnival (Bank Holiday weekend in August) in West London may have lost some of the socio-political sub-text that once defined its existence,[40] but it remains a potent symbol of Black resistance and socio-political positioning.

Carnival emerged in the Caribbean and the Americas as a codified form of resistance for Black slaves, who were permitted to celebrate once a year, as a rare act of indulgence by their slave masters.[41]

Black slaves used this opportunity of the relative freedom of carnival to design and construct elaborate costumes in order to engage in ostentatious forms of dramatic behaviour that affirmed their basic humanity while mimicking the brutal and hypocritical practices of their so-called Christian slave masters.[42]

The importance of carnival and the ritual of elaborate dress and disguise have become hugely important emblematic cultural constructs within Diasporan African contexts. Peter Van Koningsbruggen has identified the annual carnival in Trinidad as an essential cultural barometer for the quest for an authentic national identity for that island.[43]

The drama is inherent within the masks, role play, dance and communal acting that is resplendent in such celebrations as Bacchanal or Junkuno in Jamaica[44] or Vodun inspired practices in Haiti and North America.[45]

In contemporary Black Diasporan life the dramatic element of Black culture is evidenced not only in the modern incarnation of the Notting Hill carnival, but is also visible in such forms of cultural production as dub-poetry, rap and hip hop,[46] calypso,[47] and dancehall music.[48]

The dramatic impulse within religio-cultural contexts can be seen in the development of Rasta practices. Daniel Middleton's interview with Ras Benjamin Zephaniah in Gossai and Murrell's book *Religion, Culture and Tradition in the Caribbean*,[49] reminds us that theology within African contexts has always possessed an oral quality and dimension to its discourse. Zephaniah, a practising Rasta, performs a number of his poems and articulates the political agenda that is inherent within his work.[50] Middleton says of Zephaniah's work:

> [he] sees his poetry (among other things) as "an alternative news broadcast"…they demonstrate his fascination with and understanding of Judeo-Christian Scriptures.[51]

The Drama of Black Worship

The invocation of the spirit within Black worship, fused with a decorative and expansive display of "theatricality," has been one of the defining hallmarks of Black religiosity, in which ritualized drama has played a central part. Robert Beckford offers a carefully constructed Black British Pentecostal perspective on this creative dynamic in which informal drama is an important means by which the liberative impulse of Black life is expressed.[52] Dale P. Andrews notes the inherent dynamism of Black religiosity, in which the dramatic encounter with the "otherness of God" is often a common feature, particularly in the area of worship and preaching.[53]

Anthony Pinn's highly influential book *Terror and Triumph* highlights the evocative power of drama within Black religious and liturgical life.[54] Pinn contends that the elaborative, decorative display that is often exemplified in Black religiosity (many Black Christians still remain wedded to reserving their "best clothes" for Sunday worship) was a conscious attempt to create an embodied text on which to construct their own quest for "complex subjectivity."[55] Put simply, Black bodies, so often degraded, de-humanized and destroyed by White power and oppression, became the site for decorative dress and complex human emotions and expression, in order to assert the humanity and subjectivity of the Black self.

On a personal level, I witnessed the "drama" of my parents preparing themselves to attend church every Sunday during my formative years in Bradford, in the West Yorkshire region of the UK. My father, in particular, is one who loves to wear a variety of bespoke suits to worship. When I was much younger, I struggled to appreciate the significance of my father wearing a variety of hand-made suits to church, when many of the White men who attended the same church, who earned far more than he did, were content to dress casually. It has only been in hindsight that I realized that my father's sartorial eloquence was his attempt to transcend the humble position of his birth and the urban drudg-ery of the industrial engineering works where he toiled six days a week wearing a drab overall. Drama in its broadest sense (if not in the more narrow discipline of the deliberate acting out of a dramatic script) is endemic within Black reli-gious life, whether within the realm of Black oral traditions such as preaching[56] or more generally in Black worship.[57]

Reformation and Post-Reformation Ideas

The return to a more literate, cognitive approach to worship and learning arising from the Reformation led to a widespread prohibition against drama within the church. The rejection of the elaborate pageantry and liturgical embellishment reflective of Catholicism led to an increasing dependence upon cognitive, literate forms of Christian worship and nurture, at the expense of more affective and visual forms of expression.[58] The popular mythology of the Puritan regime in England between 1549 and 1558 has become almost cemented in the psyche of the nation. The Puritans' appeals against the licen-tious and frivolous nature of all forms of entertainment have somehow come to be enshrined as the normative position of the Protestant Church in Britain. Within the British Methodist Church, for example, the popular image of the Primitive Methodists has been taken to exemplify the default position of the whole Methodist movement since the eighteenth century.[59]

The constricting and minimalist legacy of this reformed movement (learn-ing happens only via the intellect, and the emotions and other senses are downplayed) has been challenged in more recent times by a number of scholars, including Gerard Sloyan,[60] John Westerhoff[61] and Byron Ander-son.[62] Each of these scholars has asserted that a more holistic and richer appreciation of God's presence in the midst of human experience will be gained when both the cognitive and the affective, the intellect and the emo-tions, are engaged in worship and learning contexts.[63]

Drama Returns to the Fore

The growing challenge of modernity in the latter half of the nineteenth cen-tury onwards led to a growth in the popularity of both liberal theology and liberal models of Christian education.[64] This transatlantic movement, particularly in terms of educational method, had proponents on both sides of the English-speaking world. In the United States, the likes of William Rainey Harper, John Dewey and George Albert Coe[65] were matched by their British counterparts, which included such figures as Basil Yeaxlee and Hamilton Archibald.[66]

A significant player in the attention and growth given to Christian drama was the Religious Drama Society of Great Britain (RADIUS). RADIUS' history dates back to the 1930s and the sponsorship of Dr George Bell, the then Dean of Canterbury. Bell started the Canterbury Festival and invited Poet Laureate John Masefield to write a poetic drama. Masefield's drama was entitled "The Coming of Christ." Following Masefield's work was the first production of T. S. Eliot's poetic drama "Murder in the Cathedral."[67] The play was a commission for the Canterbury Festival in June 1935. The work, one of only six Eliot plays, reflects his gradual transition from agnostic to Christian, and explores Thomas Becket's commitment to the will of God over everything.[68]

From the 1940s onwards, there was a growing awareness of the needs of learners, stimulated by an increased engagement with developmental psychology and influenced by the challenges presented by modernity. This led to increased experimentation in the educational methods deployed in Christian education.[69]

The groundbreaking research of Ronald Goldman in developmental psychology led to a wholesale reassessment of the role of the Bible in the Christian education and nurture of children and young people.[70] Goldman contended (controversial at the time) that too many children and young people were being exposed to the Bible too early in their emotional and intellectual development, as they had yet to master the forms of abstract, metaphorical thinking that would enable them to handle the often difficult themes and concepts in the Bible.[71] Goldman states:

> I suggest that it is impossible to teach the Bible as such to children much before adolescence, and that we must look for another approach which offers a more realistic alternative to our present ills.[72]

That search for an alternative approach or method for Christian nurture led many to seek solace in Christian drama. The emphasis placed upon Christian drama as a means of assisting young people and children in their growth in faith can be seen in two publications from the 1960s. In Elizabeth Lane's *A Pageant of Bible Plays*,[73] the author states that:

> The whole collection of plays is intended for use in Day School and Sunday School; also for any other group of young people. Although each one can be performed on the stage, they can also be used in the normal Scripture lesson, and in this case, they will provide a good basis for discussion and help the books of the Bible to "come alive."[74]

I shall comment on the plays themselves in the next section of this chapter, but at this point, it is interesting to note that in 1965 a Christian dramatist could still assume that their work would be equally acceptable in school in addition to a church setting.

Margaret Love's *Let's Dramatise*[75] is, perhaps, more reflective of the post-Goldman paradigm shift in how Christian educators presented biblical and Christian material to children and young people in the latter half of the 1960s. In her introduction the author writes:

> Dramatisation is an essential teaching technique, and Christian education in particular cries out for its inclusion in the programme. Teaching starts with experience. There are real experiences of life. There are contrived experiences, specially planned. And there are the experiences entered into through imagination. That is where drama comes into its own.[76]

A dominant theme in both publications, which is replicated in a number of texts of a more modern vintage, is the attempt to write drama as a form of Christian apologetic. The scripts seem to be written in order to defend the idea of believing in God, or to remind the reader/listener of God's essential goodness. Undoubtedly, given this general theme that runs throughout the scripts, one is not surprised to detect a distinct evangelistic sub-text at work in both books. It would appear that in response to the growing march of secularism that appeared all dominant and triumphant in 1960s Britain, some Christian educators were attempting to stem this onward march by means of Christian drama. Although I have made these comments with respect to these two texts, I should point out that neither can be said to be overtly proselytizing, dogmatic or didactic either in the theology they espouse or in the educational methods they employ.

Theological Themes at Play in Christian Drama

The following section is an assessment of the theological themes and content present in a number of Christian drama works either in print or in electronic form. Given the plethora of Christian drama texts that exist, it is impossible to provide an exhaustive survey of all of them. So in order to make this survey manageable, I have decided to confine my assessment and analysis to a number of newer, more modern examples and will look for generic themes[77] and concerns that permeate the various Christian drama texts under investigation.[78]

Using a Black hermeneutic (or interpretative framework)

When people are confronted with any form of data or information, in order to make sense of that which confronts us requires that we engage in some form of interpretation. The process of interpretation can be undertaken in light of a number of factors or concerns. The interpretative process may be undertaken with an eye upon historical issues. Alternatively, one may want to interpret information from a socio-economic or political perspective. Again, one may want to emphasize gender or class concerns. The interpretative framework I have chosen to use, consistent with the concerns I have outlined in Chapter 1, is that of a Black hermeneutic. As my task is to construct a method for articulating, doing and learning Black theology by means of drama, I want to assess these pieces in light of the concerns, issues or concepts that are central to Black theology.

My assessment of these various resources may seem particularly harsh on occasions. I am sure that many of the authors whose work I have critiqued will no doubt claim that I have done their work a disservice in terms of the comments I have made. In my defence, I would want to counter any likely challenge to my contentions by making two brief points.

First, I am not judging these pieces on their merits or otherwise as either good or bad pieces of drama. I am not a drama critic or a literary specialist, and do not consider it my place to make those kinds of judgement. Similarly, I am not making any judgement as to whether these texts are worth buying or using. The individual consumer of such work can make up their own mind on that matter. Neither am I making any form of judgement on the original intention or aim of the author(s) in terms of what they hoped their piece of work would achieve.

Second, my assessment of these resources is based upon my own subjectivity as a Black religious scholar. I am analysing these texts in light of the concerns and issues that affect me and other Black people of African and Caribbean descent, particularly those who live in the African Diaspora. I am sure that the authors will claim that their work should not be judged on these grounds for these scripts were not written to bear this kind of scrutiny or analysis.

In response I will say that as there was no statement on these texts signalling that Black people should not or could not use them, then I am correct in assuming that these pieces were written in the belief that they could be used by a variety of people. In fact, the pieces do not make specific claim as to whom they are addressed or for whom they have been written. It should be noted that they do not say that White people can use them either (even though the authors are most probably White).

My concern is to design, create and implement resources that will enable Black, often subjugated individuals and communities to assert their innate personhood and authentic selves in a world that often denies them these basic rights. With reference to my work and ministry, I have analysed these texts in order to assess their utility in assisting me to achieve my stated aims, to which reference has just been made.

Defining a Black Hermeneutic

Central to a Black hermeneutic or interpretative framework are the following concerns or issues:

1. Black experience—the individual and collective concerns and reality of Black people.[79] I have outlined some of these issues and concerns in Chapter 1.
2. Black history and narrative. What is the content and process of Black story over the past 500 years?[80]
3. A Black re-interpretation of the Bible.[81]
4. Analysing Black culture(s) and their various forms for an indication of Black selfhood, identity and the substance and reality of being human (ontology).[82]

These issues are not exhaustive, and a more detailed analysis of the themes and content of Black theology will be made in the following chapter. At this juncture, however, it is sufficient for me to alert the reader to some of the perspectives that will inform my analysis of the following Christian drama texts. While there is much one could say about these various pieces, the overarching concern that emerged from my analysis was that of context and particularity.

Context-less

What the various Christian drama scripts I have analysed have in common is an absence of any meaningful context or particularity. By this, I mean that the various scripts, aside from mentioning the setting in the initial instructions, assume a notion of general universalism in the speech patterns and subjectivity of the characters in the narrative. Reading the various pieces, there is no sense of the particularity of these people. Who are they and what do they look like?

In fairness to the various authors, they will no doubt say that they are writing for a broad constituency, and it is simply impracticable to insert culturally specific gestures, idioms or other forms of ethnic or class identifiers that might give a clear steer or indication as to the identity of the people who populate their scripts. In many respects, this generic universalism makes good marketing sense and has a clear theological grounding and rationale. It allows dramatic writers to create pieces that can notionally work in a wide variety of contexts, with the emphasis upon best practice production values and less upon particularity or social analysis.

A theology of homogeneity and unity

The theology of homogeneity runs deep within Christianity. The injunction of the writer to the Galatians (3:28) that in Christ there is no Jew or Greek, or slave or free, remains a powerful theological and societal ideal for which we all dare to dream. Biblical scholars such as Esler have investigated the attempts to surmount the seemingly endemic differences of ethnic and cultural particularity that would have faced the author of the book to the Galatians.[83]

Inderjit Bhogal, the first Black President of the British Methodist Conference, drawing upon the work of Balasuriya,[84] constructs an inclusive ideal for human interdependence based upon the notion of a "table for all" that is the embodied ideal of the Eucharist or The Lord's Supper.[85] Bhogal sees within Christ's invitation to come to his table to be fed, a model for a radical form of inclusivity that transcends all ethnic, religious, cultural, ideological, gender and class based differences.

It is my suspicion that these dramatic authors, albeit in a sub-conscious, pragmatic marketing vein, have drawn upon the language and theology of homogeneity in Christ in order to write in a somewhat abstract and context-less manner.

By sublimating the reality of contextual particularity, whether in terms of class, gender, ethnicity, class or economics, the various authors are able to address seemingly more generic, spiritual and theological concerns that would appear to transcend the differences I cited a few moments previously.[86]

This form of sublimation is not new, of course. Despite the deeply conscious embodied and contextual reality that was and is the incarnation, Christianity quickly jettisoned the desire to locate its concerns amongst the material and physical in favour of the abstract and the spiritual.[87] The church has learned to ignore the material needs and the embodied nature of human subjectivity, particularly if those human subjects are Black or people of colour.[88]

Problematic sameness

There are a number of problems with this commitment to transcending cultural, ethnic, gender and class differences. My chief problem with this theological construct and, as a corollary, the creative manifestation of generic universalism is its spectacular failure when scrutinized through the lens of Black historicity. A Black hermeneutical reading of these scripts simply reminds me of the hypocrisy of White supremacy.

Black theology came into existence as a response to the failure of White power to live out the very theology it had so carefully constructed from the earliest days of the first Christian communities in the Mediterranean. Whether in its self-conscious political form from the 1960s onwards,[89] or in its more implicit folk religion incarnated through the lives of Black slaves and subjugated Africans living under the yolk of colonialism and segregation,[90] Black theology continues, for the most part, to be a response to the de-humanizing tendencies of White hegemony.

One would be hard pressed to find much evidence for the transcending of difference as evidenced in the practice of White power when it collided with the existential experiences of Black people. So how can we ignore difference? How can we say that it should be ignored, for we are all one? In theory yes, but in practice, most definitely no.

W. E. B. Dubois in his groundbreaking book, *The Souls of Black Folk*, argued that the problem of the twentieth century would be the "color line."[91] The twentieth century came and went; we, the collective mass that is humanity, are no nearer dealing with the "color line" over a century since Dubois wrote those prescient words.

My comments may appear churlish when applied to the seemingly harmless enterprise of Christian drama, but I believe that the generic universalism of these pieces is indicative of a larger, quite pernicious, malaise that is presently exercising the minds of scholars in a number of arenas.

The unnamed power of Whiteness

In all the Christian drama sketches I have analysed, there is no attempt to locate the various characters in the scripts within any cultural or ethnic context. I have already given my reasons why the authors may feel this is unnecessary or even undesirable. As I have indicated in a previous work, this form of generic universalism (all characters speak in a universal language and are not identified by class, geography or ethnicity) only seeks to mask the assumption that these people are White.[92]

In more recent times, a branch of scholarship entitled "Critical White Studies" has begun the task of naming and unmasking the privileged construct that is "Whiteness." Whiteness operates as an overarching construct, which assumes a central place in all epistemological and cultural forms of production, thereby relegating other positions or perspectives as "other."

A relatively simple means of asserting this truth is to look at the world of literature. My sense of Black consciousness was first aroused when I began to study for my A levels. I had chosen to undertake a course in English literature. On commencing the course I was struck at once by the universal "Whiteness" of all the literature on view within the syllabus. A few months into the course I discovered the writing of Chinua Achebe. His landmark novel *Things Fall Apart*[93] was described as a brilliant African novel. Achebe writes about the social and cultural world of which he is a part. It was soon made clear to me that Achebe was *only* an African writer. His work was important, for it shed light upon a particular community and cultural reality in modern day Africa. I was intrigued that Achebe's work was limited in this way, due to the precise milieu in which he was located and the particularity of his reflections upon that specific context. And yet the same limitations and parameters were not placed upon Jane Austin and her work, which I had to endure for the two years of that course. Why was the precise, particular social and cultural milieu of Austin worthy of universal application and celebration? The world in which she is located, and which serves as the basis for her work, is no more universal and transcendent of context than that of Achebe's. Austin's world is universal because it is located within the wider framework of Whiteness. Austin's Whiteness makes her universal.

Jacqueline Battalora has challenged some of the universal notions of Whiteness in her analysis of North American society.[94] Robert Beckford, one of the leading Black British theologians, has also turned his attention to challenging the unnamed privileges and power of Whiteness.[95] Similarly Womanist religious educator Lynne Westfield challenges the inherent, unnamed privilege of Whiteness when, drawing on the fiction of Walter Mosley and his main protagonist's (Fearless Jones) encounter with a White man, she writes:

> White people still live in an isolated culture of privilege that allows them little to no contact with Black people.[96]

The unspoken assumption of all these texts is that the characters and protagonists of the drama are White. A generic universal text does not need to name its particularity. Rather, it simply assumes a normative position for the unspoken Whiteness, by resorting to generic patterns of "standard received English" and addressing abstract, context-less concerns that affect all people.

My approach to the literary task of writing Christian drama with a view to elucidating some of the central tenets of Black theology has been informed by the theory and practice of post-colonial discourse. Within the arena of literary studies, post-colonial theory has challenged the centralist positionality of Whiteness, and has initiated a process of "de-centring."

De-centring is a process of changing the point of focus for the articulation of experience and the production of knowledge. In this new epistemological enterprise, the initial point of departure is no longer the centre, but a subversive and systematic shift to the margins.[97]

Apologetics

The majority of the Christian drama resources I have investigated reject any recognition of contextual concerns that might be identified with particular communities in favour of a more evangelical concern for doctrinal exposition and general apologetics.

The main differentiation between a US and the UK perspective on the substantive theology that underpins Christian drama lies in the preoccupation with doctrinal issues within the North American context and the emphasis upon apologetics within the United Kingdom. The difference in their theological preoccupations may lie in the process of secularization, which is a live issue within many western democracies. It has been argued that religion continues to play a much more vibrant and self-conscious role within the body politic of the United States.[98] The relevance or viability of Christianity is not a major question for theologians and religious scholars within the US. Conversely, within the United Kingdom where church attendance is decreasing and the viability of the church appears in serious doubt,[99] scholars such as Marsh[100] and Lynch[101] are attempting to map out a future trajectory for the Christian faith that will be relevant in our postmodern, post-atheist and post-organized religious context.

The apparent concentration on apologetics within a number of Christian drama texts published in the UK reflects, perhaps, a desire to "win the argument" for the reality and relevance of the Christian faith.

Apologetics is often defined as the rational defence of the given tradition of the Christian faith. Given the rise of science and new forms of knowledge and truth (epistemology), the Christian faith has been challenged on all sides by a number of competing philosophies and ideas about the nature and intent of human existence. In response to these challenges, the Christian Church has often engaged in apologetics in order that the Christian faith can adequately respond to the various movements and developments in human rationality.[102] Mervin Willshaw offers a helpful corrective to this traditional and commonplace perspective on Christian apologetics.[103]

Dealing with the reality of difference

I have stated, at an earlier juncture in this chapter, that it is not my intention to belittle the quality of these Christian drama scripts. Many of them are very ingenious and imaginative ways for exploring Christian faith. At one level, I can appreciate the desire to want to write in a generic, universal fashion in order to address theological issues and concerns that affect us all. Emmanuel Lartey reminds us that juxtaposed with the particularity and sense of difference that is inherent within human subjectivity there is a clear sense of our innate sameness as human beings. In some ways we are all alike, in other respects we are like some others and yet in another sense we are unique.[104]

One of the enduring strengths of Christianity is its commitment to oneness and unity. The biblical and theological motifs of "One body" in Christ and the unity and diversity within the Body of Christ are significant emotional and psychological templates on which a good deal of ecclesial life is based. The radical inclusivity that is at the heart of the Gospel[105] is a challenge to move beyond the endemic insularity that separates "us" from "them."[106]

Black theology remains no less committed to this theological imperative to be one, but recognizes the deep fissures and power imbalances that make such pronouncements, no matter how worthy, as nothing more than cheap, hollow rhetoric if not accompanied by structural reform and the empowerment of the poor. James Cone, the founding father of the modern, political conception of Black theology, attacks the simplistic notion of the colour-blindness and alleged impartiality of God when he writes:

> In a racist society, God is never color-blind. To say God is color-blind is analogous to saying that God is blind to justice, to right and wrong, to good and evil. Certainly this is not the picture of God revealed in the Old and New Testaments. Yahweh takes sides.[107]

The God who takes sides and identifies with the poor and oppressed, particularly those whose very skin pigmentation has singled them out for oppression and subjugation, is not one who is overly concerned with correct doctrine or defending the status quo of the church.[108]

In popular parlance, it is often said that one cannot "put the Genie back in the bottle." Notions of White supremacy and the racialized stratification of humanity, deeply embedded within Christianity since the formative period in the development of the faith,[109] and in many respects, perfected during the Enlightenment,[110] cannot be overturned by pretending that they do not exist.

A Black Theological Perspective on Christian Drama—the Initial Attempt

I have analysed a number of Christian drama texts using a Black hermeneutic. In this, the final section of this chapter, I want to highlight my initial attempt at creating an approach to Black theology by means of Christian drama. The following piece was written for a group of young Black people in London. The script was written with this group in mind. It was my attempt to illustrate the dramatic elements of African Caribbean religio-cultural life in Britain through the prism of a piece of drama.

In this piece, I want to look at the different positions and values adopted by various people within Diasporan Black British communities. I have sought to do this by way of constructing a fictional social gathering—a party, or in Black speak, a "dance," at which a variety of people and voices are present. This piece was a precursor to my later efforts at combining the central tenets of Black theology within a dramatic format.

An example of this new approach

The following script was used with a group of Black young men in their late teens. The group consisted of ten people. All members of the group were born in the UK. Half of the group lived with one parent (four with a mother and one with a father). The other half of the group lived with both parents. All but one of the parents was born in the UK. All members of the group were pursuing further and higher education in a number of local educational establishments.

THE NEW ARRIVAL

The scene: we are inside a sitting room. The room is full of people. The house belongs to a Jamaican family, who are celebrating the christening of their child. There are lots of family and friends all milling around. Enter a large commanding woman who walks to where the cot is situated.

Woman 1: [*Peering down at the baby*] Is wha' de baby call' again?

Mother: Johanthro…

Woman 1: [*Indignant*] What?

Mother: Johanthro.

Woman 1: [*To another woman*] Yu hear dis? Johan… What 'im name again?

Mother: Johanthro… It's an African name.

Woman 1: [*Struggling with the name*] Jo…han…thro? But what de blouse an' skirt kin' a name dat? Johantro? Yu may as well call' de pickney John Crow.

Uncle: [*Taking issue with Woman 1*] But wha' mek yu so miserable hi? De pickney have a nice name… John… What 'im call' again?

Mother: [*Fed up*] Johanthro…

Uncle: Yes… Me like dat name… Johan… Johan… [*Gives up*]… Lovely name.

[MOTHER *is called away by someone in another room.*]

OTHER PERSON: [*Calling out, but unseen*] Delores... Delroy wants a word.

MOTHER: [*Looking at baby*] I'll be back in a minute, Jo... [*To* UNCLE]... Watch Jo Jo for me, Uncle.

[*Exit* MOTHER...*all the other characters begin to peer over the cot and stare at the baby.*]

UNCLE: Johan... What 'im name again?

AUNT & WOMAN 1: Johanthro!

UNCLE: Foolish fe true... [*Looking a bit closer*]... But what a way de pickney ugly hi?

WOMAN 1: Me never wan' sey, but really and truly; dis de pickney noh pretty at all.

AUNT: De fadder mus' a living monkey.

[*All three begin to laugh...they stare a bit closer.*]

AUNT: Yu remember when Leroy born?

UNCLE: Who Leroy again?

AUNT: Fe your eldes' bwoy. Yu noh rememba'?

UNCLE: [*Suddenly realizing*] Ah oh... Me forget 'bout Leroy... Me cyan never rememba' fe dat bwoy name.

WOMAN 1: No wonder 'im curse yu so bad...

UNCLE: [*To* WOMAN 1] Quiet yu'self 'oman, noh trouble me.

AUNT: Leroy noh so pretty at all. Me rememba' de preacher man bawl tears when 'im see de pickney. Him so 'fraid, him nearly drop de baby.

UNCLE: But wait...Wha' yu a sey? Yu a call my bwoy ugly?

WOMAN 1: Jus' like 'im fadder. Ugly as sin.

UNCLE: [*Angry, squaring up to the woman*] But... Yu fiesti...

[*Baby begins to cry...*]

WOMAN 1: Yu see wha' yu miserable self do now? Yu mek de baby cry.

[*MOTHER runs back into the room...she goes to the baby.*]

MOTHER: [*Comforting the baby*] There there... Mummy is here now... [*Looking around at the older people*]... You should know better... Upsetting poor little Jo Jo like that.

[*The other three bow their heads in shame.*]

EVERYBODY ELSE: I sorry.

[*Enter another character. She walks directly towards the party standing around.*]

WOMAN 2: [*Mouth is full of food*] Bwoy, dis chicken taste good.

WOMAN 1: Dat's all yu good for... Fill fe yu belly. Yu craven wretch.

WOMAN 2: Sticks and stones may break my bones, but names will never harm me... Yu have any more a dat chicken? Fe my belly still empty.

EVERYONE ELSE: Craven...

WOMAN 2: [*Looking at the cot*] Dis de pickney?

WOMAN 1: No, it a elephant...

WOMAN 2: [*Talking to the baby*] Cutchy coo... What de chil' call' again?

MOTHER: Johanthro.

WOMAN 2: What?

EVERYONE ELSE: Johanthro.

WOMAN 2: [*Slight pause*] Funny name fe give de baby... Yu know somet'ing? Fe 'im name soun' like John Crow.

MOTHER: [*Angry*] Will you shut up about my baby's name... It's an African name. I want my child to be proud of his African heritage. To know where he came from, and be proud of his history and culture... Now I don't want to hear another word said against that name, do you hear me?

[*Everyone is silent...MOTHER is called away again.*]

MOTHER: [*Looking at the cot*] There there, Jo Jo, I'll be back in a minute… [*Looking at everyone else*]… And don't any of you go upsetting the child, you hear me…

WOMAN 1: [*Looking around*] Dis tek me back yu know. Me rememba' when Ivan christen… Fe my mudder bawl some eye water dat day.

AUNT: It noh seem two minute since Delores little baby 'erself. Bwoy dem pickney grow up fas' nowadays.

UNCLE: Too fas' sometimes.

[*They all look down at the baby again.*]

WOMAN 2: 'im favour Uncle Myrel.

UNCLE: No sah… Myrel noh so ugly.

WOMAN 1: 'im favour Lionel… Ruby eldes' bwoy…

AUNT: Who Lionel?

WOMAN 1: De one who gwan a Panama and dead… Him was a lovely bwoy. So mannersable. How com' all de good ones die so young eh?

WOMAN 2: De lard only know… [*Looking at the baby again*]… Yu t'ink 'im go'n grow up to be like Uncle Myrel?

UNCLE: Noh put de mout' 'pon de pickney. Yu want 'im grow to be an ol' tief like Myrel? Me wouldn't wish dat 'pon me worse enemy.

AUNT: [*Nudging UNCLE*] Yu betta' hol' yu tongue… Look who a come from over deyso?… Don't look.

[*UNCLE and everyone else looks.*]

AUNT: Yu deaf or somet'ing? Me sey noh look…

WOMAN 1: It noh Myrel.

WOMAN 2: Is what dat ol' tiefing brute a do ya so?

UNCLE: Probably come fe de same reason yu come… Fe fill up 'im belly. Wherever free food dey; dey yu go'n fin' Myrel, wid 'im mout' full up a chicken.

[*Enter MYREL. The others go silent and pretend not to notice him. MYREL peers into the cot.*]

MYREL: [*Looking at the baby*] What a beautiful baby.

[*WOMAN 1 and AUNT cough loudly.*]

MYREL: [*Talking to the baby*] Hello darling... Yu know me? Me is yu Uncle Myrel... Yes, Uncle Myrel... [*To the others*]... Yu noh t'ink de baby favour me? 'im have fe mi nose.

UNCLE: Yu talk too much foolishness. De pickney noh favour yu at all.

MYREL: [*Looking again*] Is what de baby call'?

WOMAN 2: Johanthro...

MYREL: Come again?

EVERYONE ELSE: Johanthro.

WOMAN 2: [*All knowledgable*] It an African name... Delores wan' de chil' fe know 'im African heritage and all dat kin' a t'ing.

MYREL: A lovely name fe a pretty baby... Johanthro... Me like dat. [*Looking down at the baby again*]... Hello Johanthro. Yu is a lucky little bwoy. Everyone love yu. Yu Aunt, Uncle, Sister, even me. Yu be good and bring dem credit when yu get bigger, yu hear me?

[*Re-enter MOTHER...as she is walking forward WOMAN 1 walks ahead to meet her...talking to her aside.*]

WOMAN 1: [*To MOTHER*] Yu see who over deyso? It noh yu ol' tiefing Uncle. Who sey 'im can come?

MOTHER: I did.

WOMAN 1: Yu!

MOTHER: He's the baby's Uncle. He's part of the family. He has as much right to be here as anyone else.

[*MOTHER and WOMAN 1 rejoin the main party.*]

MOTHER: [*Looking down into the cot*] Hello Jo Jo...isn't he pretty?

[*All the others begin to murmur. MOTHER begins to push the pram off stage, leaving the group behind.*]

MOTHER: [*Talking to the baby*] That's a good Jo Jo… Smile for Mummy…
Wave bye bye to your aunts and uncles… [*Looking up at the group*]… Time
for his feed. I'll bring him back later on… See ya.

[*Exit* MOTHER, *with pram. There is silence. All the people in the group
look sad.*]

UNCLE: [*Sniffing*] I love dat liccle baby yu see…

AUNT: Children is a blessing.

WOMAN 1: [*Begins to cry. Pulls out a handkerchief and blows her nose loudly*]
Me wan' go to de toilet… [*Blows her nose again*]…

[*Exit* WOMAN 1…*all the other people in group look at each other.*]

WOMAN 2: Me see it, but me don't believe it. Me never know sey, she
coulda cry…

MYREL: People do all kind t'ing when liccle baby involve.

[*More silence…a few of the characters are sniffing loudly.*]

UNCLE: [*Still sniffing*] [*To* MYREL] Yu wan' play a game a domino?

MYREL: Yeah man…let's go.

[*Exit* UNCLE *and* MYREL…*leaving only* AUNT *and* WOMAN 2 *remaining.*]

AUNT: Funny how liccle baby like dat mek yu feel ol' and young all at dat
same time…

WOMAN 2: [*Pregnant pause*] Yu want anodder drink?

AUNT: Fe my mout' well dry…Come.

Reflections on the Drama

One of the challenges facing Black theologians and cultural commentators
is the necessity to develop a more honest and holistic view of Black cultures and the practices that exist within various Black communities. Too
often, Black scholars (myself included) have concentrated our efforts (quite
rightly, for the most part) on the external challenges that have confronted
us, such as racism for example, with less emphasis being given to the internal issues and struggles that exist within our own communities.

For example, when seeking to describe and illustrate Black community living, great emphasis has been placed on the examples of solidarity and community. The many examples of homogeneity or sameness have been highlighted. This is particularly the case when scholars have spoken about Black and Black majority churches.[111]

Our tendency to view Black communities as monolithic has meant that the diverse range of experiences and values that exist within the overall whole tends to be either downplayed or ignored altogether. I have addressed some aspects of this tendency to mythologize or romanticize aspects of Black culture in a previous book.[112]

On occasions, there is a type of hierarchy of "Blackness" in Black communities, where some people are judged as belonging in a more complete fashion than others. There are many Black people who have been accused of not "really being Black" or not being "Black enough."[113]

The sketch makes extensive use of Jamaican patois, which operates as a form of signifying, alerting us to the subversive and complex positionality of Black language when used within a Black sub-cultural setting.[114] In using this script with the group, I was interested in exploring the use of language amongst these African Caribbean young people, all of whom were in their late teens. To what extent does Jamaican patois function as a legitimizing code for Black self-authentication? It was interesting to note that some members of the group seemed more at ease with the language than others.

For some, this linguistic code operated as a form of familial remembering, reminded them of grandparents and older relatives, but did not function to any great extent in their daily operations. For others, the use of patois became a signifying code to alert their peers and White authority to their position with regards to the cultural and societal mainstream in British life. The attitude of the young people to the use of language in the script echoes many of the findings of Sewell's empirical work with a group of Black young men in London, and their general attitude to White authority.[115]

Theological Concerns

As I engaged with the group, having performed the sketch on six occasions over several hours, I was struck by the sense of a dialectic tension in the discourse that emerged from our conversations. Many in the group felt both attracted to and repulsed by many of the characters in the drama. When I asked why, two individuals stated that the people were "too argumentative" and "embarrassing."

I began to explore with the group what issues they felt were present in that social setting of the christening party? Most of the group felt there was a high degree of animosity and jealousy. When I asked if they saw this setting as a constructive or optimistic one, eight of the group replied negatively. The setting was not a positive depiction of African Caribbean people. When I asked if they felt there was anything that might be seen as redemptive or transformative about this scene, again most of the group (eight out of ten) said "no."

For the most part, this group did not perceive this setting as a redemptive one. I encouraged the group to look at the passages concerning the Israelites in exile (Numbers and Deuteronomy) and the accounts of early Christian communities in Acts and in the Pauline letters. I asked for their opinion on the bickering and arguments within these respective faith communities. What parallels could they see between the group of Black people in the drama and the Jewish and Christian communities from the Bible?

Interestingly, most of the group were far more tolerant and understanding of the biblical communities than of the group in the drama. The Black people in the drama reminded these young men of the unhelpful schisms and rancour within Black communities in Britain. The divide between the "righteous" members of the party and Uncle Myrel, the archetypal rogue and "sinner" who is distanced and judged by the "elect," mirrors Robert Beckford's concerns of particular aspects of Black Christianity in Britain and its restrictive self-serving brand of faith that seeks to engage only those who are saved.[116] In an earlier work, Beckford addresses the ministry and praxis of two prominent Black churches (within the Pentecostal tradition) in London. He outlines some of the essential features of a constricted form of hermeneutics. One that is unable to bridge the gap between the structural socio-political concerns that exert a disproportionate hold over those on the margins of the church and society and those who are "saved" within the faith community.[117]

The majority of these young men (from a variety of Black church traditions) were very much influenced by a common feature of Black spirituality within Black Diasporan life; namely the quest for holiness.[118] This form of holiness is exemplified in the desire to be set-aside for God and God's purposes alone, which is manifested in the constant call to reject all worldly, ungodly vices and corrupting influences.

These Black young men quickly sided with the other characters in the drama, over and against the figure of Uncle Myrel. There was no "hermeneutic of suspicion" in terms of Myrel's estrangement from the rest of the group. In response to this observation, I asked the group why they were prepared to condemn Myrel purely on the testimony of the other members of the party? After some thought, three members of the group admitted that they had assumed that the other members were being entirely truthful. Further conversation enabled the group to reflect upon the times when they had been privy to or had participated in the mis-reporting of events of another person. Can the motivations and veracity of people be assumed?

Through this prolonged encounter, the notion of subjectivity, positionality and context as hermeneutical devices for reading and re-reading texts were explored—key concepts in the development of Black theology.

The Incarnation as a Black Theological Motif

Perhaps the most striking theme that emerged from the conversation with this group of Black men was that of the incarnation. This theme emerged from the final performance of the drama. By this point in the proceedings, the young men were very familiar with the script and had begun to improvise with the written text.

In response to this final performance, I asked the group for their comments on the changing dynamics in the drama. What brought the drama to life? How is this context transformed and resolved? After some discussion in pairs, the various members of the group felt that the presence of the baby (Johanthro) had exerted a significant influence upon all the protagonists in the drama.

It was the birth of the baby and his christening that had brought the various members of the community to this context in the first instance. Johanthro's presence also enabled a number of the characters to reflect upon their own life experiences and heritage. Johanthro becomes the catalyst for changes in behaviour and attitude. His birth, and the subsequent party, provides the occasion for Myrel to return to the community, and while Myrel's presence is not greeted with approval, nor is he reconciled with his peers, he is, nevertheless, present within that social setting.

The comments of the young men offered an interesting parallel with the emotions displayed by the aged Simeon and Anna on their meeting with the infant Jesus (Luke 2:25–38).

First and second generation Black theologians have focused a great deal of scholarly attention on Christological issues. The works of James Cone and Jacquelyn Grant, for example, have examined the implications of Jesus' location amongst the agrarian poor of Galilee, for the existential selfhood and liberative agenda of Black people in the twentieth century.[119]

The theological and philosophical ground on which Black Liberation theology has established its connection with the "Jesus of History" has been by means of its identification with the very context in which Jesus was born and nurtured. James Cone writes:

> I begin by asserting once more that *Jesus was a Jew*. It is on the basis of the soteriological meaning of the particularity of his Jewishness that theology must affirm the Christological significance of Jesus' present blackness. He is black because he *was* a Jew. The affirmation of his past Jewishness is related dialectically to the significance of his present blackness.[120]

James Cone remains the most persuasive and eloquent commentator on the basic overarching theological and philosophical grounding between the historicity of Christology and the contemporary experiences and existential, psycho-social realities and needs of Black people.[121]

Jesus and Social Transformation

Central to the Christological and soteriological basis of Jesus is the belief that his very presence becomes the catalyst for a seismic transformative process, through which and after which, human affairs and the very nature of existence will never be the same.[122]

For oppressed and marginalized people, the notion of social, political and personal transformation is a highly persuasive, dare one even say romantic, ideal.[123] Whether liberation and transformation are envisaged as a political process,[124] or as a pneumatologically inspired enterprise[125] or in terms of conscientized pedagogy,[126] these themes, nonetheless, remain at the heart of the Black theological enterprise for many in the African Diaspora.

The discussion amongst these Black young men became more animated and challenging when we began to reflect upon the themes of transformation, change, healing and reconciliation, arising from the presence of Johanthro in the drama.

I reminded the group that the presence of a Black child in this drama should not be taken too literally when establishing links with the birth of Jesus. And yet, in some respects, in raising this issue, I was doing these young men a gross disservice. Many of them knew, intuitively, that most of our God-talk is suffused with metaphor and analogy. They knew that Johanthro was not the Christ child, in the same way that many Christian followers know that God is not directly male, even when the Scriptures and the Christian tradition address God almost exclusively in male terms.[127] (This issue will be addressed in the next chapter when I analyse the central piece of drama in this book, *My God!?*)

The creation and deployment of *The New Arrival* enabled me to begin to play with the possibilities of developing a new approach to Black theology by means of drama. This piece of drama was my first attempt. The resulting discourse alerted me to the possibilities inherent in this method for engaging with Black people and other marginalized peoples who reside outside of the academy, and for whom existing approaches to Black theology are not appropriate for their development.

In the following chapter, I will outline the major Black theological themes that are present in the dramatic pieces I have created for this study. I will assess how Christian drama can be a repository for Black theology, and ask what challenges does this method offer for the more systematic, scholastic orientated enterprise that resides within the academy?

3 Welcome to the Party: Christian Drama Meets Black Theology

In this chapter, I want to look more closely at some of the theological themes represented in the dramatic pieces developed for this study. The main script on which most of my analysis will be drawn is *My God!?* I will talk about the development of this piece shortly. At this point, however, it is worth stating that this sketch has been used for a number of years as a basic introduction to Black theology, in my teaching ministry across the UK.

This piece has been amended over the years and the echoes of this development will be described shortly. I have returned repeatedly to *My God!?* because I feel it encapsulates many of the nascent themes of Black theology within its few pages.

Black Theology Brought me Back to Life

The relationship between the Christian faith and Black people has always been complex and contradictory. In a previous work, I described Black people as being "incurably religious."[1] Within the overall framework of Christianity, the Bible in general and the figure of Jesus in particular, remain hugely important to Black Christian expressions of faith across the world. Scholars such as J. Deotis Roberts,[2] Peter Paris[3] and Vincent Wimbush[4] have commented on the importance of the Bible and the Christian faith as a whole to the socialization and orientation of Black people.

My own Christian formation has been within a strict Christian framework. At no point in that process of socialization can I remember the Bible in particular, or the efficacy of the Christian faith, ever being challenged. God was real, was good and was most definitely to be trusted. Peter Paris writes:

> Contrary to the opinions of many outsiders, Africans do not experience the supreme deity as capricious but as one who serves the well-being of all as their creator and preserver.[5]

In time, as I developed from childhood to adulthood, I began to question the essential goodness of the church. At no point did I seriously question the reality of God in my existential framework, but the church was definitely another matter. Kortright Davis, reflecting on the differentiation made by Caribbean people between God and the church, states:

Caribbean people make a clear distinction between "Churchianity" and "Christianity." A well-known saying in the region goes like this: "Nearer to Church, farther from God." God is real in the Caribbean, even more than the sun and the sky. God is more than just God in the Bible… Caribbean people are deeply devoted to the reality of a God who not only creates the world but who loves the world.[6]

My sense of growing distrust towards the church lay in the unhealthy and pernicious conflation of the hierarchical top-down powers of the machinery of the state and that of the institutional church. The church became the mouthpiece of the former, leading to the wholesale sanction of oppression and marginalization of those who were without a voice.[7] Noel Erskine has challenged this corrosive relationship and outlined a schema for de-colonizing theology.[8]

As I have outlined in the introduction to this book, my own growing awareness of a wider conceptualization of the Christian faith emerged during my student years at the University of Birmingham, UK. While studying for a degree in History (majoring in Church History), I studied the Reformation, and saw at first hand the failings of a reformed movement to make a substantive, cognitive leap of faith in terms of how the Christian faith might be conceived, particularly for those whose very humanity was under threat. In effect, the reformers were no more adept at recognizing the innate selfhood of people of colour than their Catholic forebears.[9]

As my heightened awareness of my Blackness began to emerge (manifested in an engagement with the writing of "Black power" authors[10]), I began to ask a number of critical questions of the Christianity I had imbibed from childhood.[11]

This questioning led to my later engagement with Black theology, via an access course in Black Christian studies taught by Robert Beckford at the then Queen's College in the early 1990s. Attending this afternoon and evening course taught by Beckford re-invigorated my deeply moribund and desultory Christian faith.

My dissatisfaction with the hypocrisies of White Christianity, and its stultifying effects upon the selfhood of those whose voices have been silenced by White hegemony, led me to question the very basis of my religious experience. Could God really be trusted, if the people who acted in God's name could be so discriminatory? I was aware, as I asked these questions, that I had actually prospered in social and material terms from my engagement with the very institution I was now critiquing. What of those who had not been so fortunate? Robert Beckford's inspired teaching, and the encouragement of a number of highly influential people,[12] encouraged me to undertake my own doctoral studies in the mid 1990s. Black theology brought my Christian faith to life. In many respects, it enabled me to remain within the Christian church in Britain.

Writing *My God!?*

The context and occasion for writing *My God!?* need not detain us at this juncture. It is worth, however, spending a few minutes detailing my original intention when I first wrote this piece of drama.

My God!? was written for a Birmingham University Meth. Soc. summer retreat in 1986. I do not recall the theme for that summer retreat. I remember that we met at St. Andrews Methodist Church, on Pump Street in Worcester, from Friday night through to Sunday afternoon. The drama was performed on the Saturday morning and was repeated in the evening act of worship at Selly Oak Methodist church by the same individuals (myself and four others).

When I was asked to write a piece of drama on our perceptions of God, I remember thinking that I wanted to write a script that would challenge the group. At the time of writing, I was beginning to emerge from the conservative evangelical biblical literalism that had, hitherto, dominated my life. As I began to reflect upon my own images and understanding of God, I wondered what might surprise the group. How might our collective perceptions of God be challenged? I cannot remember what triggered the concept of making God a woman, but once the idea had taken root the writing of the script was relatively straightforward.

Since those heady days of being a student, a slow process of redaction has been in evidence regarding the finer points of the text in *My God!?* While the substantive content has remained the same, my exposure to the central tenets of Black theology have given rise to a series of subtle changes in the text of *My God!?* The most substantial change occurred in my conception of God, at the very heart of the drama. In the initial version, God was a generic woman. In later versions, God became a Black woman. The change was made in order to reflect my growing understanding of Womanist theology, and to reflect the shift in my sense of who represents the "voiceless" on the margins of human experience.

In my original piece, I was struck by the all-embracing sexism and patriarchy at the heart of most societies in the world. At the time of the original script, I felt it was sufficient simply to identify God with the majority of womankind, who are marginalized in most economic, religious, cultural or societal codes across the world. If God was on the side of the oppressed, then God would be a woman.

My exposure to the work of Alice Walker[13] and later Jacquelyn Grant[14] led me to a broader understanding of the wider conceptions of marginalization and oppression in the world. The work of Grant and other Womanist theologians alerted me to the multi-dimensional realities of Black women's oppression, which is more acute than the corresponding experiences of their White counterparts.[15] In order to remain faithful to the original vision and intention of this piece, God became a Black woman.

In making God Black, and not just a generic woman, I had, as a corollary, to amend the reactions of the men. The reactions of the men would be more acute and vehement when confronted by a Black woman. As I will demonstrate shortly, the commitment to challenge racialized oppression within Black theology has not prevented (at best) a limited commitment to challenge the gender oppression of Black women, or (at worst) a diminution of the personhood of Black womanhood.[16]

My God!? was not conceived as a Black theology text when it was written in the summer of 1986. My subsequent development as an educator and a theologian, however, has witnessed a corresponding change in the text of *My God!?*, leading to the final (for now, perhaps?) version you have before you. I invite you to read (if you have not already done so) *My God!?* What is your perception of God in this drama? This God is neither benign nor without "attitude." Do these character traits reflect your experiences or conception of God?

MY GOD!?

Players: one woman (who is God) and four men.

Opening: MAN NO. 1 *walks centre stage, looks around, quite apprehensive. He kneels down and begins to pray.*

MAN NO. 1: [*Kneeling and praying*] Oh most merciful and all powerful God. I come before you now, in humble petition, hoping that you will take pity on me and answer my request. Oh God, please, answer me.

[*There follows a period of silence…then* GOD *appears.* GOD *is a black woman.*]

GOD: [*Smiling*] You called?

MAN NO. 1: [*Shocked*] Who? Www who, are yyyy you? What are you doing here?

GOD: You called.

MAN NO. 1: [*Frightened*] I called?

GOD: Yes, you did call. Now what do you want me to do for you?

MAN NO. 1: [*Confused*] Do! Do for me?

GOD: [*Beginning to lose patience*] Yes do. What do you want me to do for you? Look, I'm very busy and you did call, so you must obviously want me to do something for you. So just tell me what it is you want and I'll see what I can do. Alright?

MAN NO. 1: [*Still confused*] But I called for God... [*Trying to make sure*]... Yes, that's right, I'll called for God... [*Speaking to himself*]... Oh most merciful and all powerful God... That's what I said... I called for God. I definitely called for God.

GOD: And here I am. So what do you want from me?

MAN NO. 1: [*Perplexed*] But you're a woman!

GOD: [*Sarcastically*] Well you obviously don't want the gift of healing on your eyes, do you?

MAN NO. 1: [*Very confused*] But you're a woman. And a Black one at that.

GOD: Give the man a prize, let him enter Mastermind and give him some more carrots. Look, of course I'm a Black woman, what did you expect? Now for the last time of asking, what is it you want?

MAN NO. 1: Since when have you been a woman? And so Black as well?

GOD: [*Irritable*] What sort of stupid question is that? You obviously want the restoration of your brain as well, don't you? Look, I've always been a Black woman... Who did you think God was? A White man?

MAN NO. 1: Well... As a matter of fact, yes... I was told by my Sunday school teacher that God was a middle-class, pinstriped suited stockbroker from Surrey who was a Conservative and now I'm confronted with this... I think I'll come back another day if you don't mind. You know, when things have sorted themselves out a little bit more.

GOD: [*Very angry*] Look, there is no one else, just me. I am God. It's no use coming back tomorrow because that won't change anything... Now for the last time of asking, what do you want?

[*At that moment in comes MAN NO. 2... he walks centre stage, bends low and begins to pray.*]

MAN NO. 2: Oh God my father... [*Interrupted by MAN NO. 1*]

MAN NO. 1: [*Sarcastically*] I'd knock that on the head for a start-off, if I were you. God sure isn't your father... Come to think of it, God isn't anyone's father.

MAN No. 2: [*Indignantly to* MAN No. *1*] What are you doing here? I asked for God and, besides, how dare you interrupt my prayer.

MAN No. 1: [*Nonchalantly*] I only wanted to warn you before you went and put your big size ten foot in it.

MAN No. 2: [*Still aggrieved*] Well, I don't want your interruptions thank you very much… Now push off… [*Resumes prayer*]… Dear God my father… [*Looks across at* MAN No. *1 and grimaces*]… I call upon you now to help me during my darkest hour of need. Oh please be with me, God my father.

GOD: You called?

MAN No. 2: [*Mortified*] Who the hell are you?

GOD: I'm God and there's no need for such language.

MAN No. 2: But you're a woman. A Black woman!

GOD: There's nothing like an intelligent and perceptive man, is there? Now what do you want from me?

MAN No. 2: [*Still aggrieved*] But you're a Black woman.

GOD: What's upsetting you the most? Me being Black, or the fact that I'm a woman?

[*MAN No. 2 looks puzzled. He does not say a word.* MAN No. *1 looks on at* MAN No. *2.*]

MAN No. 1: [*Smug*] I did try to warn you old bean, don't say I didn't try… [*Begins to laugh*]…

MAN No. 2: [*Indignantly*] How can you possibly be a Black woman? It's, it's disgraceful, that's what it is, disgraceful… You, God, being a woman… I've been misled, I want my money back. I'm going to relinquish my church membership for this. In fact I'm even going to write to the highest authority in the land. I might even write to the Pope. I'm not Catholic, but he must have something to say about this. God, a Black woman, I ask you, it's not even scriptural.

GOD: And where does it say that God is a man?

MAN No. 2: Well…well, it is severely implied and that's good enough for me.

MAN No. 1: [*Trying to wind up* MAN No. *2*] Touchy touchy, we're not taking this too well, are we?

MAN NO. 2: [*Turning on* MAN NO. 1] Look, I'll fill your face in if you're not careful, sunshine.

[*God steps in and separates the two men.*]

GOD: Stop it both of you... This is getting us nowhere. Now, not withstanding that I am a Black woman, is there anything you two want from me?

[*Both characters look at each other, make faces and think... About three seconds elapse and* MAN NO. 3, *a black man, enters the fray. He lies prostrate on the floor and begins to pray aloud.*]

MAN NO. 3: [*Lying on floor, arms outstretched*] Oh magnificent potentate, maker of all is seen and unseen. I ask your presence to be with me now, Oh Lord of all.

GOD PLUS MAN NOS 1 & 2 IN UNISON: You called?

MAN NO. 3: [*Very surprised*] Yes, I did, but what are you three doing here?

MAN NO. 1: I was here first.

MAN NO. 2: Then there was me.

GOD: And I'm God.

MAN NO. 3: You're having me on... You God? But you're a woman. A Black sister, if I'm seeing it right.

GOD: Men!

MAN NO. 3: Well, if you're God, prove it to me, do something.

GOD: Thou shalt not test the Lord your God.

MAN NO. 3: I don't believe in any of that rubbish, I read another book.

MAN NO. 1: [*Curious*] Oh and what book is that?

MAN NO. 3: The Koran.

MAN NO. 2: [*Up in arms*] I protest, God, he shouldn't be here, he's not one of us.

MAN NO. 1: [*Equally angry*] Yeah, he's one of them, he should be somewhere else. Throw him out, God, tell him to step off.

MAN NO. 3: [*Mischievously*] Is this a Black thing? Cos, you know, I can report you for that kind of thing!

MAN NO. 1: He's not one of us. Tell him to leave, God.

MAN NO. 3: [*Hurt*] I've got as much right to be here as you two. I worship God as well.

MAN NO. 1: Yeah, but not our God.

MAN NO. 2: You must worship another God, go and speak to him then.

GOD: There is only one God and here I am. Now what is it all three of you want?

MAN NO. 1: [*Being petulant*] I refuse to be served at the same altar with him over there… [*Pointing to MAN NO. 3*]… Unless he goes, then I go.

MAN NO. 2: [*Equally petulant*] Well I don't want anything from you anyway. You're a woman and until I get written confirmation from some higher authority, then I can no longer worship you.

MAN NO. 3: Well I don't want anything until you make those two blasted idiots apologize for their out-of-order-ness. Telling me to leave. Jumped up White…

GOD: [*Interrupting*] No one threatens God. I will do nothing of the sort. I am God and I will not be coerced into doing or changing anything… Now the rest is up to you three.

> [*All characters stand around motionless, thinking…occasionally one looks across at the other and then quickly looks away…no one is saying a word… Enter MAN NO. 4 who walks centre stage. Still standing, he utters his prayer.*]

MAN NO. 4: [*Standing casually, eyes to floor*] I just don't know… These exams, I just can't do them… What am I going to do? Oh God!

GOD PLUS MAN NOS 1 & 3: [*Cheerfully*] You called?

MAN NO. 4: [*Extremely surprised*] What's going on here?

GOD: I'm God.

MAN NO. 1: And we were in the process of praying.

GOD: Now what is it you want?… [*MAN NO. 4 stands aghast and doesn't say anything*]… Cat got your tongue? Don't tell me, you're surprised because God is a woman? Yeah, and before you say it, I know. I'm gorgeous and Black! You're stunned, I can tell.

MAN NO. 4: [*Apprehensive*] Well, ya see… It's just that… Well, you see… To be honest, I don't even believe in God. I'm an atheist.

MAN NO. 2: You called out to God.

MAN NO. 1: Yeah, I heard you.

MAN NO. 4: I was only blaspheming.

MAN NO. 3: [*Horrified*] Lord have mercy! Taking the Lord's name in vain? My God!

MAN NO. 2: [*Interrupting* MAN NO. *3*] Not your God, our God.

MAN NO. 1: [*To* MAN NO. *2*] I thought you wouldn't accept a woman God until you got written confirmation from on high?

MAN NO. 3: Does it matter whose God it is?… [*Pointing to* MAN NO. *4*]… This man must be punished for blaspheming… Burn him in oil and throw him into everlasting damnation.

MAN NO. 2: I agree.

MAN NO. 1: Burn him Lord, burn him up.

MAN NO. 4: [*Nonchalantly*] Who cares? God doesn't exist anyway.

GOD: Who am I then? The invisible gorgeous Black woman? Look, I'm very busy OK? Now unless you lot want anything, I'll be on my way. If you want to bicker, then that's your business, but I've got things to do… Now what is it you lot want?

MAN NO. 4: You can't do anything for me as you don't exist, and if you do, then you're most certainly not a woman, but an existential extension of our super ego and, as such, a sub-conscious creation of man's own being.

MAN NO. 3: [*Talking to* GOD] Unless you discipline… [*Pointing at* MAN NO. *4*]…this reprobate, then I refuse to worship you.

MAN NO. 1: [*Pointing at* MAN NO. *4*] You can't talk, you shouldn't even be here. God, I demand that you throw him out, or else I too will have to step out of here. You are my God and my God only.

MAN NO. 2: You're not even a God, you're a woman and a Black one at that, and as such I refuse to accept you as my God, so there.

GOD: [*Tapping feet impatiently*] Is that it? That's your final offer? Nothing else to add?… [*Slight pause*]… Then it looks like it's time you lot were leaving. I will not and, I repeat, will not be dictated to by you mere mortals. Either you accept me as I am and worship me accordingly, or you must reject me. I make the terms around here, not you… So what is it going to be?

> [*All the other characters begin to grumble amongst themselves underneath their breath…eventually they all decide to leave. Exit all other characters except GOD.*]

GOD: Typical. They all think they can construct me to fit into their own image. Make me appear as their imaginations would have them believe. There is only one God and here I am.

Theological Issues Arising from *My God!?*

Black people's belief in God—Whose God?

The most basic question that arises from my re-reading and analysis of *My God!?* relate to the very title itself. You will have notice that in the title I have inserted an exclamation mark, followed by a question mark. These insertions are obviously deliberate. I have included them in order to call to mind the inherent ambiguity and tension in this statement.

In the midst of their ongoing oppression and marginalization, those who I have termed the "voiceless," most often poor Black people, have clung tenaciously on to the belief that a benevolent God is with them in their struggles and hardship.[17] This was certainly the case for the slaves in the Caribbean and the Americas in the eighteenth and nineteenth centuries.[18]

In many respects, the assumed relationship between Black suffering and Christian faith expression has led many scholars to adopt a reductionist perspective on Black religion. Joseph Washington in his classic *Black Religion* argued that the Christianity of the Black church in America was devoid of any significant theology in its own right, and should be understood as purely compensatory, and seen as a form of religious orientation solely concerned with protest and survival.[19] Washington writes:

> The religion of the negro folk was chosen to bear roles of both protest and relief.[20]

In effect, Washington is asserting that Black religious faith is mainly compensatory, attending to the loss of personhood and the dehumanizing contexts in which the Black self is housed. While there is a great deal of this thought within the literature of the Black experience and that of other groups and communities who might be described as the "voiceless," there is, none-theless, an alternative perspective on how one might conceive Black reli-gion. Anthony Pinn argues that Black religion is not merely compensatory or an existential reaction to the realities of deprivation and oppression. Pinn argues that there is an inherent search for the transcendent within the religious experience of Black people, which accords with the more generic studies on religious phenomenology. Black religious faith in God is not purely reactionary or survivalistic[21] (although how one untangles the modes of religious experience from the actual history of Black suffering is a moot point).

Peter Paris argues against the reductionist perspective on Black religi-osity, which asserts that theistic expressions of African people are purely compensatory or reactive. He points to the religious orientation of African peoples prior to their enslavement in the so-called New World.[22] Many of these people had a highly developed religious cosmology, which accorded with the central tenets of Christianity, to which they were soon to be coerced into believing.[23]

This assumed relationship between voiceless Black people in the world and religious faith has been challenged by a number of scholars. It is the strident challenge against an assumed religiosity of Black people that prompted me to insert the exclamation and questions marks at the end of the title of the drama. In asserting the words "My God," one has to ask if this is an assertion of fact based upon hope or is it a sceptical, even quizzi-cal, question?

Challenges to Black Theism

William R. Jones' classic *Is God a White Racist?* challenged the, hitherto, accepted orthodoxy of Black theism. Jones argued that the notion of a benevolent God who is sympathetic to and actively involved in the affairs of oppressed and suffering Black people was at best overstated, and at worst, totally erroneous.[24]

Jones believes that if God is actively on the side of Black people, then where is the evidence for this belief? If God is all-powerful and has any form of preferential option for the poor and the oppressed, then why do Black people suffer disproportionately in the world? Perhaps the answer to this fiendishly difficult question lies in the notion of a God who is not on the side of Black people at all? God in effect actively sanctions Black suffer-ing. Therefore, God is a White racist.[25]

If, conversely, we argue that God neither sanctions nor actively involves Godself in Black suffering, then God is benign and irrelevant to Black struggles, in which case, God is irrelevant to Black life.[26]

In more recent times, the likes of Pinn[27] and Ware[28] have continued to probe the complexities of theodicy, with reference to Black suffering. Pinn argued for an increased engagement with humanism as an important source and norm for Black theology. He challenges the assumption that theism, particularly Christian faith, is the normative default position for Black religious orientation.[29]

It is beyond the scope of this study to detail the differing perspectives outlined by Black theologians regarding the nature of Black suffering and theodicy. Clearly, as a Black theologian, I have outlined my own position in terms of *My God!?*, as God actually exists in the drama and interacts with humankind. My position, in many respects, mirrors that of James Cone who writes:

> To summarize Black Theology's perspective on suffering, we can say it is based on the Scripture and the black Christian experience which claim that the God of Jesus is the Liberator of the oppressed from oppression. Although the continued existence of black suffering offers a serious challenge to the biblical and black faith, it does not negate it.[30]

In my brief theological schema within *My God!?* God is an active presence in the lives of the four male protagonists. God responds to their calls (please pardon the artistic license at this point) and is present in their immediate context, but whose God is this God? Can we make God particular in this way?

Black theology argues for a particular intent in God's actions and presence in human history. Cone, once again, states:

> The God in black theology is the God of and for the oppressed, the God who comes into view in their liberation. Any other approach is a denial of biblical revelation.[31]

Hopkins argues that a "commonsense wisdom" within the life experiences of enslaved Blacks helped them to realize that God's liberating presence within the midst of their suffering offered an important antidote to the seemingly insoluble problems of their current situation.[32] Within the more folk-orientated conception of Black theology (as opposed to the more ideological assertions of James Cone, for example), Black people have never doubted that God takes sides.[33] Andrews states:

> God's activity in human history on behalf of the oppressed and disadvantaged constitutes the formative properties of a black biblical hermeneutic.[34]

It can be argued that there is little direct evidence within *My God!?* to suggest the ideological or particularized emphasis of God's agency on behalf of the oppressed, in particular the voiceless presence of Black humanity. While this is true in some respects, I would argue that God in this drama, if not directly taking sides, reminds the mainly White male protagonists[35] that "She" will not be controlled by White assumptions of Divine co-operation.

This may appear to be a semantic point, but I would argue that within Black theological thought it remains, however, a key concept. Black theologians have long argued against the wholesale colonization of God at the behest of White hegemony. Within distant and more contemporary history, the God of the Christian faith has been used to justify the oppression and subjugation of people of colour across the world—the voiceless presence in human history.

Within *My God!?* the Divine presence is tangible. God exists. As J. Deotis Roberts reminds us, the "Death of God" movement so popular within parts of liberal White Euro-American thought never took root with the faith construction of Black people.[36] Roberts writes:

> The Death-of-God theologies are bred in deep yearning for meaning and fulfilment in the secular city of affluence and technology… Secular city theology is characterized by the fact that man has come of age, cut the umbilical cord, and in all honesty has decided that God is not "up there." It is a theology of strength—it is for the suburbs, for the "haves"—it does not know powerlessness, injustice and bondage. Black theology is "inner-city" theology.[37]

Historical and contemporary experience would seem to suggest that White hegemony working from a position of power and authority has either sought to deny God's existence (on the grounds that God is no longer necessary), or has attempted to co-opt God in support of its own socio-political and economic ends.[38]

As far back as 1964, Bob Dylan wrote of the predilection of the US to invoke the notion of God, and God's approval to sanction the activities of White authority, both internally and internationally, in his protest song "With God On Our Side."[39] Of a more recent vintage, George W. Bush's "War on Terror" after the 9/11 atrocity invoked the language of "crusade" and divine support for American actions. Walter Mosley has argued that African Americans, given their internal struggles for dignity and personhood within the US, have always viewed White-inspired American imperialism with a mixture of suspicion and hostility.[40] The sense of the manifest destiny of White corporate America continues to be challenged by Black theologians and religious scholars.[41]

My God!? challenges the assumptions of White hegemony. God cannot be enlisted to do the bidding of White power. In the drama, God refuses to be dictated to or re-constructed in order to fit the dictates of White male normalcy.

The challenges to White patriarchy that arise from *My God!?* are amplified when one considers the major theological theme at play within the drama.

The Challenge of Womanist Theology

The major theological theme within *My God!?* relates to God's depiction as a Black woman. I have explained my thinking in creating the image earlier in this chapter. What I hope to do now is to reflect theologically upon the meaning of this image and symbol. Why is the depiction of God as a Black woman of importance? What does it suggest for our own understanding of God and the nature of God's purposes in the world?

Womanist theology is both a method and a conceptual approach to theology that arises from the experience of Black women. In more introductory texts on Womanist theology reference is made to Alice Walker, for it is her work and thought that gave rise to the term "Womanish."[42] Walker identifies many of the formative notions of Womanism. These include self-determination, self-definition, the love of oneself, a commitment to holistic living, solidarity with other women and a respect for the experience and knowledge claims that arise from the reality of being a Black woman.[43]

The growth and development of Womanism since the early 1980s has led to an overarching methodological and philosophical branch of study that straddles a number of diverse disciplines, including theology, gender studies, cultural studies and sociology. Black women are utilizing Womanist epistemologies as a means to interrogate contemporary life and experiences in order that greater understanding of self and the world can emerge.[44] Womanist theology is the attempt to construct God-talk that arises from the particularity of Black women's experiences.[45]

The re-writing process that gave rise to this, the latest version of *My God!?*, was greatly influenced by the work of Jacquelyn Grant. In *White Women's Christ and Black Women's Jesus*, Grant outlines the central problem of male patriarchal theology and White Feminist theology.[46] Grant acknowledges that Womanist theology and Feminist theology share not dissimilar aims.[47]

It is important to note that Womanist theologians are not unique in wishing to challenge both the normative status of male images of God in particular and the privileging of male perspectives on theology in general.[48] From the ranks of White feminist scholars, I am particularly indebted to Sallie McFague's *Models of God* for initially inspiring me to conceive of God in feminine terms. McFague writes:

> The essence of metaphorical theology, however, is precisely the refusal to identify human constructions with divine reality… Thus the fundamentalist's assertion of univocity between human language about God and God

or "God's word" fails to appreciate the most basic characteristic of religious and theological language: its inconoclastic character, what the tradition calls the *via negative*. All language about God is human construction and as such perforce "misses the mark."[49]

My formative introduction to Feminist theology enabled me to surmount the patriarchy of the Christian faith and the underlying theology of my childhood and adolescence. If God could be conceived in female terms, it did not take a huge leap of imagination to move one step further, and construct an image of God as a Black woman. Jacquelyn Grant critiques feminism for its refusal to adequately engage with the experiences of women who are not White or middle class.[50] Grant offers a corrective to this myopia by outlining an alternative construction emanating from Black women's experiences.[51] The work of Delores Williams[52] and more recently Linda Thomas[53] has assisted in refining this drama.

God as a Black Woman

Revisiting *My God!?* in light of Womanist theology forced me to consider a number of important themes and concerns in my own life. The re-writing process occurred while I was engaged in my doctoral studies at the University of Birmingham. Travelling around Birmingham, engaging with a number of older Black people, many of whom had travelled to the UK from the Caribbean in the mass post-Second World War migration, I was struck by one inescapable thought. The majority of these people I met were older Black women. Many of them were not dissimilar to my own mother in terms of life experiences and faith.

While Black women have made significant strides in British society since the landing of the *SS Empire Windrush* on these shores on June 22, 1948, the majority of Black women, in particular those older ones of our communities, have not made any great progress. My attempt to honour all these older stalwarts, particularly the women, is detailed in a previous publication.[54] Stephanie Mitchell summarizes the structural, societal and cultural norms that limit and objectify Black women. She writes:

> Even though celebrity icons like Oprah seem to signify that "success is possible," Black women who are not Oprah daily become invisible; they are expected to be workers: expected to hold the broom or care for the child or type the memo or cook the meal. Often Black women who do not work in service or pink-collar occupations are viewed as an oddity.[55]

In writing this dramatic piece it was not my intention to assert that God is *literally* a Black woman. Rather, my continuing engagement with this piece arises from my desire to create a dramatic approach to theology that speaks to and reflects the needs of the voiceless—dispossessed and marginalized Black people in a world of rampant White power and authority.

As Mitchem reminds us, the vast nameless and faceless mass of Black women represent the ultimate voiceless presence in our world today. Black women are usually nameless and faceless save for those moments when they are objectified as sexual constructs to satisfy the lust of a patriarchal world.[56] Lorraine Dixon in her interpretation of the Book of Esther, particularly the first four chapters, writes of Vashti:

> The maintenance of the social order is a perspective that can be drawn out of the biblical narrative in question... What little we are told is that Queen Vashti gives a banquet for the palace women. There is a sense that these women's lives and destinies are not their own. Their bodies are certainly not their own either. This is emphasized by the King's request to have Vashti display herself in front of him and his nobles. But here is the rub! Vashti refuses outright.[57]

Dixon's Womanist interpretation is similar in many respects to the highly influential study of Hagar by Delores Williams and her retrieval of Hagar and her wilderness experience as a paradigm for Black women in the slavery and post-slavery epoch.[58]

In order to represent and establish the dignity of all Black women—the voiceless presence in the world—it was imperative that God become a Black woman. By making God a Black woman, the concerns and needs of the mass of dispossessed and marginalized Black women become the central, defining element in God's relationship with humankind.

Reflecting upon the drama, how can Black women be rendered totally invisible and without a voice, if the basis of all that is (i.e. God) is representative and represents these very marginalized people? Just as Cone is able to assert that God is Black, for Black represents the most oppressed and marginalized of all peoples in the world, then *My God!?* goes even further by asserting that God is a Black woman.

The Blackness and femininity of God forces us to make a number of significant readjustments in terms of how we conceive God's agency in the world. Where do God's interests lie? Clearly, for Womanist theologians and the overarching discipline of Black theology, greater emphasis must be given to the inherent sexism within Black cultures and within the practices of the Black church.

Kelly Brown Douglas, reflecting upon the limitations of the Black theology movement prior to the emergence of Womanist theology, writes:

> Shaped by the Black Power/civil rights movement out of which it emerged, Black theology focused only on one dimension of Black oppression—White racism. Its failure to utilize Black women's experience further prevented it from developing an adequate analysis of Black oppression. It did not address the multiple social burdens, that is, racism, sexism, classism,

heterosexism, which beset Black men and women. Consequently, it presented an image of God and Christ that is impotent in the fight for Black freedom. A Black God, one concerned only with the battle against racism, could not sustain and liberate the entire Black community. This God could not affirm or empower Black women as they confronted sexism. My recognition of Black theology's limitations set me on a quest for a theology more reflective of Black women's as well as men's efforts to "make do and do better."[59]

The construction of a female image of God is not simply an act of so-called "political correctness." Construing God in terms of the most vulnerable and marginalized enables us to not only see these people as visible and valuable in the sight of God, it also challenges us to bring the concerns of these voiceless people to the forefront of our thinking. By focusing upon the concerns of the most oppressed and marginalized, we are enabled, in partnership with God, to rectify a whole host of other fractured and impaired aspects of the world that stem from systemic disadvantage and the uses and abuses of power. As Paulo Freire reminds us, it is only the (most) oppressed, who possess the power (derived from God, with whom we are in partnership) to free themselves and those who hold power.[60]

Recognition of God as a Black woman would challenge many religious communities to address the inherent sexism within their existing practices, much of which reputedly rests upon divine sanction.[61]

Similarly, a focus upon a Black female image of God might redress not only the institutional failings of patriarchal faith communities, but may also address the sexism of individual male attitudes and their accompanying behaviour. Dwight Hopkins, influenced by Womanist thinking, argues for a new "heterosexual male" who is not bound by the stereotypical conventions of Black masculinity.[62] Hopkins amplifies his general thesis on reconstructing Black masculinity by sharing the fruits of his attempt to put this emerging theory into practice through co-teaching with his wife, who is an eminent Womanist scholar (Linda E. Thomas). Hopkins writes:

> Indeed, the black male has to learn a gender that opens itself to challenges and transformation in all areas of what it means to be loved by a God who wants liberation for the poor. Some of these inclusive and holistic areas are vulnerability; protection; intimacy; political protest; self-critique; new forms of leadership both in the home, church, and broader civic society; and other frontiers.[63]

The challenges posed by a female image of God are self-evident within the drama. The male protagonists appeal to tradition, ecclesial authority and even scripture in order to justify their antagonism to God, who is the Black woman stood before them. God as a Black woman subverts the very heart of White male patriarchy that has governed Christendom and indeed the whole world for the past two thousand years. If God is intensely committed to the liberation of the whole of creation, with particular emphasis given to the blighted and subjugated humanity of the poor and the oppressed, it is my belief that this self-same God must be understood through the interpretative lens of Black and Womanist theologies. A theology from the top-down,[64] propagated by White men with power, does not possess the structural force to give up power in order that others might live.

The surrendering of power by Jesus on the cross serves as the theological paradigm by which salvation and liberation are often conceived.[65] The challenge presented by Jesus' supreme actions serves as a constant reminder and an indictment to White hegemony, whether of the secular or religious variety. I cannot recall from history any significant example where White male authority has voluntarily given up power (as opposed to being coerced and forced to do so), in order that others might live.

Many of us who once marched in support of universal suffrage in South Africa will recall the courageous and costly actions of the African National Congress (ANC), in order that the White Apartheid regime might be "persuaded" to surrender their exclusive hold on political power.

My God!? challenges us to look towards the silent voices of the mass of poor and marginalized Black women in order to discern the liberating presence of God who is at work in the world.

Additional Themes Arising from *My God!?* and the Other Pieces of Drama

Black theology and other faiths

On a final note regarding *My God!?* it has been interesting to note the reaction of participants to character no. 3 in the drama. Character no. 3 is not only a Black male, but implied within his first speeches is the sense that he is a follower of the Islamic faith. This seemingly minor point brings into sharp focus the issue of Black theology's relationship with other faiths.

Since its inception in the late 1960s, Black theology has always incorporated a distinct Christological basis to its overall system for doing theology. James Cone writes:

> Christian theology begins and ends with Jesus Christ. He is the point of departure for everything to be said about God, human-kind, and the world.[66]

Black British theologian Robert Beckford utilizes an African Caribbean, Rastafari Christological motif as the basis for his first major work in Black theology.[67] The pivotal role of Jesus in Black theology, while offering a highly personalized, focused point for realizing God's relationship with humankind,[68] nonetheless has the potential for closing dialogue with other faith traditions.

Recognizing this possibility, Cone has widened his appreciation of the possible sources and norms for undertaking Black Liberation theology.[69] In more recent times, Dwight Hopkins has continued the quest to broaden the sources that inform the practice of Black theology. Hopkins states:

> To believe in Jesus is to walk the way of Jesus… Consequently, to be with Jesus will mean, in many cases, not ever being in a Christian institution or context. Furthermore, this divine revelation, which dwells among the poor in their struggle for all humanity, is not contained only in the way of Jesus. If God is the spirit of freedom for the vulnerable in society, then this spirit has to be active as an event and process of struggle even where the name of Jesus is not known. We cannot confine our experience of God within human-made doctrines or beliefs.[70]

The dramatizing theologies for the voiceless outlined within this text are committed to an ongoing conversation between the various faith traditions and philosophies of the world. Their point of departure is the fractured, marginalized and dispossessed humanity of Black people across the African continent and the Diaspora. This enterprise is contained within the overarching discipline of Black theology, influenced by a particular and distinct Womanist perspective. And yet, despite its precise starting point, the God who is depicted within the drama at the heart of this work is not limited to the Christian tradition.

In *My God!?* God engages with character no. 3 in the same manner as with the previous two male protagonists. God's partiality is not based upon faith constructions, but upon justice and dignity for the poor and despised.

The next piece of drama that forms a part of the substantive content of the process of "dramatizing theologies" is *The Wisdom of Solomon*. This piece was first written for a Black religio-cultural celebration at my home church[71] in the late 1990s. The full text of the sketch is reproduced in the following pages.

THE WISDOM OF SOLOMON

The scene…the stage is empty. A Black man/woman walks centre stage and begins to call out.

SERVANT: [*In a loud voice*] Hear ye, hear ye, hear ye. Be upstanding for the entrance of King Solomon, the most high, the most gracious and the most magnificent King of Israel. Oh hear ye, King Solomon is the hostess with the mostess. He is the man. The dude who knows where it's at, and if he don't, then ain't nobody saying nut'ing, ya know what I mean?… [*Looks to the side*]… All stand for King Solomon.

[*Enter* SOLOMON *who is a Black man. As he walks centre stage, the* SERVANT *begins to bow.*]

SERVANT: [*Bent very low*] Oh your most magnificentness. Your Holy brilliantness. You most handsome Black man I have ever seen... [SOLOMON *is looking on impatiently*]... Sir, that is a boss suit you have on there sir, if I could only be so lucky to be able to wear a suit like that... Sir...

SOLOMON: [*Irritated*] Hush up bwoy... Quiet nuh? Mi cyaan even 'ear fe myself t'ink... Cho... Man cyaan 'ave no peace, a so it go?

SERVANT: No sir... You can have all the peace you want... Yu is a man who deserve a whole heap a peace... You sir, you deserve more peace than any body. You work so hard sir... But I shall tell dem... Leave poor Solomon alone, because he is a man who need some peace.

SOLOMON: [*Cuffing* SERVANT *across the head*] Wha' wrong wi yu? Mi nah go'n tell yu again... Now 'tan' up.

[SERVANT *gets to his/her feet.*]

SOLOMON: Now what are my appointments for the day?

SERVANT: [*Opening up a large ledger*] Well sir... Your most magnificentness.

SOLOMON: [*Looking at* SERVANT] Yu start it again?

SERVANT: Sorry sir... Well... You have an appointment with the King's Council, at twelve noon. Then at one, you're meeting the Royal Chronicler. He wants to look at the latest draft of your Book, the Song of Solomon. You are a great writer sir.

SOLOMON: You're too kind... Go on.

SERVANT: Then you have to write some more of your Proverbs. The publishers want to make it into a book.

SOLOMON: Yes... Next.

SERVANT: Then you have an adjudication session. Two women are claiming that a particular baby belongs to them. They want you to decide. Then there are three men, who are all arguing about a plot of land, out beside the bush, over deyso. They want you to sort out the will. Then...

SOLOMON: Laard have mercy 'pon fe my soul... Why am I so busy?

SERVANT: Well sir, you are the most famous Black man in the world. The people look up to you. You are their inspiration. The people see you as a role model. You are their hero. Heroes are busy people, sir... And you sir, are a hero... And then there's Sheba.

SOLOMON: Sheba?

SERVANT: Yes sir, the Queen of Sheba. It was her birthday yesterday. You were meant to take her out. You do remember sir?

SOLOMON: Laard have mercy... Sheba go'n kill me.

SERVANT: You didn't forget did you sir?

SOLOMON: Hush up... Me been so busy lately... Wha' wid de book, de meetings an' t'ing... [*Looks to audience for support*]... Mi couldn't 'elp it?

SERVANT: [*Looking to the wings*] I hope Sheba understands... She's coming this way, right now... Mi garn.

> [*Exit* SERVANT. *As* SERVANT *exits, enter a furious* SHEBA, *who is a Black woman. She marches straight to* SOLOMON. *She stands in front of him, tapping her feet. She does not say a word.*]

SOLOMON: [*Embarrassed*] Yu alright darlin'?... [SHEBA *is silent*]... Lovely day, hi?... [*Still silent*]... Me deares' yu look sweet an' nice... [*Still silence*]... Com' nuh? Yu nuh 'ave fe handle me so rough... Look babe, it wasn't my fault. I had meetings all day. People to meet, deals to make, hands to shake, babies to kiss, books to write... Darlin' my time's not my own. I'm a Black hero. The people love me. I'm pressed on all sides... [*Tries to stroke* SHEBA's *face*]... Sorry darlin'.

SHEBA: [*Walking away furiously*] Yu sorry? Is dat it? Is dat all me go'n get? Yu is sorry... [*Kisses her teeth*[72]]... Yu know how long me did wait lars' night?

SOLOMON: Well ermmm...

SHEBA: Six hours... Six long hours. I put on my criss clothes. My most expensive perfume. My best wig. De expensive shoes I get fe lars' birthday... An' fe wha'... Lover bwoy, never com' at all... See yu? Yu wort'less and selfish wretch.

> [SOLOMON *walks across to the side of the room. He picks up a small package and returns with it. He hands it to* SHEBA.]

SOLOMON: [*Handing package to Sheba*] Darlin', fe yu.

[*Sheba pretends to ignore it... Solomon pretends to throw it away.*]

SOLOMON: Well, if you don't want it.

SHEBA: 'ey, hol' on a minute... Whey yu a go wi me present?

SOLOMON: So you want it now?

SHEBA: Gimme nuh?

[*Solomon hands over the present... Sheba quickly opens it.*]

SOLOMON: Fe yu darlin'... Yu lik' it? Expensive yu know... Dis nuh cheap, dibby dibby, Brixton market t'ing... Me get it from Harrods.

SHEBA: Expensive?

SOLOMON: Yeah man... Cost nuff money.

SHEBA: Fe me?

SOLOMON: Yu is de only one for me, darling.

SHEBA: T'ank yu darlin'.

[*The two begin to hug...while they are hugging, re-enter Servant. He/ she walks tentatively across to the hugging couple. He/she taps Solomon on the back, but the two are not to be moved. He/she continues to try and gain their attention, but still nothing...finally, he/she taps Solomon on the head rather hard. The couple break off their clinch. Neither of them are happy.*]

SOLOMON: Is what yu want? An' it betta' be good, else me go'n kill yu?

SERVANT: Well... Your brother Adonijah, is plotting to overthrow you, and there needs to be an emergency Government council, as soon as possible. You are needed, King Solomon.

SOLOMON: Now?

SERVANT: Right now.

SOLOMON: [*Turning to look at Sheba*] Darlin'...

SHEBA: Yu ain't doing this to me again, Solomon.

SOLOMON: Sheba darlin'... I don't want to go.

SHEBA: Don't go den.

SOLOMON: But darlin', I've got responsibilities. I'm a professional Black man.

SERVANT: Might I interject here?

SOLOMON & SHEBA: Shut up.

SERVANT: Alright den... I will be waiting sir. What shall I tell the council?

SOLOMON: Mi nuh know... [*To SHEBA*] Sheba darlin', I have to set a lead. The people need me.

SHEBA: But I need you.

SOLOMON: I'm a hero... I have to set a lead.

SHEBA: Gwaan nuh...

SOLOMON: You mean I can go?

SHEBA: Yu is de King... Yu can do what yu like.

SOLOMON: You're vex, aren't you?

SHEBA: No.

SOLOMON: Will you be here, when I've finished?

SHEBA: What do you think?

SOLOMON: You love me darlin'... We're a successful Black couple. We support each other. We give each other strength. We're role models. You'll be here, won't you darlin'?

SHEBA: Try again.

SOLOMON: But darlin', you cyan handle me so?

SHEBA: Watch me...

> [*SHEBA begins to walk away...she takes a few steps, stops, and turns to look at SOLOMON.*]

SHEBA: Solomon... Me lef' yu... Me garn.

> [*SHEBA begins to walk off stage, SOLOMON is calling out to her.*]

SOLOMON: But Sheba darlin'... Yu cyan do dis to me. I love you babe.

[*Exit* SHEBA… SOLOMON *is alone…after a few seconds, re-enter* SERVANT.]

SERVANT: [*To* SOLOMON] I'm back sir… You're most Royal Magnificence.

SOLOMON: Nuh bodder com' wid dat stupidness again.

SERVANT: Has Sheba gone sir?

SOLOMON: Gone, gone, gone… And she won't be coming back.

SERVANT: Oh, I don't know sir.

SOLOMON: Is what don't you know?

[SERVANT *gives* SOLOMON *a note from* SHEBA.]

SERVANT: [*Handing* SOLOMON *the note*] Read this sir. Sheba gave it to me, as she was leaving.

SOLOMON: [*Reading the note*] I forgive you Solomon. Give me a ring when you get in tonight. We'll mash it up big time, when you get back. Love Sheba.

SOLOMON: Yu 'ear dat? Fe me Sheba love me fe real… Yeah man… [*Looking at* SERVANT]… Com' nuh? We 'ave a meeting to go to.

SERVANT: Very good sir.

[*The two of them begin to walk off stage.*]

SOLOMON: Being a successful Black man is a tough job you know… Pressure, pressure everywhere… But I can take it… Yeah man, I can take it. I won't let my people down. Not now, not ever… [*Looking at* SERVANT]… Come… We have work to do.

SERVANT: Anything you say sir.

[*Exit both characters.*]

Relections on the Drama

This piece of drama was initially written for a group of Black young people in Birmingham. The theology within the drama accords with the central tenets of Black theological thought. *The Wisdom of Solomon* in tone and form reflects a number of important features that have been expressed in both *The New Arrival* and *My God!?*. *The Wisdom of Solomon* is influenced by the rise of Black biblical scholarship. Black biblical scholars have attempted to engage with Hebrew and Christian scriptures in order to both correct the previous distortions of White Eurocentric scholarship, and to unearth the liberative potential of these sacred texts.

When conceiving and writing this piece of drama, I was influenced greatly by Cain Hope Felder's landmark edited publication *Stony The Road We Trod*.[73]

Stony The Road We Trod inspired me to think in terms of re-contextualizing biblical narratives in order that they should both reflect and inform the Black experience. A key figure in enabling me to develop this form of creative Black theological approach to drama has been Randall Bailey. Bailey is, arguably, the key scholar of his generation for his development of an ideological approach to the biblical text. Bailey brings the ideological suppositions of Black theological thought into direct "confrontation" with the biblical text.

One of Bailey's techniques is to establish a connection between the text and Black experience by means of identifying a Black presence within the narrative itself. Writing with reference to Old Testament scholarship, Bailey states:

> The treatment of Egypt is another example of the tendency to minimize African influences on the Hebrew Canon. This has been achieved by a twofold strategy. On the one hand, there are those efforts to move Egypt out of Africa by arguing for a sharp distinction between Sub-Saharan Africa and Egypt. On the other hand, there are those efforts that argue that the Hamites were not Africans.[74]

In a later essay, Bailey highlights the attempts by Euro-American scholars to "de-Africanize" Moses as he is depicted within the Book of Exodus.[75] In a more recent publication, Bailey has recruited an impressive array of Black biblical scholars to continue the Afrocentric engagement with the Bible.[76] J. Deotis Roberts asserts that a form of Afrocentric hermeneutic is at the heart of the Black biblical enterprise within Black theology.[77] Roberts' assertions echo my own preoccupations when I created *The Wisdom of Solomon*.

The Theology at Play in *The Wisdom of Solomon*

Black language

One of the most notable features of this drama, in common with *The New Arrival*, is the use of the idiom of Jamaican patois. On the many occasions when this piece has been performed, it has been interesting to note the reaction of the mainly Black participants to the linguistic traits at play in the script. The intimations of Black identity and selfhood have been enhanced by envisioning this biblical narrative within a Black cultural context. The dynamics of Black cultures, and the accompanying expression and production, are reflected in the linguistic patterns of these Black protagonists.

The importance of re-casting biblical narrative within a Black cultural context through the medium of Jamaican patois is becoming an increasingly important feature of the missiological enterprise of such international agencies as the Bible Society.[78] A close friend, who resides in the UK, but who spent a significant part of his formative years in Jamaica, describes patois as the "language of the heart." For many Black people of Caribbean descent, Jamaican patois, in particular, represents the authentic language of passion and authentic selfhood. Cone describes Black language within Black theology as "passionate language."[79]

In deploying this linguistic code within the drama, I am signalling a belief in the engagement with God through the interpretative lens of Black cultural expression. Hopkins reminds us that one of the sources for undertaking Black theology is by means of Black culture.[80]

In addition to utilizing Black idioms, *The Wisdom of Solomon*, in keeping with aspects of ideological, Afrocentric biblical interpretation, seeks to locate a Black presence within the sacred narrative itself. While Bailey *et al.* have utilized the cumulative exegetical resources of the African American biblical community in order to re-discover the hidden presence of Black people within the biblical text,[81] I as a Christian educator have re-imagined this narrative within a contemporary Black, African Caribbean setting.

Re-setting in a Black context

The setting of the drama is crucial to its theological underpinning. By relocating the drama to inner-city London (Solomon establishes the location by informing Sheba that her present is not from "Brixton Market") I have chosen to make the largely structural poverty-ridden locale of Black Britain the centre for God's performative action. Brixton in South London has often been perceived as being the capital of Black Britain. By establishing Brixton, and South London, as the setting, Black British people become centre stage in God's drama.

For Black British people who are often rendered invisible by the media save for largely stereotypical representation (sporting activity or criminality)[82] this "moment in the sun" has proved remarkably cathartic. "We" have come into the spotlight, but not as exotica or for our romanticized physicality, but because we are valuable in our own right, simply for who we are in the sight of God. In a previous publication, I critiqued the "White-washing" tendencies of British film makers to edit out a Black presence from their depiction of contemporary Britain in their films.[83]

It is interesting to compare and contrast the differing levels of recognition accorded Marianne Jean-Baptiste and Kristen Scott-Thomas. Both are British actresses, but the former is Black and the latter White. Both were nominated at the 1996 Oscars, Baptiste for Mike Leigh's *Secrets and Lies*, Scott-Thomas for Anthony Minghella's *The English Patient*. What was instructive about their respective treatment at the hands of the British press (and Hollywood for that matter) was the almost obscene refusal to acknowledge the achievements of Baptiste. The Black actress was virtually ignored, while the White Scott-Thomas was lauded as the "English Rose." Clearly roses are never Black! At the time of writing, Baptiste's film career appears to have hit a plateau, and she is currently to be seen on US television. The invisibility of Black people, so clearly evident in the annual BAFTAS (British Academy of Film and Television Arts) and in many other forms of the media and British public life, is critiqued in this drama.

Black visibility

Having previously acknowledged the relative shift away from a Christo-centric focus within Black theology in more recent times, I am forced at this point to acknowledge that the self-conscious Black presence within this Old Testament drama is, nonetheless, a reading back of that narrative through the focusing lens of Christology.

The necessity of a "Black Christ" who is deeply located within Black human affairs remains a central theological motif in Black theology.[84] Jesus' location amongst the urban poor, where he adopts the concerns and the plight of those who are voiceless and shares in their Blackness, has led a number of theologians to speak of a "theology of presence."[85] Jesus is involved in the daily concerns of Black folk, getting his hands dirty, as he engages in our context, undertaking the dangerous, divine work of salvation.[86]

My reverse reading (reading the Old Testament, by way of Jesus' actions in the Gospels) of this text from Chronicles 2:9, led me to construct a Black cultural reading of this narrative.

One of the methods for undertaking Black theology necessitates a recognition of those Black forbears whose battles highlight the ongoing struggle for Black selfhood and liberation. Anne Wimberly's *Soul Stories* utilizes this approach of remembering and rehearsing the narratives of liberation as they have been displayed in the (s)heroes of the past as a means of promoting holistic forms of Christian discipleship in contemporary Black life.[87] Similarly, within some of my past work, I have sought to identify "Black heroes" as a means of indicating God's redemptive work through Black struggle and defiance.[88]

Once again, in these particular approaches to Black theology, Jesus remains a pivotal figure, even when his name or presence is not directly invoked. By locating Jesus as "one of us," in effect, a "Black hero,"[89]

Jesus' actions assist Black theologians to identify the work of the Divine presence in the hearts and minds of all Black people whose commitment to justice and righteousness echoes "the way" of Christ.[90]

Black leadership

Within the context of *The Wisdom of Solomon* we see the two central protagonists as pro-typical Black heroes. Solomon and Sheba display contemporary attitudes and modes of behaviour that are reflective of Black British life. Solomon in particular is aware of the politics of "race" and the pressures of being a "professional" Black man with power. Within the drama, Solomon in accordance with his depiction within Scripture is a deeply fallible, but intensely intelligent man. Solomon is in possession of inspired divine knowledge. By making Solomon a Black man, wisdom and brilliance are now located within Black cultural experience. Solomon is a wise Black man.

In a world where intelligence, brilliance and achievement are still perceived as being the exclusive attributes of White Euro-Americans, the perception that Blackness can be the receptacle for divine wisdom and leadership carries a highly social, political and cultural charge.[91]

The reluctance, for example, of White-dominated democracies in the West to elect Black men and women to ultimate positions of political leadership[92] is no doubt challenged by the recognition that a highly influential leader within the biblical narrative is Black. The exegetical work of Black biblical scholars has identified the Black African identity of Solomon and Sheba.[93]

Repressive representation

It is interesting to note from the drama that Solomon is deeply aware of the pressures and vulnerability of his role as a king and a leader. He recognizes the representative role he carries as a Black male leader. One of the stultifying and limiting pressures that are exerted upon Black people, in order to curtail their potential for leadership within White-dominated institutions and the broader society, is by means of "repressive representation." By this, I mean the externally and internally imposed pressure to be a representative for the entire community of which one is a part.

This form of "repressive representation" removes any sense of choice for the individual concerned to effectively construct their own positionality, *vis-à-vis* the wider community from which they have emerged. In effect, individuals are forced to carry the burden of wider representation, irrespective of their personal propensity or inclinations. In more colloquial terms, this pressure is manifested in the often-used aphorism of "When one fails, we all fail."

This form of representative pressure, alluded to by Solomon in the drama, is spared White men with power. When one individual White man fails (in whatever profession or position of responsibility), one never hears the cry "Well there you go; you see, you simply can't trust White men to do the job!" Such are the constructs of power within White-dominated societies that the "repressive representation" of which I speak has exerted similar (although not the same) pressures upon White women. In a previous piece of work I argue that many of the societal norms in Christian influenced contexts are shaped by collapsing Whiteness with Divine agency. In effect, Jesus becomes White, which, as a corollary, legitimates White male power, thereby creating a seemingly indestructible norm from which Black people in particular and Black women especially are excluded.[94] By defining "the norm" in White male, patriarchal terms, White men are able to establish the normalcy of their own subjectivity.

By locating the legitimacy of their power with the Divine self in terms of a White Christ, White men are able to deflect any structural or systemic critique away from their collective identities. In effect, no one seriously challenges the legitimacy of White men to rule! And such is the power of this construct, failure of any individual is not a failure of the norm (that has already been established and has Divine sanction in a White Jesus sent by God to save others), but rather, is a failure of the individual.

Conversely, when non-White men fail, because the norm has not been established (and also because it lacks Divine sanction), the negative verdict falls upon all who share a similar background or identity of the failed individual. It is for these reasons that a White Jesus is essential, and why God in *My God!?* and Solomon and Sheba in *The Wisdom of Solomon* are Black, and need to be so.

It is interesting to note the relatively few White women, and Black men and women, who have surmounted the greasy pole of social and occupational mobility to occupy the highest positions in most western democracies.

As I will demonstrate to even greater effect, when analysing the final piece of drama, the internalized pressures that emerge from "repressive representation" often lead to self-imposed forms of limitations on what Black people think and feel they can achieve. Black people become so self-conscious of the fear of failure and the burdens of "making all of us look bad," that we often fail to avail ourselves of the opportunities that present themselves.

This is certainly the case within the candidating procedures for ordained ministry within the White-dominated historic-mainline churches in Britain. I have met a number of very able, devout and eminently qualified Black Christians who could (and in many cases should) candidate for ordained ministry in their church (predominantly Anglican, Catholic, Methodist, Baptist and United Reformed), but often fail to do so, due to the pernicious dynamic I have just described.[95]

Sheba, on the other hand, represents a form of Black female assertiveness that has been the bedrock upon which many Diasporan Black communities have attempted to surmount the systemic hardships that have faced them.[96] In this respect, the character of Sheba in the drama reflects the tenacious presence of many Black women and their contribution to the ongoing battles for liberation and economic self-determination.[97] Sheba sits within the wider pantheon of Womanist (s)heroes and, with respect to the previous drama *My God!?*, reflects many traits of the Divine presence in whose image she has been created.

The next piece of drama in this dramatic theological scheme is *Love is the Answer*. This piece is one of the more recent scripts I have written and was created for another religio-cultural celebration at my home church in Birmingham, in the West Midlands region of the UK. The script is one of the most ambitious short dramatic pieces I have attempted, and in many respects is a drastic departure from many of the previous pieces I have written up to this time. The complete script is reproduced in the following pages.

LOVE IS THE ANSWER

We see a person standing centre stage. The individual looks at the congregation/audience and begins to speak.

No. 1: A strange thing happened to me the other day. I was standing there in front of this J.P. and I was steaming. I was mad. I was mad mad mad. I was madder than a mad thing in a mad place where very mad things happen. You might say that I was little… [*Slight pause while he/she thinks for a moment*]… A little. Mad I guess. Well, I'll tell you. [*Points to the other side of the stage*]

[*Enter No. 2 on the opposite side of the stage. No. 1 points at No. 2.*]

No. 1: [*Pointing at No. 2*] That's me last week. That's the person playing me in the flashback. I know I look different, but that always happens in flashbacks. You always look uglier somehow.

No. 2: [*To No. 1*] Hey, watch it. We'll have less of that. I'm doing you a favour playing you in this flashback. If it weren't for me, you'd be playing both parts yourself and wouldn't that be confusing?

No. 1: Fair enough. Yep, that's me last week, when this happened. There I was shouting and railing against the world. I was seriously vex. Nah man, I was bex.[98]

No. 2: Why? Why huh? It's a disgrace. That's what it is, an absolute disgrace. There was no excuse for it. That man should be shot. No, he should be hung up by the neck, half killed, then they should take him down, put him in some stocks, all manner of nastiness should be thrown at him, then they should lash him ten thousand times and then they should kill him.

No. 1: I admit it, I was kinda angry.

No. 2: Mad I think the word was.

No. 1: Thank you. It is good when your self can correct you. Yep, that was me. I was seriously mad. It was not a pretty sight.

No. 2: Eh, I've told you about that kinda thing before. Hold off on the ugly stuff.

No. 1: I was talking about the situation, not you. Touchy touchy. Well, there I was. I admit it, I was angry.

No. 2: I think the word you're looking for is mad!

No. 1: Yeah yeah yeah, whatever. Look, who's telling this story, me or you? You're just the flashback remember. Ugly so and so.

No. 2: Eh, watch it! What have I told you about that ugly thing?

No. 1: Whatever! Anyway, when I had finished shouting against the whole world, this seriously weird person came and stood next to me.

[*Enter No. 3. They walk and stand next to No. 1.*]

No. 3: I'm the seriously weird person. Hi. I'm seriously weird.

No. 1: He is seriously weird. And over there.

[*No. 1 points to No. 4. Enter No. 4 who stands next to No. 2.*]

No. 1: [*Pointing at No. 4*] That new person is the flashback of the seriously weird person.

No. 2: [*To No. 4*] So you're the flashback of the seriously weird person?

No. 4: Yep, that's me.

No. 2: It's great being a flashback isn't it?

No. 4: You reckon? Looks like the short end of the straw to me.

No. 1: [*To Nos. 2 & 4*] Do you two mind? I'm trying to tell a story here? This is my story, remember? You two are just the flashback people. Don't be getting above yourselves. [*To No. 3*] These flashback people. Who do they think they are? If it weren't for us, they wouldn't even exist.

No. 3: Yeah.

No. 1: Any road up. I turned to this seriously weird person who was looking at me and I said to him…

[*There is a moment's silence as No. 2 does not react.*]

No. 1: [*To No. 2*] Ey, soft brain, it's you. We're in flashback mode. It's time for you to speak. [*To No. 3*] See him? Ugly so and so.

No. 2: Watch it, you. Less of the ugly stuff. So I said to the seriously weird person. [*Turning to face No. 4*]… I said, what do you want? Can I help you?

No. 4: No, but can I help you?

No. 2: Come again?

No. 4: Can I help you?

No. 2: You can help me? Seriously? How are you going to do that then?

No. 4: Give me all that anger you have.

No. 2: You mean that mad mad mad stuff?

No. 1: I think we get the picture.

No. 2: That mad stuff. All my railing against the world. All that nasty pain and stuff. All that?

No. 4: All that. Give it to me.

No. 2: Why? What you gonna do with it?

No. 4: I will take it away. You don't need it. All that anger and pain is hurting you. It is making you bitter and twisted. You are becoming selfish and nasty. You are not the person you were. Revenge is eating you away from the inside. You need to let it go.

No. 2: [*Speechless*] Right.

No. 1: [*To No. 3*] You are seriously weird aren't you?

No. 3: What can I say? I was made that way. I am here to do things completely differently from the way they have been before.

No. 1: You really are a seriously weird person. [*Looking at Nos. 2 & 4*] At least your flashback is good looking.

No. 2: [*To No. 1*] I'm warning you.

No. 4: So what do you say? Are you going to give me all that anger?

No. 2: Madness.

No. 1: Whatever.

No. 4: Well, are you?

No. 1: I don't know. It's a part of me. I've carried it for so long, I wouldn't know what to do without it. It sort of keeps me going. I feed off that anger.

No. 2: The madness.

No. 1: [*Looks at No. 2 disapprovingly*] What am I going to do without that stuff inside of me? [*Slight pause. To No. 3*] Go on then, seriously weird person, what do you have to say to that? What am I going to do without all that stuff?

No. 2: The madness!

No. 1: [*To No. 2*] Shut it you, you're only the flashback.

No. 2: You stop calling me ugly then.

No. 3: You will become a better person. You don't need all that pain and hurt. It doesn't fuel you or keep you going. It holds you back. You cling on to it like a crutch. Now it's time for you to throw away the crutch and walk unaided. I can heal the pain inside of you.

No. 1: Then I said… [*Looking at No. 2. Pretends to clear his/her throat*]

No. 2: So I said to the seriously weird person, so what do you want in return for all this madness… [*Looks at No. 1*] hmmm, anger inside of me?

No. 4: I want you.

No. 1: You what? I said.

No. 2: You what?

No. 1: [*To No. 2*] That wasn't necessary.

No. 2: This story is in the past tense, remember?

No. 1: I was fair struck dumb I was.

No. 2: Yeah, that I was.

No. 3: I could tell that this person was in pain. It was a struggle. Trying to contain all that hurt, disappointment and frustration. I offered them a new way.

No. 1: [*To No. 3*] And what way was that?

No. 3: The way of love. Loving your enemies. Loving those who hurt you and cause you pain. Love is harder to do, but it costs you much less in the long run. The more love you give, the more peace and freedom you will feel inside yourself. You will become a better person for loving. Love is the answer.

No. 1: I didn't know what to say. So I looked at the seriously weird person and I said…

No. 2 What do you want with me?

No. 4: I want to take over your life, if you will let me. I want to help you to become all that you could be, should be and were meant to be.

No. 2: You can do all that for me?

No. 4: If you will allow me to come into your life. All that bitter stuff inside will go away. It will take time. But you will become a new person. With my love within you, I will change you. My love is making all things new.

No. 2: I see.

No. 1: Now that was some heavy-duty stuff. Not the kind of thing that confronts you every day. I was thrown. I was scared to give up all the stuff inside of me. I had gotten used to it. But what the seriously weird person said was true. Deep down, I wanted to get rid of it. But could I?

No. 3: It's the big decision that confronts all of us. Are you willing to let go of your past and allow me to transform your present and reform your future? I can make you whole. You will no longer be at war with yourself. Look at yourself.

[*No. 1 looks across at No. 2.*]

No. 3: You've spent so long being angry, you can't even bear to see or be with yourself. Your flashback is you. No part of you is ugly. You are a beautiful person. I made you, so I should know. No part of you is ugly.

No. 2: No one had ever said that to me before.

No. 4: You've never met me before. I am making all the difference. Love will make all the difference. Trust me.

No. 3: I can be trusted. Go on, let it all go.

No. 1: I suppose so.

No. 2: Will this love change everything?

No. 3: Things will never be the same.

No. 4: Love is making all things new.

Reflections on the Drama

This piece was written for the seventieth birthday of a much loved and respected former minister of the church. When I was approached to write a piece of drama for this occasion, I was busy undertaking some research and writing on Black identity and Black theological method.[99] The title for the celebratory act of worship was "Love is Making All Things New." With this theme in mind, I began to reflect and plan for the short piece I was to write.

Love is the Answer is different in form and method than the previous pieces of drama I have analysed. In the first instance, it is more of a dramatic reading than a piece of drama *per se*. Secondly, unlike the other pieces it does not contain an explicit Black hermeneutic within the text. None of the characters are identified as being Black, and the themes at play within the drama cannot be said to explicitly represent aspects of Black culture or cultural production.

The New Arrival and *The Wisdom of Solomon* contain visibly recognizable Black characters. *My God!?* has the central character of God as a Black woman. In contrast to the previous pieces, *Love is the Answer* is more implicit or even generic in its treatment of the various characters and the themes at play in the drama. And yet despite its seemingly generic treatment (something which I critiqued in the previous chapter), I would argue that the central thesis of this sketch remains, nonetheless, true to the major tenets of Black theology. Reading this drama in light of Black theological thought emphasizes a number of the major themes at play in Black theology.

Love is the Answer was written for what I knew would be a predominantly Black congregation/audience. Although I realized that the commissioning of this piece was made by a White minister, and was intended for an inclusive, inter-cultural context, I approached the writing of this piece as a self-consciously driven Black religious scholar. The drama, while not as explicit as some of the other pieces I have written,[100] remains faithful to the dramatic interpretation of Black theology within this study.

The Theology at Play in *Love is the Answer*

One of the central concerns of Black theological discourse has been the desire to challenge and surmount the damaging psychological fault lines that have been implanted in the Black psyche arising from the era of slavery. In the first chapter, I outlined some of the seeds for the negative portrayal of Black people, which arose from the falsehood of White supremacist thought. The wholesale negation of Black selfhood has led to the internalization of racialized oppression, and the fostering of pathological levels of self-hatred.

One of the most important scholars within the wider field of African-centred studies is W. E. B. Dubois. Dubois cannot be described as a Black theologian in any easy or convenient sense, but his penetrating analysis of the "Black condition," nevertheless, has provided many Black religious scholars with the necessary tools to interrogate Black ontology.

One of Dubois' most important theories was that of "double consciousness."

Dubois and *Double Consciousness*

The notion of competing realities is not a new phenomenon for Black people. This was first detailed by the great W. E. B. Dubois in his now classic text *The Souls of Black Folk* first published in 1903. Dubois detailed a phenomenon he termed "double consciousness." In using this term, Dubois was speaking of the struggle evinced within African American people to reconcile two opposing realities at war within the Black psyche.[101] This dialectical struggle was one between competing notions of truth, whether determined by a self-affirming internalized form of subjectivity, what Pinn calls the quest for "complex subjectivity,"[102] or an all-embracing externalized form of negation and objectification. Dubois' most memorable comment in this book, that has to a great extent helped to define Black

Diasporan discourse over the course of the last century, was that the "the problem of the 20th century is the problem of the color line."[103]

In the first instance there is the internal vision of a self that is positive and clothed in the garment of belonging and self-affirmation. This internalized vision is juxtaposed alongside the external world of White hegemony in which that same Black self is denigrated, demonized and disparaged. These two "unreconciled strivings"[104] have continued to fight their tumultuous struggle within the battlefield of the Black mind.

The struggle for dignity and affirmation, although given sharp focus by the externalized factors of racialized oppression and White supremacy, also contain, however, subjective internalized dimensions. Doreen Morrison has challenged Black theologians and religious scholars to attend to these internal dimensions as opposed to a seemingly sole preoccupation with the externalized factors of racism.[105]

Fred Smith, an African American religious educator, details the work he has undertaken with Black boys in order to counter the negative self-image of these individuals. A consequence of such poor self-concepts is the greater propensity to resort to violence as a means of dealing with one's problems.[106]

Struggling to Exist in an Inhospitable Environment

The notion of exile has always been a prominent theme within Black religiosity and the theology that has arisen from it. The notion of exile, whether in terms of physical estrangement from a specific geographical location,[107] cultural and communitarian estrangement[108] or spiritual estrangement,[109] remains a powerful motif within Black religious thought.

Love is the Answer contains a dramatic dialogue in which the central character is challenged by a "Seriously Weird Person" to re-engage with his or her inner self. The central protagonist is fuelled by a deep torrent of self-negation and anger, which seems to strikes a chord with the notion of "low level rage," articulated by Robert Beckford. Reflecting in part upon his own experiences as an African Caribbean British male trying to deal with racism, Beckford writes:

> I stayed quiet because I feared being pathologised as the "angry Black male with a chip on his shoulder." As a Black man, I was conscious of wanting to limit my aggression and assertiveness in response to injustice. A long time before, I had made the conscious decision, in response to inner-city comprehensive schooling, to suppress my rage and find other ways to negotiate racism.[110]

The rage that Beckford and many Black people feel in trying to negotiate life in a post-colonial world, where the all-pervasive spectre of racism stalks our consciousness, lies at the heart of the multiple traumas that bedevil the central protagonist in this drama. This individual is burdened by many ills, personal and societal, systemic and individual, physical and spiritual, which are met by the healing resources of the "Seriously Weird Person." The "Seriously Weird Person" does not identify him/herself, nor reveal any significant details that might help us, the viewer or reader to know him/her in any sense. Rather, this individual is known by their deeds—the healing ministry that transforms the inner life of the troubled central character. The praxis of this stranger destroys the old vestiges of the negated and self-destructive self, and brings new life possibilities to the central character. The power of love proves to be the emotive fuel that transforms this troubled individual.

Black theology has often been characterized as a polemical, iconoclastic theology committed to changing the systemic and structural abuses that oppress subjugated Black people who are denied their authentic voice. Yet in spite of this overarching perception and seeming pre-occupation, one must never minimize the importance of the personal emotional transformative power of Black theology. The spirituality at work in such scholars as James Cone,[111] Emile Townes,[112] Renita Weems,[113] Josiah Young[114] and Robert Beckford[115] continue to juxtapose the structural and the external with the internal and the subjective.

Conclusion

In this chapter, I have attempted to demonstrate how many of the central themes of Black theology can be illustrated and "brought to life" within a dramatic structure. In the three pieces I have highlighted in the chapter (in addition to the previous piece towards the end of Chapter 2), there exists a means of articulating Black theology, in addition to a method for presenting this discipline in a more accessible form, for those who reside outside of the academy.

Naturally, given the limitations of drama (some of which will be explored in the following two chapters) I cannot claim that the version of Black theology created within this study can encapsulate the finer points of a systematic treatise on this discipline. Rather, what I have presented is an alternative means of undertaking Black theology, in which the central ideas of this enterprise are distilled into a dramatic form in order that those who are the "voiceless" can find their voice within an interactive, participative format.

In the following chapter, I will seek to delve behind the facility of drama, in order to uncover a method by which the educator and theologian may construct relevant dramatic pieces that engage with the repressed selfhood of the voiceless.

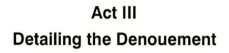

Act III
Detailing the Denouement

4 What Lies Behind the Façade?: Developing an Underlying Method for Bringing Drama and Black Theology Together

In the last chapter I demonstrated the means by which Black theology can be carried in a dramatic form in order to represent the concerns of marginalized and oppressed Black people who represent the voiceless presence in the present world order. In this chapter, I want to investigate the means by which these and other dramatic materials can be created in order to present and reflect an authentic theology of the voiceless.

In order to analyse the process that enabled me to create these pieces of drama (in addition to imagining the newer pieces that might emerge), I have sought to utilize concepts and epistemologies that arise from a range of disciplines.

Being in Solidarity with Those who are the Voiceless

One of the primary faults of many theologians and cultural commentators, who work on behalf of the voiceless, has been their inability to inhabit the "world" of those individuals and communities. Within historical and more contemporary discourse there has been a noble tradition of scholars speaking on "behalf" of and rarely "with" those who might be considered the voiceless. I have detailed some of these ongoing tensions in the first chapter of this book.

How can theology and the mission of the church speak with and enable others to find their voice, rather than speaking for them? In my area and context, I am aware that it has been a relatively recent innovation for Black scholars and authors to document the Black religious experience in Britain. Prior to the determined efforts of Black religious scholars to "name" their own experiences,[1] it was not uncommon to find the bulk of religious and cultural analysis of Black people undertaken by White European academics.

It is not my contention that those from outside of the Black experience cannot write accurately or act in solidarity with those who reside within an African and Caribbean framework. Such a contention, although espoused by some commentators,[2] is not one I wish to pursue at this juncture. As I hope to demonstrate shortly, talking about "insiders" and "outsiders" in the representation and analysis of any discourse is not a simplistic affair. It is made complicated by issues such as context, the ontology of the people under discussion and the positionality of the scholar attempting to document that particular phenomenon.

I want to eschew any seemingly simplistic notion of "outsiders" and "insiders," which carry the restrictive refrain of essentialism and the notion of hard and fast boundaries that seem to "police" cultural experience and their accompanying production. As Lartey reminds, culture is a dynamic, human construction, which rejects any sense of fixity.[3] In some respects, human beings are very different from one another, in terms of ethnicity, gender, class, geographical location or historical experience. Yet in other ways, the common experience of being human remains the ultimate unifying concept for all people. Lartey sums this up beautifully when he writes:

> Every human person is in certain respects:
> 1. Like all others
> 2. Like some others
> 3. Like no other.[4]

Clearly, it is both difficult and, in some respects, dangerous to create fixed lines detailing who belongs to (and presumably can speak for) a particular group or community and who does not belong, with the opposite being the case. When I speak of scholars being in solidarity with the voiceless, I am conscious of the complexities and philosophical and cultural nuances at play, as I invoke this term. How can any scholar authentically live within the world of the voiceless?

My analysis of Black theology in the previous chapter was largely done by means of accessing the rich literature of largely African American scholars. While there is no doubt that scholars both identify with and consider themselves to be a part of the wider community and cultures of Black people in the US, to what extent can they be said to inhabit the worldview of those who are the poorest and most dispossessed of their number? Surely, the very fact that many of them are professors within the theological academy renders them a distant presence from the very subjects who might be described as being the voiceless?

Perhaps Victor Anderson is correct in reminding Black theologians of their ongoing tendency to collapse significant differences within the Black experience through their refusal to address significant issues aside from "race" and racism?[5]

Aspects of this seeming contradiction confronted me in a previous piece of work. When writing *Faith, Stories and the Experience of Black Elders,*[6] I was conscious of the privileged position I occupied as a Black religious scholar. I was accorded the privilege of entering into the experiences of a group of Black elders, who, due to the pernicious, silencing tendencies of racism, have been rendered mute in post-colonial Britain. And yet, here was I, as a Black scholar, creating a book based on the silence of others! The irony was crushing.

The task of trying to act in solidarity with those who are voiceless is a seemingly impossible task. Writers such as Laurie Green,[7] Kenneth Leech[8] and John Vincent[9] have attempted to inhabit and act in solidarity with those who are marginalized and oppressed. While there is a great deal that is commendable about the work of these scholars, I remain unconvinced about the extent to which the voice of the voiceless emerges from the pages of these very fine books. The writers speak for their subjects. I am aware that my comments may appear somewhat harsh and unfair.

How can the voiceless speak for themselves in a manner that will enable them to be heard? The academy works on the basis of text. Publishing remains the medium of choice for the articulation of new knowledge. How do we persuade the voiceless to write their stories? Do they want to write, and indeed, why should they? As I have intimated previously, I have been conspicuously unsuccessful in enabling the voiceless to speak for themselves in my past work.

What I hope to demonstrate through the facility of drama is that Black theology can be undertaken with voiceless, oppressed Black people, as a means of enabling them to discover and verbalize their authentic experiences. In order that this method for undertaking theology can reach its optimum potency, it is necessary that we create an appropriate mechanism for bringing the self-defined experiences of the voiceless to light. How can drama accurately reflect a theology that is both for and of the voiceless?

In short, how could I convert the often serendipitous developments of the dramatic pieces highlighted in the previous chapters into a consistent method for articulating a process of dramatizing theologies that ultimately can be owned by the voiceless?

Before I outline the methodological framework that has assisted me in this task, let me first outline, briefly, a number of factors that should inform this approach.

Preliminary Issues Prior to Being in Solidarity with the Voiceless

Critical openness

The concept of the term "critical openness" has, in many respects, become synonymous with the work of John Hull, who for many years was Professor of Religious Education at the University of Birmingham.[10] I have referred to the work of Hull and his concept of "critical openness." If the voiceless are to be enabled to discover their authentic selfhood, the educational processes within the overarching structure of theological discourse must contain an embedded commitment to this cause.

Black theology since its earliest inception has been in the business of constructing new ways of thinking about God in the service of Black liberation and wholeness of life. It has recognized that the Christian faith has always been policed and controlled. This can be seen by the use of creeds and concomitant denominational doctrinal standards. There has always existed a high importance attached to internal orthodoxy and consistency of belief. Emphasis has been placed upon the necessity to observe the orthodox truth claims of the meta-narrative. This naturally leads to the need for authority, training and education to expound upon it. Can the seemingly uneducated (in the eyes of White authority, that is) voiceless mass of Black people be trusted with this story?[11] Jeff Astley, speaking on the issue of lay theological education, states:

> One gets the impression sometimes, not least from some clergy, that adult Christian education is a dangerous thing, that adult church members are to be protected from and indeed ministers themselves need to be protected from exposure to an educated laity.[12]

While Black theology has remained committed to articulating a view of God that challenges the top-down patrician conception of the Christian faith, we should be in no doubt that Black church practices need reforming in addition to those tendencies within White hegemony. As I have shown from my analysis of *My God!?*, patriarchy and androcentrism remain deeply embedded within Black religio-cultural practices. The radical freedom of Christ is often compromised within conservative social mores and restrictive doctrine. Grant Shockley details the means by which the Black church in the US has linked a conservative educational pedagogy to a top-down clerically dominant perspective of ecclesial life.[13]

In these contexts, the poorest, most disenfranchised, inhibited objects are still denied voice in favour of those who are better educated and more "respectable."[14] Beckford argues that one manifestation of an uncritical perspective on Christian tradition and the Bible is an enforced rigidity on issues such as jewellery (the prohibition on wearing wedding rings, for example) and women wearing hats in church.[15]

A number of scholars have asserted that a key component in the development of an inclusive, non-restrictive means of articulating Christian faith is by acknowledging the importance of "critical openness." This term within the context of this study refers to a process of theological reflection that takes the autonomy of the individual seriously, and encourages them to engage critically with the inherited story and tradition. The Christian story is not necessarily a closed or a fixed entity.[16]

Pedagogy

The Roman Catholic religious educator James Michael Lee has challenged the neo-orthodox notion of reflection within Christian thought as being principally a theological and not an educational affair. He has been dismissive of pneumatological perspectives on Christian reflection, denouncing them as the "Blow theory."[17] It is interesting to note that, in the development of Black theology on both sides of the Atlantic, relatively little cognizance has been given to the need for effective pedagogy. Is pedagogy important? Relatively little of the aforementioned concerns are in evidence either in Black theological discourse or in the Black church, particularly in its efficacy with lay people. (Clergy, of course, need to be educated.)

Critical questions of pedagogy include the types of models we employ within Black theological discourse. Are these connected with inducting people into existing communities of faith? In this particular approach, emphasis is placed upon models of socialization that will assist individuals to learn the cultural, societal and religious frameworks that govern that particular community of faith.[18] Alternative approaches include the faith/spiritual development model, a liberationist perspective (my own preferred model and one employed in this study) or the interpretative approach.[19]

In constructing a pedagogical framework for working with the voiceless, from where does one start? Who oversees the process? Where is the most effective location for this reflection and learning to take place, and what are the social norms for this construct? Are they inside, within, or beyond the church? These issues will be addressed in the latter part of this chapter and in Chapter 5.

Within the context of this study, particular attention has been given to the efficacy of attempting to work in a participatory manner. There has been much written on the importance of critical shared reflection as a means of undertaking theological reflection.[20] I was also cognizant of the literature, which while supportive of the general tenure of Black/Liberationist approaches to pedagogy and learning, seeks to problematize and critique many of the basic assumptions of these approaches to participatory reflection. Can an inclusive, participatory pedagogy cope with the dichotomous, transcendent epistemology of many Black people, where their resulting discourse may be heavily censured as a form of signifying. The religious forms of knowing and truth of Black people are often identified and categorized by scholars as modalities of subterfuge and disguise.

Cognizance of these helped to nuance the alacrity with which I adopted the facility of drama as an inclusive and participative pedagogy for undertaking Black theological discourse.

Self-actualization

Theological reflection recognizes the importance of realizing one's personal potential as an important aspect of Christian discipleship. Christian maturity is in essence a reversal of humanist perspectives on actualization, that is, people achieve their highest form of personhood through *a denial of self* and an ongoing process of imitating Christ. Pauline theology stresses the necessity of losing oneself in Christ. (See 2 Cor. 10:5 and Gal. 2:20.) Within the related areas of practical/Pastoral theology, the literature pertaining to faith development theory (whether Fowler,[21] Nipkow[22] or Westerhoff[23]) stresses the importance of faith/spiritual growth. Self-actualization through reflection offers a critical challenge to the wholesale fragmentation and self-absorption of post-modernity. It is the quest for authentic, critical living and believing.

Much of the aforementioned has been largely absent in Black religious thought. The work of Grant Shockley[24] and Anne Wimberly[25] needs to be supplemented by newer scholars, particularly in Britain. This method for articulating and engaging in praxis-driven approaches to Black British theology offers a critically constructive and interactive means of engaging with issues of process (methodology and pedagogy) in addition to the usual concerns surrounding content. The work of Philip Richter and Leslie Francis[26] has shown that people are more likely not to attend church due to the lack of appropriate pastoral care and the ineffectiveness of the Christian story to accord with their story and less because the "content" does not make sense.

If Black theology in Britain is to achieve one of its stated aims, namely, the re-energizing of Black faith communities in this country, we must not be afraid to throw off the often stultifying constraints of orthodoxy. We must not pretend that the meaning of Christian theology is uncontested. On the contrary, from its inception there has been an internal (and external) conversation regarding the import, necessity and meaning of the Christian faith. Bhikhu Parekh makes some interesting points regarding the internal dialogue and self-understanding of Christianity from a cultural perspective.[27] The process of Black theological reflection must be multi-sensory and bi-focal. This process is one that attends to the cognitive and affective domains of human experience.[28] Such a process is also aligned with attitudinal and behavioural changes, leading to a belief in Jesus as Christ and saviour.[29] Can this heavy burden of attempting to democratize and free Black theology from the academic prison in which it has languished since the late 1960s be achieved by means of recourse to drama?

Using a Participation Observational Model for Engaging with the Voiceless

In order to engage with those who I have termed the voiceless, in a manner that would emphasize their autonomy and subjectivity, it was essential that a theoretical and practical framework was found, which would foster consistent "truth-telling." I was unconvinced of the efficacy of traditional theological discourse in this regard. It is interesting to note the general drift in Black theology amongst what might be termed the "Third Generation" of Black scholars. The emphasis has moved from doctrinal or systematic concerns into more inter-disciplinary avenues, often risking the charge of being merely self-indulgent entertainment for its own sake, shorn of the need to engage with the contextual needs of a wider community. The work of Pinn,[30] Dyson[31] and Beckford,[32] for example, has alighted on the area of Black popular culture as an arena for pursuing Black theological discourse. Influenced by these scholars, and more recently, by the work of Thomas,[33] I have chosen to use the arena of ethnography and participant observation as a means for distilling the issues and concerns of Black people. This method of interrogating Black experience enabled me to gain valuable insights into the world of the voiceless, in order that I could then create critical dramatic pieces that would become the conduit for a theology for those without a voice.

Participant observation is viewed as a distinct and important element within the wider area of ethnographic study. Participant observation requires that researchers engage with the ongoing life experiences of the people that they are attempting to study. While the philosophical roots of participant observation are to be found in social anthropology, the origins for the practical application of this discipline lie in the Chicago school of social research in the 1920s and 1930s. This rise of observational research in Chicago led to a whole arena of study that found expression in diverse social and cultural milieus such as criminology, "race," and urban studies.[34]

The importance of participant observation as a methodological tool has been charted by, amongst others, William Whyte. Over a prolonged period, utilizing this method in a variety of contexts Whyte attests to the efficacy and contribution of participant observation to social-scientific research.[35]

A number of anthropologists, cultural and literary theorists, sociologists and researchers have found that the seemingly simple art of observation is a very grave misnomer. Writers such as Hammersley,[36] Glaser and Strauss,[37] Pryce,[38] Bryman[39] and Silverman[40] have commented on the complexities of researchers observing social situations. Concerns that arise from this literature surround the conceit and deceit in the theoretical assumptions of the observer in relaying their perceptions of what might be termed observed reality.

Getting involved

An assumed maxim of ethnographic work, particularly in the use of participant observation, is the notion of social interaction with the context and significant others within that specific milieu. Participant observation avoids value-free data collection and observation.[41] The researcher is expected to become a part of the social world that they are investigating and attempting to document.

The realization that the researcher is immersed, inextricably, in the social milieu they are attempting to document leads us into the difficult area of subjectivity. How far does the very presence of the researcher influence the social situation they are observing?

Given the presence of the researcher as participant and observer, one would expect a degree of influence to be exerted upon the social situation by the individual conducting the research. Some researchers have poured scorn upon the notion of naturalistic[42] forms of ethnographic research. This particular stance is seen by many as a myth. Accounts that purport to describe any situation on these grounds are often over simplistic in their analysis.[43]

Insider versus outsider accounts

There is an ongoing encounter between the researcher and the environment in which he or she is operating and seeking to document. At issue, for many, is not the question of engagement and influence. Rather, their concerns are focused upon the reflective nature of that engagement and how this relationship is reflected in the documentation of that situation by the researcher. Writers such as Clifford Geertz, for example, have discussed at length the methodological issues involved in interpreting the reality of people's diverse cultures, and the nature of one's own interpretation upon the writing of ethnographic accounts.[44]

Researchers and writers working within an ethnographic paradigm are expected to engage with the social situation in which they are operating. This, in turn, leads to the corollary of how one attempts to document that particular milieu. Can the researcher undertake this task with greater accuracy and integrity, if they are insiders or outsiders? How do they belong? Can they belong?

The issues that underlie these questions have been confronted by a number of researchers and writers. Robert Jackson details some of the historical and contemporary issues in the field of social anthropology, citing the work of Geertz and his hermeneutic method. Jackson contrasts Geertz's approaches with those from the deconstruction school, who are suspicious of text and the interpretations of the researcher/writer.[45]

The adequacy of ethnographic accounts is questioned from a philosophical perspective, concerning the veracity of various forms of descriptive writing. Additional questions surround the subjective bias and power of the ethnographer,[46] which are influenced largely by our notions of location and space.

In an earlier book Jackson and Nesbitt outline the fruits of their research with Hindu children in Britain.[47] In their work with Hindu children the authors contend with the issue of being outsiders to the group with whom they are working. In such situations, difficulties in understanding certain concepts or values may arise given the cross-cultural nature of the engagement between researcher and informant.[48] One of the primary difficulties in this type of discourse, particularly from an inter-cultural perspective, is the issue of "experience-near" and "experience-distant" concepts.

Jackson and Nesbitt describe this issue in the following terms. Experience-near concepts are those

> [w]hich insiders use naturally to define their thoughts, feelings and so forth. "Experience-distant" concepts, on the other hand, are those (in this case) employed by ethnographers often as analytic terms.[49]

Experience-distant concepts usually represent attempts by external researchers to develop theoretical frameworks that permit them to categorize and delineate the behaviour, feelings and thoughts of the people with whom they are working. There is the temptation upon the researcher to use his or her power to impose these external conceptualizations on to the people who are the focus of their study. Often, these conceptualizations are made without sufficient recourse to the internal, experience-near concepts that connote meaning for the informant.

Geertz outlines a means of overcoming the inherent tensions between the internal subjectivity of those within the social situation and the external researcher seeking to describe, analyse and document. His method utilizes both experience-near and experience-distant concepts in order to provide a wider vista that contains the nuances of that particular milieu.[50]

A number of researchers have reported their difficulties in the documentation and understanding of a social situation, particularly when that understanding appears to be at variance with those who would describe themselves as official insiders.[51]

In contrast to the work of Jackson *et al.*, others have sought to engage in ethnographic work from the perspective of the insider. While this may seem desirable on a somewhat assumptive level, as Dhadeka Sashadi Raj has shown, the dichotomy between insider and outsider, and the alleged superiority of the former, can be a false one.[52]

Similarly, Lubna Nazir Chaudhry details her own research amongst the Muslim community in Northern California. In her work, she details some of the stresses and tensions of being an insider undertaking ethnographic research amongst people with whom she has an intimate knowledge and empathy.[53] Chaudhry explains the pressures she felt being pulled between two competing perspectives that informed her role as an ethnographer. In the first instance Chaudry is influenced by post-colonial and post-structural leanings in her anthropological work. This perspective, however, is juxtaposed with a sense of wanting the approbation of her peers, many of whom are suspicious of her presence and the role she exercises within that setting.[54]

In the context of this study, it has been hoped that I have inhabited the role of "critical insider." In using this term, I want to draw attention to the dialectic struggle at the heart of my attempt to construct an overarching theological framework that can reflect and become an empowering presence for those who are rendered voiceless.

Putting Ethnography to Work in the Service of the Voiceless

My hope in utilizing the method of participant observation is to enable a more critical and honest assessment of the religio-cultural context and experience that has shaped and continues to influence the subjective selfhood of Black people. How does being (for the most part) poor, Black and without influence or positive visibility affect one's immediate outlook in post-colonial Britain?

As I have outlined in my analysis of *The New Arrival* and *The Wisdom of Solomon*, Black cultures and the cultural production that arises from this phenomenon have proved vital tools in the ongoing work of Black religious scholars.[55]

What I propose to do in this section of the study is to use the overarching framework of ethnography and participant observation, to reflect on and analyse the socio-cultural and religious context of voiceless Black people in Britain. This analysis will serve as the backdrop to my ongoing attempts to create an approach to doing theology in partnership with the voiceless through the medium of drama. I hope to draw upon the insights of educationists, cultural theorists and developmental psychologists to assist me in this analysis.

Post-modern Game Playing—Time for a Barn Dance

The challenge to accurately distil the central characteristics and features that inform the experience of any community has been documented in the previous section on participant observation. Much of the aforementioned discourse has been my understanding of some of the literature pertaining to the overarching methodology of ethnography. If I wanted to work alongside Black voiceless people in an act of solidarity, it was imperative that I devise a means of making the fruits of the aforementioned discourse more accessible in order that these people can assess its veracity for themselves.

In a previous piece of ethnographic research, I investigated the whole area of Christian education and nurture of African Caribbean children in inner-city churches in Birmingham.[56] At a mid point in the research, I analysed a number of religio-cultural festivals in the differing churches. I was interested to see how these churches celebrated "Harvest Festival" and to what extent Black religious and cultural expressions of faith were in evidence within these settings. On one occasion, I was amazed to find myself in a Black majority setting with a number of Black young people, trying to participate in a very traditional barn dance. The idea of Black people engaging in a barn dance intrigued me.

Constraints of time prevent any significant description or definition of a barn dance. Some have described the barn dance as follows.

> A Barn Dance (sometimes called a Ceilidh) is a collection of dances which can be done by anyone who can walk, and knows their left from their right hand! The dances are usually fairly straight forward and can be learnt on the night of the dance with the help of the caller. No previous knowledge is required.[57]

Barn dances have their origins deep within the folk culture of village life in England, and in other parts of the world, particularly North America. Observing these Black young people smiling at the sight of their parents and grandparents, attempting to join their White peers in learning the steps to a traditional White (British) cultural practice, implanted in my mind an idea that would assist me many years later.

Why not combine the insights of ethnography with an experiential learning model based upon an imaginary construct—namely a barn dance?

Constructing the Imaginary Barn Dance

Working with three groups of Black young people in London (although in the final analysis, only data from group one was used in the development of this work),[58] I invited the various participants to construct an imaginary barn dance. Group one consisted of eight Black young people, between the ages of eighteen and twenty-one. All the participants were born in Britain. Five of the group were male and three were female. Of the eight participants, five had grandparents who were born in the Caribbean.

The other three were born in Africa. The parents of these young people were, for the most part, born in Britain (six of the eight). All group participants belonged to a Black majority church of some form (Church of God of Prophecy, New Testament Church, Adventist, Methodist, Anglican and the Baptist churches).

I met with the group on three occasions. The task I set them was to make an exhaustive list of the various approaches one would undertake in order to "discover the truth" of the barn dance. What approaches would enable them to learn the central features and issues at play in this fictitious barn dance? What were the different ways one might interrogate the reality of the barn dance?

The only rules for undertaking this exercise in self-actualization was that the young people should imagine themselves as being present at the barn dance, both as a participant and an observer. This thought, quite naturally, generated a good deal of levity, as many of the young people could not imagine themselves ever attending a "dry" event like a barn dance.

The various group members were encouraged to adopt the position as the "critical friend" at this imaginary event. Their presence was to imaginatively join in with the whole phenomenon of the event. They should dance and interact with the imaginary others, but juxtaposed with this participation was the critical element of observation. In their capacity as participant and observer, what questions would come to mind? What would emerge from their engagement with others in the barn dance? Extracts of what emerged from this exercise is detailed below.

The subsequent responses of the group to these questions included the following lines of inquiry. The list below is an indicative one. The order of the questions in the list does not imply any level of importance, but simply reflects the order in which the various queries arose.

- Who decides when and where the barn dance should take place?
- Who decides (and how) what kind of dance is undertaken at the event?
- Are there rules or instructions as to how the dance should be undertaken? If yes, then how are these rules learnt?
- Who first devised this event? Is there a historical record documenting its development?
- Who does the "calling" (of the instructions or moves)?
- How is this person chosen? Is there a training course you have to attend?
- Is this position (and other roles within the dance) open to both genders?
- What type of music is played at the dance? Who decides this? Is it one person (the caller?), a group of people or the whole community?

- Does the community that holds the barn dance meet up only for these particular events, or do they meet on other occasions? If the latter, then where and for what purpose?
- What kinds of people attend the barn dance? (Ethnicity, age, gender, class).
- Does any one ethnic group dominate the dance (either in terms of office holding, leadership roles or simply in numerical terms)?
- Do you need an invite to attend, or can anyone come to the dance?
- How long has the dance been in existence?
- Has the nature of the dance changed in all those years? (Styles of music, dance steps, the customs and culture of the dance, etc.).

What was most impressive about this exercise was the means by which the group quickly became aware of the metaphorical basis of this imaginary construct. Clearly, we *were not talking about a barn dance per se*. The group saw the barn dance as a metaphor for church, or in more macro terms, Black people in Britain as a whole.

In order to explore these ideas further, I asked the various individuals to reflect upon the imaginary barn dance, with particular emphasis being placed upon those questions that seemed most intriguing or relevant to them. Which of the various points raised in their previous discussions were the most important?

The young people were mainly concerned with issues of "style and interpretation." There appeared less concern with the particular factual elements of the dance, such as the history or the development of the event. What concerned the group to a much greater extent were those questions pertaining to how the dance was constructed, and who got to decide what style of music or moves were permitted at this cultural event.

My intention in devising this exercise was to see whether in using the method of participant observation in an imaginative, dramatic form, one might enable these young people to interrogate their reality more critically. I was not concerned, to any great extent, with the content of their responses.[59] Rather, I wanted to assess the process of thought that might emerge from this exercise. In what ways did this exercise, which incorporated many of the salient features of participant observation, enable these young participants to reflect upon aspects of their own culture and identity?

In using this creative and dramatic device, I wanted to create an affective dissonance between the subject and the wider cultural environment. Previous research with Black young people had alerted me to the fact that learnt behaviour and the strictures of religious socialization often create a level of inhibition and constricted thought in any resulting discourse arising from the encounter with a researcher.[60] In short, people learn the correct language and terms to use, which often lead to an ability to speak a more explicit truth arising from experience.

In using this device, it was my hope that these Black young people would be enabled, through a distancing process, to critically engage with their wider environment and context. The semantic "game playing" was very much embedded within the framework of the exercise. As the young people began to imagine themselves dancing and participating in this barn dance, they realized instinctively that this exercise was both real and imaginary. The exercise was both about the barn dance and concerned with greater issues external to this event.

This sense of a dialectic consciousness is a staple ingredient of a number of approaches within Practical theology. This dialectical consciousness can be seen in the work of Jerome Berryman and his approach to undertaking theological reflection with young children,[61] or the Womanist-inspired pedagogy of Lynne Westfield.[62] In both schemas, the ability to dialectically hold two competing notions of truth, and allow them to interplay with each other, is central to the methodology of their work.

The fact that these Black young people were very much concerned with the style and interpretation of the dance calls to mind the research of Janice Hale-Benson and her pioneering work into the learning styles of Black children in the US.[63] Hale-Benson argues that one of the characteristic features of the learning styles of Black children is their ability to improvise and create new meaning from established norms or templates, rather than attempting to replicate those existing patterns.[64] These young people were not overly concerned with the possible rules of engagement within this imaginary construct. Rather, their primary interest lay in how they might express themselves within this cultural context. Particular emphasis was given to the covert or implicit rules within the barn dance. How could one know if what was stated about this phenomenon was the whole truth? What if "certain people in power were chatting long talk (empty rhetoric) but were hiding their true motives"?

This theme became a re-occurring one in the final section of the three meetings. How could we know the truth of any situation? Would we recognize the truth if and when it confronted us?

The contemporary resonance of this discourse for the religious and theological sensibilities of the various participants was stark and self-evident. A number of participants spoke of the restricted nature of their church and the limitations imposed upon them by church leadership often out of touch with the needs of young people. The suspicion levelled at ecclesial authority echoes the much vaunted "hermeneutic of suspicion," based on commonsense experience that is at the heart of Black theological discourse.[65]

"Just because they say it goes like that, doesn't mean to say it has to go like that!" There speaks the words of one of the group participants.

Issues Arising from the Exercise

Amongst the number of factors that emerged from this exercise was the sense that these young people were enabled to reinterpret their reality by means of a distanced, yet engaged dramatic metaphor. Upon the conclusion of the second of three sets of meetings, I asked the group to identify a central theme or concern around which I could write a drama that might explore these issues.

After a great deal of conversation and hilarity, it was felt that the issue that most came to mind was that of "truth telling." Can people be trusted when they make particular pronouncements? Is it not the case that "everyone has something to hide"? Further discussion led the group to consider the life and ministry of Jesus. Could he be trusted? Were his motives clear and unambiguous?

In the midst of this ongoing discussion, I was at pains to remind myself of the disparity between myself and my research subjects. I was a male academic in my late thirties. There existed some twenty years between this group and myself, and a significant gulf in our social status. I am a recognized scholar within my church and the theological institution in which I work. These young people were largely anonymous. Five of the group were unemployed. Two members of the group were at university, with large overdrafts from the bank and no certainty as to their future employment. Another individual was working for the local authority. It was his first job, and he was twenty-one years old.

I was conscious of the tendency amongst Black people to "signify" when in the company of authority figures. Beckford describes signifying as

> [t]he ways in which African Caribbean cultures "play," "manoeuvre" and "conjure" a subject, issue or event so as to arrive at "direction through indirection." Signifying can be a form of trickery that enables oppressed people to negotiate or manipulate the dominant power.[66]

Given the tendency of Black people to signify, I was determined to exercise some caution in terms of the discourse that emerged from my encounters with the group. Might they be guilty of telling me what I wanted to hear? The challenges of engaging with this group of largely voiceless Black young people (very much reminding me of myself when I was their age) were very real and clearly apparent. As a Black religious scholar, was I working at the behest of their church leaders, in order to convince them of the efficacy of attending church and believing in God in a more orthodox manner? My assurances that I was working independently were largely heeded, but to what extent they were internalized and believed is a moot point.

Creating the Next Piece of Drama

In order to further the discussion, I felt I needed to write a piece of drama for the group to perform in and reflect upon. Time was short, and I had many other pressing tasks to undertake, so the resulting piece was very impressionistic and very much a "first attempt." I was struck by the fact that the group expected me to write something that would be seen as "the usual Christian stuff. Telling us what to believe." In response to their cynical jibes, the following piece was created. *Style and Fashion* attempted to resonate with the deep ambiguity and concern of the group with regard to issues of truth-telling and integrity. To what extent could people in power or those holding office be trusted? I sensed that the group had a number of obvious targets in mind when they shared these concerns—their ministers being one target and elected politicians being another.

STYLE AND FASHION

The scene…we see a Black militant woman, dressed in a combat jacket, Doctor Marten boots and wearing a very old, tatty bobble hat. She is member of a very millitant left wing group. She is stood next to a bus stop. She is shouting out slogans and handing out tracts and pamphlets.

WOMAN: [*Shouting out*] Death to White people and all they stand for. An end to White capitalism. End the oppression of Black people. Black is the rock and roll of the future. Nuff respec' to the brothers and the sisters of the struggle.

[*A neatly dressed Black man walks by and is approached by the woman.*]

MAN: [*To* WOMAN] Carol, is that you?

WOMAN: Join the struggle, comrade. We need to grab the means of production for ourselves. To unchain the shackles of Babylon that has burdened the African people since Whitey came and stole our t'ings. We need…

MAN: Carol, it's me… Giles…

WOMAN: Giles? Is that you?

MAN: How goes it?

WOMAN: I'm OK. And you? What have you been doing since Oxford?

MAN: Been working in the City. Advertising. The industry's been a bit rough of late, but I'm still scratching a living. Making 30k, or thereabouts. And you?

WOMAN: I'm into international struggle against Babylon and capitalism these days. You want to join the struggle, my brother?

MAN: [*Looking Carol up and down*] I don't think so. I dig the struggle, I really do. I once wore a dashiki and sported a beard like Bob Marley and hung out with a funky sister from Somalia when I was at Uni, so I'm down with you sista, I really am.

WOMAN: So what about going the full way, and dedicating your life to the abolition of the exploitation of the working class?

MAN: [*Looking Carol up and down*] I'd love to, Carol… But I couldn't hack the clothes. I love the working class, I really do, and I've always been sympathetic to wippets and outside toilets; but do you have to look like a pile of crap when you go out? Look at those threads, my sista? I'm getting a headache looking at you, Carol.

WOMAN: But Giles, clothes are a materialistic construct. They signify the inherent class structure that has strangled this country for centuries. Throw away your clothes.

MAN: And walk stark-bollock naked? I don't think so, Carol. I prefer to parade my genitals to one woman at a time, not the entire population of central London.

WOMAN: [*Shaking head*] You're lost, comrade. The system has dulled your mind.

MAN: And you sold your bedroom mirror. How could you even leave the house wearing trousers that were not Ferruchi? … [*Shaking head*]… Horrid man, simply horrid.

WOMAN: I'm free… I'm a liberated woman.

MAN: So what happened, Carol? Someone stole your credit cards? Your designer left the country? I can help you, my sista, I know the name of a sweet designer in central London who could restore your image overnight.

WOMAN: Marx came into my bedroom one night and gave me enlightenment.

MAN: I hope he was wearing a condom at the time.

WOMAN: I've been set free. I want to set the working class free.

MAN: By dressing like a hobo?

WOMAN: My clothes are an expression of solidarity with the oppressed of the world.

MAN: They're a symbol of your bad taste... [*Looking down at her shoes*]... That combat jacket and the hat. Lord have mercy on my soul. That is simply too hugly[67] for words.

WOMAN: Are you going to join the struggle, comrade?

MAN: Not this side of the grave, Carol, sorry.

WOMAN: What would your colleagues at work say, if they knew you were once a rasta? ... [*Begins to sing in a very bad Jamaican accent*]... "I'm jammin'. Yeah jamming. And I hope you like jammin' too. Yeah, jammin' oh, jamming."

MAN: [*Quickly putting hand over Carol's mouth*] Hey Carol, you promised... You did destroy the negatives?

WOMAN: Those locks all down your back, plus the khaki pants and the baseball boots. All very cultural and stylish. Is wha' yu ha' fi sey fi yourself, fi my yout'?

MAN: Now look, Carol. I've got influence. I can help the cause, my sista, I really can.

WOMAN: [*Beginning to sing and dance like Bob Marley again*] "Natty dub it inna Zimbabwe. I and I a liberate Zimbabwe. Africans a liberate Zimbabwe." "Exodus, movement of Jah people. One more time, my yout. Old pirates yes, dey rob I..."

MAN: [*Stopping Carol again*] You want money? How much? I've got lots of money. You want some of my credit cards? Here... [*Opens his wallet and takes out a few cards*]... Visa, Mastercard, Access, a Liddle store card, Netto's as well! What do you want? Name your price! Say the word they're yours ... You can't do this to me. You can't ruin my credibility. I was young in those days. I was experimenting. Taking drugs. I even voted for the SDP. Please sis, give me a break.

WOMAN: How much were you going to give the cause?

MAN: [*Pulling out a cheque book*] You name it, I'll write it.

WOMAN: [*Thinking*] Hmmmmmm… Now let me see… Two grand should be in order. Can you manage that?

MAN: Fine, fine. Anything else I can help you with?

WOMAN: Well … I do like to shop at Liddle and Netto. Mi love de cheapness.

MAN: Liddle, Netto? No problem. Here, take the cards. Shop like you're a mad woman on supermarket sweep. No problem. Here… [*Hands over the cards*]… Take them. Anything else?

WOMAN: Just a couple of things?

MAN: You say it, I'll get it.

WOMAN: Can you get hold of the latest issue of *Marie Claire* and *Essence* magazines?

MAN: [*Slightly taken aback*] *Marie Claire* and *Essence* magazines? Not very proletariat? A touch decadent if you ask me… What about this freedom from capitalistic materialism?

WOMAN: That's for the plebs. I was educated at Oxford, remember. I appreciate the better things in life. I'm a better class of socialist.

MAN: I see… So you're going to share these possessions with your comrades?

WOMAN: After the revolution. They can make do with Billy Bragg and margarine for the time being.

MAN: [*Relieved*] Thank heavens for that. You really had me going for a moment there, Carol. You still like a drop of the old Bollinger?

WOMAN: Don't all good socialists? And I know just the place to drink it as well. The Groucho club should be pretty empty this time of the morning.

MAN: Spoken like a good socialist…

[*WOMAN dumps the large bundle of pamphlets into a nearby bin and the two of them begin to walk away.*]

WOMAN: You still got your Big Yout' album?

MAN: Got them? I bought his greatest hits CD last year.

WOMAN: You and ten other people… You've still got the fake stick-on locks?

MAN: Don't tell anyone, but I dress up in my old rasta clothes in my bedroom when I'm alone.

WOMAN: You never…

[*The two continue to walk into the distance … ad-lib to fade.*]

Reflections of the group on *Style and Fashion*

The two characters in *Style and Fashion* were juxtaposed with Jesus as depicted in the four gospels. To what extent do all people have hidden motives? The ideological battle between two apparently opposing views at the heart of the sketch seem to offer a useful counterpoint to the encounter between Jesus and the religious leaders in the gospels.

Within Black theology, distinctive claims are made for Jesus. Jesus is located in very firm and precise ideological terms. The various Christologies of Black theology may differ,[68] depending upon the exact perspective employed in their reflections on Jesus, but they all, nevertheless, contain a real sense of Jesus Christ as counter-cultural agitator. The liberative qualities of the Jewish Jesus of history, who confronts the Roman hegemony and occupation of the first century, serves as the interpretative lens through which Black theology identifies the Jesus of faith as a primary resource for the Black struggle for freedom in the twentieth and twenty-first century.[69]

The distinctive, counter-cultural Jesus, who stands against the vested interest of Roman hegemony on the one hand and yet challenges the hypocrisy of the Jewish religious establishment on the other, is central to the formulation of Christology within Black theology.

This distinct and oppositional Jesus as depicted in Black theology is countered, however, by a number of scholars. There are those, who in light of Jesus' ethnicity and practice, view him as critical friend to, rather than an implacable enemy of, the first-century Jewish establishment.[70]

For many in the group, the fact that Jesus might have been a member, and perhaps a "critical friend" of the Jewish establishment, brought echoes of the ambivalence they felt to the two characters in the sketch. For these young people, the fact that Jesus might have been a colleague of these religious leaders was akin to the woman and man being reconciled on the same side, having formerly been opponents, in *Style and Fashion*.

I do not intend to analyse *Style and Fashion* in the manner undertaken with the previous pieces. In highlighting the piece, I simply want to present what was the end product of a prolonged piece of analysis and reflection that arose from my engagement with participant observation. In reflecting upon the culture of the young people, using the insights of participant observation, I was able to gain a clearer sense of some of the underlying issues at play in their identity construction. This, in turn, when allied to an experiential, exercise-based approach to participant observation, enabled the young people to identify significant issues arising from their own reality. This self-naming process provided the raw materials for the resulting piece of drama. Further reflections on the drama gave rise to a series of Black theological reflections. It is my contention that these reflections form part of a wider tapestry of thoughts and concerns that contribute to an overarching process of dramatizing theologies for the voiceless.

Listening and Critiquing the Voices of the Voiceless

Utilizing the framework of ethnography and participant observation, I was able to devise a means of enabling young, voiceless Black people to reflect upon aspects of their experience. This process was achieved by constructing an experiential, participatory activity in which these subjects were at once distanced from, but yet connected to, their ongoing reality by means of this extended metaphor.

At an earlier point in this chapter, I mentioned the habitual facet of signifying within Black cultural life. To what extent can any discourse by Black subjects (when confronted by authority figures) be entirely trusted? The ways in which Black people "play" with reality, often invoking metaphysical elements, such as the "spirit," creates very real tensions for the researcher.[71]

For many Black people, their general theism and theology enables them to hold a dialectical perspective on reality. The concrete and explicit is not all there is. According to Theophus Smith one of the means by which African Americans play with reality is through a process he terms "conjure."[72] Conjure is the practice of magic in order to seek power and influence over one's environment.[73] Reflecting on Smith's work, Frederick Ware states:

> Smith makes clear that African Americans are not the only group who use magic. Non-Americans in Western civilization also use conjure, and so he believes magic or conjure is a suitable category for the study of not only African American religion but the religion of other groups seeking empowerment.[74]

Ware's assessment of the generic qualities of conjure within Black religious traditions and sensibilities call to mind the work of such scholars as Albert Raboteau[75] and Robert Hood,[76] both of whom have investigated the religious traditions of Black people of the African Diaspora. Their work is characterized by a pervasive sense of the work of the spirit(s) within Black life.

The spirit offers alternative ways of knowing,[77] and provides an alternative, parallel reality to the concrete nature of the immediate built environment that most commonly confronts us.[78]

I am aware of the tension within Black religious and theological discourse surrounding the relationship between the spirits and the Holy Spirit. The latter is contained within a distinct Christian framework that is often seen as being an anathema to or simply distinct and separate from the former.[79] Recent ethnographic research, in Africa for example, is beginning to tease out some of the complexities of this discourse.[80]

As I have stated in a previous publication, when working with Black elders in Birmingham,

> For Black elders, the secular and the religious meet and co-exist in the one time and space. The "here and now" and the "hereafter" exist in the one continuum. The spirit world and the material world meet... Theirs is a world of miracles and the ordinary—often, miracles within the ordinary, a world of the spirit and the flesh.[81]

This dichotomized and dualistic perspective in Black experience and ontology, often the result of a deep-seated, implicit religiosity, offers very real challenges and opportunities for the religious educator and theologian. The challenges arise from the difficulty of taking any Black discourse at face value. Within the generic, non-confessional arena of country schools in the UK, for example, Christine Callender notes the role of signifying within the broader linguistic and cultural repertoire of Black children and young people.[82]

The challenge of moving beyond the façade of Black discourse means that no researcher can take what they hear or observe at face value. The penetration of Black subjectivity requires a depth of analysis that engages with the multi-dimensional nature of Black religious and cultural expression.[83] This form of analysis constantly asks questions of the subject and the wider environment in which they are housed.

This complex nature of Black subjectivity requires that the scholar/ researcher (whether religious or otherwise) adopt the role of the "critical friend." The position is that of the slightly distanced participant and observer. One needs to maintain a critical distance between oneself and the subjects with whom one is engaging. That distance has to be carefully realized, for if one is too far removed from the experiential realities of the Black subject, the facility of signifying or the subordinate elements of "cultural dissonance" will leave the scholar floundering in a cultural vacuum.[84] Cultural dissonance in a Black post-colonial experience in Britain

> [m]anifests itself in a wide variety of social settings. Cultural dissonance is felt when one feels out of place in a cultural setting that is different from one's own. For instance, a Black person feels at home where Black tradi-

tions, values, belief systems and practices are the norm, and feels cultural dissonance in the wider socio-political environment where White, Eurocentric norms hold sway.[85]

I have written in the past on the difficulty of White authority figures gaining access to the inner lives and subterranean subjectivity of Black people due to the ongoing issues of signifying and cultural dissonance.[86] In effect, in order to work alongside and in authentic solidarity with the voiceless, one needs to engage in a delicate balancing act of not being too close or distant from those with whom one is hoping to engage.

The role of the slightly distanced participant and observer requires a commitment to multi-dimensional analysis. This form of analysis does not seek to simply gain access and interrogate the discourse of the Black subject (the voiceless). Juxtaposed with the analysis of the subject is the necessity of critically reflecting upon the wider context in which the Black self is housed.

As I outlined in the first chapter when outlining the broad contours for my definition of the voiceless, Liberation theology has provided the much needed methodology for this form of structural, situational analysis.

Structural, situational analysis seeks to place the experiences of the individual or community into a larger contextual framework, in order to shed light on the issues and factors that are exerting an adverse effect upon the selfhood of the oppressed.[87]

On both sides of the Atlantic, a new generation of Black theologians have begun to re-appropriate the work of Segundo and his method for contextual theological analysis. In the United States, Harry Singleton has attempted to unite the differing but complementary works of James Cone and Juan Luis Segundo, in order to discern the most appropriate method of doing theology in light of the ongoing oppression of the poor and people of colour.[88]

Within the British context, Robert Beckford utilizes Segundo's method in order to create a contextual theological framework for addressing gang violence and gun crime in Britain.[89]

I have utilized ethnography and participant observation in order to gain access to the complex subjectivity of the voiceless. This internalized form of socio-cultural analysis has been juxtaposed with the situational analysis of Liberation theology in order to create a broad external framework in which to house the internal subjective voice.

In my work with these Black young people, I was anxious that their reflections and comments regarding truth-telling and integrity should be placed within a broader context. What were the factors that influenced their notions of truth-telling? When is it inappropriate to "tell the whole truth, so help me God?" Beckford, in his theological reflections on gang violence in Britain, challenges the urban church to engage in this internal and external form of analysis.[90]

By juxtaposing the internal dimension of Black subjectivity and urban experience with a penetrating historical and biblical form of analysis, Beckford reminds us that telling the whole truth is not always appropriate.[91] He calls to mind the incident in Exodus 1:15–21, when the Hebrew midwives defy the might of Pharaoh (the law and power of the establishment) in order to effect God's will.[92] Beckford states that:

> Here, the midwives are presented as subversive agents challenging the genocidal actions of a ruthless dictator and an oppressive regime… What excites me here is that salvation is a social, political and physical act; saving male children who face complete extermination.[93]

The reflections of the young people on the issue of truth-telling and integrity were juxtaposed with the actions of Jesus, and those of other contemporary and historical people, within the Black Diasporan experience. Their reflections and comments had inspired me to create *Style and Fashion*. In order to encourage a further level of analysis and reflection, I brought the short drama back to the group in order for them to interact with the two protagonists—which their very own reflections had helped to create. Further conversation arose from the many performances of this short piece. Why did the group remain hostile to the rapprochement between the two characters? When was it not appropriate to change one's mind or to change sides?

The group remain wedded to a seemingly doctrinaire demarcation between "right and wrong" and "good and bad." In this respect, their theology echoes the broader strains of Black Christology and the sense that Jesus' counter-cultural image marks him out as a theological iconoclast.[94] The Jesus that emerges, with reference to the drama *Style and Fashion*, is the high Christology of John's Gospel, who seems to eschew any sense of continuity with the Judaism of his birth and heritage.[95] Jesus is set apart and wholly different from all that preceded him. The characters in *Style and Fashion* function as negative archetypes for the kind of truth-telling and sense of integrity for which these Black young people yearned. The process of dramatizing theologies is housed within dialogically constructed forms of drama, in which the negative voice of the characters display an apophatic notion of God—(i.e. God is to be known by asserting what God is not).[96] The virtues of God as manifested in the integrity and resolute nature of Jesus' praxis are not to be found in the behaviour of the two characters in the drama.

Yet, their reflections, as firm and resolute as they may appear to be, were still countered on my part by the externalized, structural analysis which cites the actions of numerous Black people from Diasporan African history whose often covert subversive actions in defying White hegemony demanded the kind of flexibility apparently eschewed by these young people. The work of such scholars as Bush,[97] Burton,[98] Campbell,[99] Dadzie,[100] Hart[101] and

Sewell[102] have all charted the complex and often seemingly contradictory ways in which Black people attempted to subvert, play and manoeuvre within oppressive contexts.

The strident binary discourse of "good" and "bad" as articulated by these young people is countered by Victor Anderson in his highly influential book *Beyond Ontological Blackness*.[103] Anderson challenges the preoccupation within Black religio-cultural expression to concentrate on the notion of "heroic genius"—those archetypal, pivotal figures (such as Harriet Tubman, Marcus Garvey or Martin Luther King) whose exemplary actions somehow are taken as emblematic of all Black people.[104] Anderson critiques this preoccupation, and challenges Black (African American) religious and cultural thought to give greater attention to the "monstra" and the "grotesque" within our various communities.[105]

These latter categories are ones that alert us to those facets or characteristics of human behaviour that are not necessarily viewed as being heroic, wholesome or the stuff of role-modelling. Yet these very facets or characteristics are very much a part of the complex tapestry that makes us human. Often times, we can learn more from, and in all truth, have more in common with, the "villains" and the characters of dubious moral virtue, than the so-called "heroes" that populate mythic Afrocentric inspired Black history.

While not wanting to revoke the validity of the discourse of these young people, I was able, by drawing upon a broader range of sources (in addition to their personal experience), to provide a critique of their theology and theologizing.

What I want to stress at this juncture is not the substantive content of their dramatizing theologies (although this remains important), but rather the process that enabled this discourse to emerge. This process, which utilizes ethnography and liberationist situational analysis, has given rise to a potentially exciting and radical method for doing theology with the voiceless. In the next chapter, I shall look in more detail at the dynamics of this approach to doing theology. As I have hopefully demonstrated in this chapter, this approach is one that holds in tension the dialectic of action (dramatic performance) and reflection (theological thought and analysis). This model of action-reflection is at the very heart of this process and content of dramatizing theologies of and for the voiceless.

5   Theology from the Bottom Up: Developing an Inclusive Methodology for Engaging with the Voiceless

In the last chapter I outlined an approach to constructing and developing dramatic material as a repository for a theology of the voiceless, which utilizes the methodology of participant observation and ethnography.

In this chapter, I want to outline some of the philosophical and methodological issues in drama theory, which lies at the heart of this approach to articulating and doing theology. I am sure that, for some, I have approached this process sequentially, in the wrong order. Surely, I should have outlined methodological and theoretical issues prior to the practical task of creating the material that houses aspects of a process of dramatizing theologies? Is it not usually the case that theory gives rise to practice?

While I am aware of the conventions that would seem to suggest that theory should take precedent over practice, my own work as a Black practical theologian means that praxis—action based on critical reflection[1]—was always going to be my preferred means of operating. As I have stated in my last book,[2] I am invariably motivated by a desire to find what works first, and then analyse how and why it works, as a secondary, subsidiary question.

In this chapter, I want to outline the process of using an action-reflection paradigm for undertaking research and reflecting upon pastoral/practical ministry that enables marginalized, voiceless people to become a part of the very process of how theology is constructed. This process is one that seeks to fuse action and reflection, not only as theoretical paradigm, but also as a practical means of doing theology.

In the previous chapter, I outlined how making use of the methodology of participant observation enabled me to find a means of analysing and critically reflecting on the salient issues in the lives of the voiceless. This process enabled me to create relevant drama that might be a repository for their theology.

Through interacting with groups of voiceless people, the educator and theologian gains the necessary insight into the relevant themes that will provide the raw material for the drama that will house their theology. Yet, it is through the accompanying process of action and reflection that the participants are encouraged to respond and dialogue with the text in order to help re-make it, and refine it. Consequently, the dramatic text becomes increasingly real and more accessible to the participants, whose own experiences and critical thinking have formed it and the theology contained within. In effect, the theology becomes one they can own—it becomes theirs!

Philosophical Background to Using Drama as a Means of Raising Critical Consciousness

The social sciences as a dialogue partner for Black theology

It could be argued that the development of Black theology in Britain despite its burgeoning strength has, like its more established transatlantic cousin in the US, yet to develop a praxis to match the potency of its ideas and theological formulations. Part of this failure, to my mind, has been a reluctance or a difficulty in engaging with diverse epistemologies from other disciplines, which would enable Black theology to discover new ways of engaging with those who reside outside of the academy. The following discussion, although somewhat theoretical, has nonetheless proved invaluable in my ongoing research, which has always been of an interdisciplinary nature, working alongside Black lay people in local churches and community settings in Britain.

The overarching tool of reflective practice has informed my use of drama as a method for inculcating Black theological ideas and concerns. By locating myself within the research paradigm, through becoming an actor and participant within the reflective process, it is my hope that one is able to construct new ways of thinking and being for Black lay people who would not consider themselves to be theologically literate.

Utilizing an action-reflection approach to doing Black theology—an exercise in democratization

The main methodological tool I have utilized in this research has been the often controversial area of "action research." I am conscious of the associated difficulties and controversy that has attached itself to the whole area of reflective practice that lies at the heart of the action research paradigm. One of the leading practitioners and theoreticians within the field of action research is John Elliot. Elliot writes:

> Action research might be defined as the study of a social situation with a view to improving the quality of action within it.[3]

Cotton and Minion define action research as being an essentially focused small-scale intervention into a specific social setting with the aim of improving the practice in some way within that setting.[4] Carr and Kemmis describe action research thus:

> Action research is simply a form of self reflective inquiry undertaken by participants in social situations in order to improve the rationality and justice of their practices.[5]

The individual often seen as being the originator of action research is Lewin[6] in 1946. Irshad and Imrie, writing on Lewin's new form of research, state:

> His model for change was based on action and research. It involved researchers, and teachers or other practitioners, in a cyclical process of planning, action, observation and reflection.[7]

The work of Lewin has been further developed by Lawrence Stenhouse, who in his 1975 book outlined a method for teachers to use their own practice as a basis for empirical research within the classroom.[8]

A central feature of the various proposals as outlined by Elliot *et al.* is the use of the word "improve." Action research is not theoretical abstraction divorced from any contextual reality. The impetus, motivation and ethical stance that is a feature of the action research paradigm is grounded within the imperative to act. The desire to commit oneself, rationally and experientially, within a specific situation is guided, for the most part, by the existential desire to improve the practice within that given milieu.[9]

Christine O'Hanlon with great clarity expresses the need for research and the role of the researcher to be guided by a moral responsibility to "act." The researcher perceives the role they exercise, as being one for ethical, democratic change.[10] The principle of wanting to improve the practice within a given social setting has its roots in the old-style secondary modern schools in the 1960s. Elliot argues that the necessity to create a relevant curriculum for comparatively large numbers of low achievers was an important factor in the impetus to adopt the action research paradigm within British state schools.[11]

Action research, aside from its commitment to action in the service of improving practice, also carries within its framework a rationale that takes seriously the reality and concretized nature of practice. In this respect, practice is not seen as subordinate or subservient to theory. This dialectic between theory and practice is one in which the major result is the production of better practice, not abstract knowledge.[12]

With the imperative to "act" being a major determinant on the course and nature of the research, it should not be too much of a surprise that I should wish to use the methodology of action research.

Discovering more effective ways of undertaking one's work is often a central motivation for any practitioner in seeking relevant and appropriate models or opportunities for personal and professional development. Indeed McNiff *et al.* have identified the area of professional development as one of the primary utilitarian functions of action research, particularly in the area of teaching.[13]

The motivation to "act" in order to change or improve the practice within a particular setting[14] must be synthesized with a desire to reflect critically upon one's action. Simply "acting" without recourse to the self-critical guidance of reflection will not necessarily yield any of the hoped-for improvements.

Reflection is a prerequisite alongside the necessity for action. At this point, I am reminded of the salient words of Paulo Freire, whose dictum that action without reflection is mere activism, and reflection without action is pure verbalism, rings very true.[15] More recently, McNiff *et al.* have written:

> To be Action research, there must be praxis rather than practice. Praxis, informed, committed action that gives rise to knowledge rather than just successful action.[16]

Within the scope of my previous and current research, McNiff's words are apposite. Action research incorporates a framework that emphasizes a personal, ethical rationale for informed, reflective action. This method afforded me the necessary scope to align myself alongside others, in the collaborative effort to change the practice of being church and the resultant elements of Christian praxis that exist within all faith communities.

The final point that needs explication is the central importance of collaboration. Integral to the methodology of action research is the concept of collaborative action, coupled with mutual reflection. The notion that the "professional" researcher is the final arbiter on issues of knowledge and the veracity of any resulting discourse is at variance with the central philosophical ideals that govern the action research paradigm.

It is not only necessary but essential that the views, opinions and hypotheses of the researcher are not only influenced by the encounter with significant "others" in the research, but are shaped by them also. For ethical reasons, but also for the quality of understanding and potential development, it is imperative that significant others within the research are convinced that their opinion is important.[17]

The temptation for researchers to use their own power and influence to impose their notions and perceptions upon "their subjects" can often overcome all ethical concerns to act to the contrary. The use of the term "their subjects" is entirely intentional for it highlights the underlying possessive maintenance of control that can become a feature of the central role exercised by the researcher in the midst of the research study. The necessity to control all variables, particularly within a scientific, positivistic paradigm, may lead the researcher to view any individual within the study as yet another inanimate object to be manipulated or controlled. One should not disguise the many difficulties of attempting to work in a truly collaborative fashion.

Yet, as Altrichter *et al.* have commented, the desirability to work in a collaborative fashion is essential if one is to break the "hierarchy of credibility" that tends to prevail in academic discourse. In using the term "hierarchy of credibility," the authors are speaking of a social rank that confers a greater degree of credibility and a sense of reliability upon certain persons.[18] In order that this "hierarchy of credibility" can be dissipated, it is essential that a process of "triangulation" be incorporated into the methodology of the research. Elliot makes it clear that action research is a collaborative enterprise, not a positivistic paradigm that is grounded in a technical process where the means justify the ends which, in turn, control and shape the practices of teachers. It is a paradigm that is rooted in context, recognizing the reality and the constraints of that which can be changed and those elements that remain beyond the realms of change.[19]

McNiff *et al.* contend that the desire to share evaluations and interpretations of the data is essential to prevent a purely subjective reading of any social situation in which the research is located.[20]

The desire to work in a collaborative, ethically democratic fashion was an important component in the decision-making process when attempting to locate an appropriate methodology on which to construct this research project.

The final feature of the action research paradigm to which I should refer is the ongoing cycle of reflection and action, which moves through a series of distinct phases. The different stages, moving from "investigation," through "planning" and "action," towards "reflection" is an important feature of the methodology of action research. The four-stage description I have given is by no means an exhaustive or overly sophisticated account of the ongoing spiral or cycle of action and reflection that is action research. A number of researchers have written at length on the continual process of planning, implementation, action, evaluation and reflection. Within more formal models of theology one has witnessed recourse to similar notions of reflexive cycles or spirals.[21] The developing arena of Practical theology has witnessed an explosion of writing, a good deal of which is addressing the central question of methods for undertaking theological reflection.[22]

One could describe a plethora of models, some quite complex and sophisticated in design, detailing the ongoing process through which one attempts to implement planned initiatives that give rise to improved practice. Arising from this process is the production of new knowledge and a developed theory.[23] Given the fluid and often-contradictory nature of action research, it is incumbent upon the researcher to develop a means of operating that is adaptable and amenable to what may be drastically changing social milieus.[24] Morwenna Griffiths describes this necessity well when she writes:

> Research proceeds by doing and by making mistakes in a self-reflective spiral of planning, acting, observing, reflecting, planning etc. This spiral is one in which feedback is going on in many ways at once. This is recognizable as the messy real world of practice.[25]

By utilizing the central ideas of action research as the dominant paradigm in my conceptualization of Black theology, one is able to create a process towards the democratization of theological reflection, thereby enabling those from the underside of history to discover their authentic voice and so name their subjective realities. I believe this process for undertaking Black theology is essential, for it enables a more concerted engagement with the messiness of context and the frailty and contradictory nature of human life and experience.

Putting an "Action and Reflection" Paradigm to Work for the Benefit of Empowering the Voiceless

Some preliminary thoughts

In the previous chapter I outlined some of the preliminary issues with which the educator and theologian had to engage in order to create a participative process for enabling marginalized and oppressed voiceless people to both articulate and undertake their own theology. I defined these issues as being ones of "critical openness," "pedagogy" and "self-actualization." By adopting an action-reflection model for undertaking theological reflection, coupled with the methodology of participant observation, it was my hope to create a participative model of engagement that would assist in overcoming these tripartite concerns.

In order that an action-reflection framework might be utilized for the benefit of the voiceless, it was imperative that I attended to a number of salient issues. These issues concerned questions critical openness, pedagogy and self-actualization. In order to address those important underlying, substantive issues, I have created the following dramatic exercise. This exercise utilizes Black theological discourse and juxtaposes these reflections with some of the salient issues within my conceptualization of a process of dramatizing theologies.

The exercise addresses issues of self-worth, encouraging participants to reflect critically on their positionality in a world where the voiceless are often reduced to marginal spaces and are constantly ignored. The exercise was designed to aid participants in their reflections following several performances of *The Wisdom of Solomon* and *Love is the Answer*. The exercise, which is comprised of some initial thoughts, followed by some Black biblically based reflections and some concluding questions, is intended to supplement the re-enactment of the two sketches, to which reference was made in Chapter 3.

The following piece is reproduced in the original form in which it was written and used with a group of Black people from South London. This group was the second of the three cohorts I had identified as being appropriate dialogue partners from the previous chapter. The piece was written to be an accessible and creative means of enabling the various participants to reflect upon their identities and subjectivity with reference to a process of dramatizing theologies. I have highlighted this discourse in the text in order to emphasize the different form of writing in evidence at this point in the book. The following piece was created to supplement the dramatic sketches.

Offering what we are and can be to God— a critical assessment of selfhood

The Action (the exercise)

- Give each individual a copy of the template at the back of the book (see Appendix, Diagram 1).
- Each individual is encouraged to use the template to do the following:
  - *Looking back on your life, how would you assess the various development and issues or concerns as they have arisen over the years? One way of doing this is by working with a timeline.*
  - *To do this you need to look at the template I have given you. I want you to think in terms of positives and negatives. The more positive an event has been in your life, that event is represented by a small cross (x) situated near the top of the template (towards the letters at the top of the page). Of course, the opposite is true in terms of negative events. For each negative event, place a cross (x) towards the bottom of the page.*
  - *I want you to begin in the box at the left hand side and begin to think of the most significant events that have taken place in your life, in the order in which they happened.*
  - *The bottom line from left to right represents your life. So the earliest events will be placed towards the left and will move, as the years move on in your life, towards the right.*
  - *As you think of each significant event, give that event or incident a cross (x) and depending upon whether it is a positive or negative experience, place the cross towards the top or the bottom of the page.*
  - *Boxes 'A', 'B' and 'C' represent the different stages of your life. When you think your life changed direction significantly, then put the next cross into the next box. So stage 1 of your life is 'A', the second stage is 'B' and the third stage is 'C'.*

- Many of you will be tempted to say that there have been more than three stages in your life. Undoubtedly, this is true, but for the purposes of the exercise, I want you to think in terms of the biggest or most significant changes in your life. This may mean having to push two or three changes together in order to make one stage, and ditto with later periods of your life.
- As you begin to plot your life, marking the most significant events in your life with a cross, your page should look something like the diagram in the Appendix, Diagram 2. (Remember that this is only a suggestion.)
- Now I want you to join up the various crosses on your template in order to create a timeline. Note the various "highs" and "lows" of your life.
- As you look back on your life, remembering the different events or incidents that are represented by the various crosses (you might want to put a code by each cross and then write down below the box what event or incident that particular cross represents), how do you remember these events? What is your interpretation of them now? How do you make sense of that event? Where was God in that situation?
- The fourth box (D) represents what you **hope** will be the events or incidents in the future. Dare you give these things a value by placing your cross somewhere in this box?

The Reflection (the narrative)

- Having completed the exercise, read the following set of reflections in light of the timeline you have created on your template.

That the church is in something of a crisis is all too apparent. It does not require a sage or a prophet to discern the clear signs of struggle and decline that presently stalk the church like a ravenous, eagle-eyed bird, watching intently as the slowly dying body is about to breathe its last breath. We are not in good shape. The causes for this decline and struggle are myriad and are way beyond the scope of this ever so humble exercise. The parlous state of the church does, however, present itself in a variety of "easy to discern" ways. Falling congregations are one obvious manifestation. The difficulty to find lay people to accept positions of responsibility in the church is another.

It is unnecessary for me to repeat the now all too familiar scenario. The exasperated grimace as no raised hands of acceptance are forthcoming at a church meeting, and yet another position in the church goes unfilled. The church can still, of course, find ministerial "volunteers." The promise to accept the will of the church hierarchy can still concentrate minds. But there are no such sanctions for lay people. To put it bluntly, there is very little they can make poor, marginalized lay people do.

In fairness, it has to be remembered that many of us have hugely busy lives. Very often, those the church prioritizes as being the best people to accept responsible roles in the church are precisely the people with least amount of leisure time to undertake the varied tasks that need to be done. Young adults, in many contexts, have the scarcity value usually accorded to a giant panda or a highly prized mountain tiger. When we find such rare creatures, the temptation to "love it to death with grateful entreaties," or to smother it in exaggerated delight, or for some, to kill it for the expensive rarity value that accompanies it, can be an all too real dilemma.

In an age when people no longer possess the same deference (a good thing to my mind) or selfless dedication to the cause, how can we persuade, cajole, plead or beg (there are numerous terms one could use, take your pick) people to take up positions of responsibility?

It seems to me that there are two possible means of engaging with the pool of latent talent that exists amongst the laity in the church. First, like many other institutions and bodies, we can appeal to self-interest and the "something for something" culture. One of the ways in which volunteerism is popular in our present age is by means of a utilitarian ethic. To paraphrase Machiavelli's old dictum, people will prove themselves trustworthy (or helpful) when they see there is something in it for them.[26]

There is no doubting the effectiveness of voluntary work as a way of developing new, marketable skills. I am sure that for some, who would want to venture down the line of professional youth work, children's play work or nursery nursing, a spell undertaking youth and children's work in the church can do no harm. We can and no doubt have already appealed to the utilitarian and functional motivations of lay people to accept positions of responsibility, including working with children and young people. Offering to work with children and young people is not the end of the matter. Of course, there is the question of preparation and training—often, not so popular an enterprise.

It is not my intention to disparage the often pragmatic attempts to solicit volunteers to discharge particular duties in the church. It is my belief, however, that we need something more resolute and in keeping with our traditions and understanding of God, than mere recourse to utility and pragmatism.

Some Theological Reflections Based on Matthew 25:14–30: *The Parable of the Talents*

Having re-read this text again quite recently, I am struck by the parallels that seem to exist between it and that of the wider church in Britain today.

I do not want to make the parallels between text and context too firmly or literally. What I am hoping to explore is the spirit that resides within the text, and to compare that with the experience of being church (corporate and individual) at this moment in time.

I believe that this text, and that of our wider theology and traditions, speak clearly against the "something for something" culture that seems to pervade our society. It is this clear disparity between the God of creation and the workings of an individualized and self-centred ethos, which renders any appeal for service solely on the grounds of utility and reward to be deeply flawed. In prosaic terms, we are all the recipients of grace. God loved us and willed us into being long before we were conscious of that reality. God loved us long before we were in a position to respond. God redeemed us, and through the mission of Christ we have been changed and inspired, before we could and were able to respond. That some of us have responded to God's unfailing love does not negate the central importance of God's primary first act.

This is basic theology. Not much that is contentious here, I would imagine. But I think it needs to be stated repeatedly, for, in the final analysis, we have all received not "something for something," "but a great deal for free." This basic fact should and often does change our perspective. It may well be the case that harassed young parents do not necessarily become less harassed and busy through acknowledging the very basis of their existence—but it can't do any harm?

In the passage from Matthew, I am struck that the master gave the talents to his servants. I have to admit that I have never given it that much thought, prior to my writing this piece. The servants were given their talents. We have no way of knowing whether they deserved the talents or not. What had they done to obtain them? We do not know. What we do know, most clearly, is that they were given them. On a few occasions, when leading workshops for local churches, I have asked them to conduct a skills audit. On large blank pieces of paper, I have asked individuals in small groups to list all the things they do and what they would like to do. It is always a cathartic experience for all concerned. It is a cliché, I know, but we have all been given myriad gifts. We may be aware of them, or we may not. We may have worked hard to develop those gifts; we may not have done anything to deserve them. We have been given them, nonetheless.

As the passage is known to many of us, I will spare you a line by line examination of the text. We are all, I am sure, aware of the actions of the three servants. The first two invest their talents well and are rewarded. The third does not invest his talents at all and is punished. The punishment inflicted upon the third servant has caused a number of us some very real difficulties. There is not sufficient time for a lengthy, in-depth study of this

text. The Bible scholars amongst us will have some definite pronouncements to make on it. My concern at this point is not on the exactitude of
this text, but upon the spirit that seems evident within the text.

As I reflected and meditated, I was drawn to this passage, but did not allow
myself to be deflected from the very real, inherent difficulties in this text.

Without wishing to ignore the implications of the master's judgement
on the third servant for his lack of initiative or consideration[27] (and besides,
post-colonial scholars would see his actions as very exploitative), I want to
concentrate on the actions of the first two, and the implications of this text
for them and us. What is not in doubt is the desire of the master to see the
talents he has dispensed grow and multiply. Hence, the first two servants
are rewarded. In vv. 21 and 23 the master congratulates the first two servants for their actions. The servants are rewarded.

I am often intrigued about what is not said in a text, rather than relying
solely on what is stated explicitly. (This is a common practice of liberationist approaches to interpreting the Bible.) We do not know if the first two
servants expected to be rewarded. I doubt their actions were motivated
solely by altruism. Whatever their motivation, they were rewarded for their
actions. It would appear that the author of the text wants us the readers to
be aware of the importance of maximizing the talents/gifts we have been
given. I suspect that the mistake the third servant made was not even to
attempt to make something of the gift he was given.

I do not want us to try to exact an uneasy photo-fit link between the text
and our present situation. In this society, I am sure that people are using
their talents in a variety of ways. Many will be undertaking invaluable voluntary work in their local communities, well away from the church. I do
not want to give the false impression that voluntary work in the church
is worth more than the important work we do elsewhere. Nor do I want
people to feel guilt ridden, and therefore, emotionally coerced into service.
There are very real and valid reasons why people cannot serve the church
in a voluntary capacity.

On the other hand, I wonder about the priorities many of us have in
our lives? In a society where we often operate on the reciprocal "something for something" model—careers for financial and emotional satisfac-
tion and reward; larger mortgages for nicer homes; pension payments for
more comfortable retirements. Where is the "something for nothing or very
little" model manifested? As I have stated at an earlier juncture, we do
not know what motivated the first two servants. Fear? Reward? Or was it
expectation? Having been given the talent did they know the expectations
of the master? I.e. that having been given something they were expected to
make the best possible use of it.

I am quite sure that I do not like the image of the master in this text.
He appears to be something of a bully. I am not sure about the efficacy

of his behaviour or his attitude to the servants. He does, however, expect much with what he has given and is prepared to reward those who meet his expectations. I am not wishing to make any determined comparisons between the master in the story and the God of love in Christ, who calls us into a loving relationship with God's self. In an age when the church is struggling to help people explore their vocations for service, it is timely, I believe, to remind us all that (a) we have been given the greatest gift free of charge, i.e. "something for nothing"—a rarity in this materialistically driven society—and that (b) our talents will grow and expand when we put them to use profitably.

Taking this passage in conjunction with the remainder of the gospel, we are reminded that reward is not self-interest. The Christ who challenged his followers to put all aside and follow him and was killed on the cross is not one who speaks to self-interest.

Yet, it is the case that even a harsh task master such as the one in this passage rewards his servants for using the most of what they have been given. Not to use our talents for the one who has given us the gifts in the first place is the real crime here, not necessarily the size of the profit the third servant failed to accrue.

The exciting aspect of this passage when applied to our present situation is the exciting challenge that confronts us, to enable others to realize and maximize their talents. The irony of this passage for me lies in the fact that a hard master rewards those who try, or are seen to make an attempt. I am not viewing this passage as an endorsement for capitalistic enterprise and the free market as many have done. This passage is very problematic in many respects.

Rather, I am thinking about the plethora of individuals who are marginalized and disparaged by a society that rewards only the few and ignores the many. I am thinking of Black people, people with disabilities, women and those whose sexuality does not conform to the norm. People who may not have a utilitarian value within this society, but individuals who with training, encouragement and empowerment may be strengthened to use what (suppressed and hidden) talents they may possess in service of the church, to the ultimate glory of the Kingdom of God. As in the passage where those who attempted to make the most of what they were given were rewarded, these marginalized and forgotten individuals will equally benefit from the opportunity to make the most of what they have been given, freely by God. If the church is not about empowering and transforming the outcast and the poor with the love of God in Christ, I am not sure what is our mission?

If we can tap into this large reservoir of talent (which are not the likely or usual candidates, often educated and career-orientated) that exists in this country, our struggle with the seemingly outdated concept of volunteerism will be dispelled. In order to do this, we need to possess the courage to fly in the face of conventional thinking, which asserts that all things or people need to be useful and no one does "something for nothing." We know this is a false dictum. Our experience of the living God tells us otherwise.

- Points to consider from the Action (the exercise) and the Reflection (the narrative).

1. The gifts you have to bring for the enrichment of others and which are your invaluable contribution to God's Kingdom are the product of the timeline you have just created.
2. No matter what the nature of that timeline, such is the nature of your experience you will always have something to contribute to the greater whole.
3. Often, for many people who come from disadvantaged backgrounds or communities, society or the world has a way of trying to make your experience and knowledge (the latter often arising out of the former) irrelevant. What are the gifts and graces you bring to the table of humanity that are the product of your experience?
4. By reflecting critically upon our life and assessing it for the gifts and graces that emerge from our experience (and are gifts from God), we can be enabled (in conjunction with others and, of course, God) to learn from our past, in order to remake our futures.
5. What excites you about box D? What are your fears for the future as you look at your crosses in box D?
6. Where would you like to see yourself? Where would you like to be?

The aforementioned exercise and the reflections that accompany it were first written in order to attempt to actualize some of the latent themes that relate to issues of critical openness, self-actualization and pedagogy. These serve as preludes to a process of critical advocacy for engaging with and enabling voiceless marginalized peoples to be actively involved in the creative process towards creating their own theology by way of drama.

Creating a Philosophy of Education for Engaging with the Voiceless

It was my desire that marginalized and oppressed, voiceless people should be enabled to play an active part in the process of shaping and reworking the drama in which their theology is housed. For this to become actuality, it became imperative that an interactive, participative philosophy of education be developed in order to facilitate this intent. Working within the broader framework of an action research methodology, and being cognizant of the issues thrown up by critical openness, self-actualization and pedagogy, I wanted to find an educational philosophy that would equip marginalized peoples.

In the first instance, the work of Paulo Freire as outlined in Chapter 1 became an important underscoring for identifying a philosophy of education for engaging with the voiceless.[28]

Freire has quite recently been seen as the progenitor for the utilization of the Marxist tools of critical, social analysis that lie at the heart of liberation theologies. Black theology, while remaining critical of aspects of Marxist thought, has nonetheless borrowed heavily from the liberation theology frameworks, bequeathed to it by the likes of Sobrino,[29] the brothers Boff[30] and Gutierrez;[31] all of whom, I would argue, owe much to Freire and his work in the early and mid 1960s.[32]

While I remain hugely indebted to the educational philosophy as laid down by Freire, I was not entirely convinced of its efficacy for this project and the desire to develop an interactive, participative method for doing theology with voiceless people by way of drama. Cheryl Johns has highlighted some of the inherent flaws in Freire's educational methodology for engaging with the oppressed.[33] Chief amongst these is Freire's notion of "conscientization" and the notion of "false consciousness" amongst oppressed peoples.[34] Freire's epistemology argues for a hierarchy of consciousness, and that oppressed peoples need to move from beyond their existing modes of thinking, to new higher and more critical levels of consciousness, which are commensurate with the ongoing task of affecting their existential liberation.[35]

Yet, as Johns makes so patently clear, despite Freire's claims that by undergoing a "death" to the first world and a "re-birth in the third world," the educator can overcome the distinct strains of paternalism,[36] there are, nonetheless, clear echoes of a top-down, authority-driven sense of imposition onto the lives of the oppressed.[37] Commenting on Freire's relationship with the poor and oppressed, she writes:

> Furthermore, Freire discounts "magic" and "myth" among the oppressed. For him, such a perspective on reality is often coupled with a distorted view of God and leads the oppressed to see their suffering as the will of God. Freire is, therefore, discounting any type of knowledge which is not a critical perception of reality. In doing so, he exhibits a bias against other ways of viewing reality, especially by delegating the thought processes of the oppressed to a lower, less than fully human perception of reality.[38]

Freire's failure to engage with the metaphysical elements in the spirituality of oppressed peoples, particularly those of African descent, means that his educational methodology is not wholly conducive to providing an overarching macro theory for enabling the voiceless to find their voice. The work of such scholars as Theophus Smith, and his notion of "conjuration" (i.e., how people of African descent work with and manoeuvre the spirits in an effort to gain strength over and insight into their present-day realities), have shown the extent to which Black people are deeply theistic people, whose spirituality is "this worldy" and "other worldly."[39]

In addition to Smith's work, one can cite the research of such scholars as Hood[40] and my own previous work.[41] In *Faith, Stories and the Experience of Black Elders* I state that older Black people are incurably religious.[42] At a later juncture, this point is amplified when I write:

> To work effectively with Black elders one has to realise the importance of, and become conversant with, the Christian religious discourse that flows through their lives. God is both immanent and transcendent. In effect, God is close at hand, assisting believers in their daily struggles. Yet that same God is far away, beyond the immediate struggles of the world, over-seeing the created world order, beyond all space and time... The "here and now" and "hereafter" exist in the one time continuum.[43]

In fairness to Freire, I have acknowledged the difficulties of trying to sur-mount the dialectical challenges of both respecting and critiquing the nor-mative consciousness and spiritualities of the oppressed, in the previous chapter. By utilizing ethnography, in the form of participant observation, I have attempted to find a means of both acknowledging and respecting the integrity of the theologizing of those who are marginalized and oppressed, while also being able to critique and challenge that discourse.[44]

The limitations of Freire, particularly as they apply to Black and other marginalized and oppressed peoples, did not negate my engagement with his work. Rather, it simply meant that I had to find an alternative basis for engaging with the salient features of his work, in order to meet the chal-lenges of trying to create an underlying educational methodology for the nascent developments of a process of dramatizing theologies.

Discovering the Work of Augusto Boal

The work and legacy of Paulo Freire has been such that many scholars have been inspired to dialogue and engage with his ideas, as an initial point of departure on the journey towards their own preferred means of operation. Scholars such as Thomas Groome,[45] Schipani,[46] Hope and Timmel,[47] plus myself,[48] have all gained inspiration from our exposure to the brilliance that was Paulo Freire.

Given that the theology I am advocating is carried within the seemingly egalitarian and accessible medium that is drama, I was interested in finding an educational approach that was committed to raising and critiquing the critical consciousness of the oppressed, but also workable within a dramatic format.

In the context of this study, the work of Augusto Boal was to prove invaluable. Augusto Boal's ideas on drama as a means of consciousness raising and problem solving owe much to the pioneering work of Paulo Freire. Like Freire, Boal was born in Brazil. He was raised in Rio de Janeiro.

Boal was formally trained in chemical engineering and attended Columbia University in the late 1940s. Despite the formal interest in engineering, Boal's true vocation was the theatre, and while still in his early teens, he began to display an aptitude for performance that would mark him out for the remainder of his life.

Like Freire, Boal's work has proved highly influential to liberationist theorists and practitioners across the world. Whereas Freire's work has been in the arena of education and critical consciousness, Boal's input has found expression in the theatre. Like Freire's, the political dimensions of his work drew unwanted attention from the military authorities in Brazil. In 1971 he was arrested, tortured and eventually went into exile in Argentina, and then Europe.[49]

Boal's approach to theatre is to collapse the emotional and conceptual distance between the performer on stage and the observer in the audience. In one famous incident, Boal stopped a performance in order that a disgruntled woman spectator could mount the stage and offer an alternative version to the untruth she was witnessing in the stage performance.[50] This incident was to prove a pivotal moment in the development and career of Boal, for from it emerged his notion of a theatre of the oppressed.

His 1971 book of that name was to usher into being a self-conscious and deliberate re-conceptualization of theatre in the name of assisting oppressed poor peoples to name and construct alternative realities to the subjugated and inhibited versions that confronted them daily, by means of participatory theatre.[51] The link between theatre and politics, argues Boal, is not a new phenomenon. Boal traces the roots of theatre as a response and a mirror to contextual realities back to the Greeks and the writings of Aristotle and Plato.[52]

The political dimensions of theatre have been explored by a number of scholars, in addition to Boal. Scholars such as Harris,[53] Milling and Ley,[54] and Schlossman[55] have utilized critical theories and liberationist themes in their approach to conceptualization of drama and theatre as a tool of exploring socio-political constructs and prevailing societal norms.

The Relevance of Theatre of the Oppressed for this Study

The concept of theatre of the oppressed gained international prominence when Boal organized the first international festival of theatre of the oppressed in Paris in 1981.[56]

Boal's 1971 book (republished in 2000) remains the most detailed explication of the conceptual ideas that underpin the theatre of the oppressed. One important dimension of Boal's concept is the identification with the character in the play as subject and the extent to which they are "free" and are able to exercise a sense of their self-determination, and are not purely objects, onto which external factors are grafted.[57] In this respect, Boal's ideas echo some more recent thoughts expressed by Anthony Pinn in Black theology and his notion of the Black self's response to religion as a search for "complex subjectivity."[58]

Writing with reference to the critical question of the character as subject, Boal writes:

> Art in general and dramatic poetry in particular play with concrete realities and not with abstractions: it is therefore necessary that the *particular* be seen in the *universal*. Philosophy deals with abstractions, mathematics with numbers, but the theatre deal with individuals. It is necessary, then, to show them in all their concretion.[59]

In *Theater of the Oppressed* and in later works,[60] Boal has not only refined the conceptual basis of his ideas around participatory theatre, but has added a number of practical training elements to the whole panoply of techniques and workshops that have grown out of his original theory.

Boal's work is concerned with helping participants in the theatre, whether performers or spectators (he collapses the separation between the two, talking instead of "spec-actor"[61]) to interrogate truth by means of inhabiting a character and exploring potential new concepts within the confines and structure of the play.[62]

This blurring of the lines between the actor and spectator, leading to the "spec-actor," finds concrete expression in the ability of the observer to interrupt the performance and to mount the stage in order to offer an alternative or corrective mode of action to that which was previously in evidence in the existing scenario.[63] The improvisatory action that then ensues carries within it the potential to be a cathartic and therapeutic space in which the pain and restricted selfhood of the oppressed can be rehearsed and examined.[64]

In order that this concept of participative, liberative theatre might come alive and deliver fresh insights into the lives of the oppressed, it is essential that the general underlying themes or subtexts for any performance be concrete and of contextual relevance to the potential participants. Writing with respect to this issue, Boal states:

> The chosen subject must be an issue of burning importance, something known to be a matter of profound and genuine concern for the future spec-actors.[65]

The importance of located key themes that speak to the experience of marginalized and oppressed peoples resonates with one of the central ideas of the work of Thomas Groome, one of the most influential liberationist practical theologians in the world.[66] Groome's concept of "generative themes," which he describes as:

> [s]ome historical issue, question, value, belief, concept, event, situation...
> That is likely to draw participants into engagement.[67]

is an attempt to locate substantive subtexts on which to develop an overarching approach to critical shared theological inquiry. In the context of this study, the various pieces of drama, created by myself, have been attempts to encapsulate substantive theological themes within a dramatic format, in a manner not dissimilar to that advocated by both Groome and Boal.

Going Beyond Boal—In Effect Learning to Deal with the God Stuff!

Boal's theories for and practical developments in using theatre as a means of enabling the oppressed to explore critical issues in their ongoing liberation has proved highly influential in this study. Boal's work has proved an invaluable link between the pedagogical concerns of Freire and the performative methodology in my emerging process of dramatizing theologies.

Simply working within the framework created by Boal, however, did not seem realistic, following further reflections on the nature of his approach to consciousness raising. In the first instance, like Freire, Boal's work operates within a humanistic framework, with little or no appreciation for notions of the transcendent ultimate reality that can mediate on the nature of human consciousness. In effect, my process for dramatizing theologies is, to state the obvious, theological. It is an exercise in talking about God and God's relationship with humankind. How do our ideas and experiences of God affect one's notion of self? What does it mean to be a human being; and in what ways do these most profound of existential questions lead to particular forms of behaviour and action?[68]

My theological exploration by way of drama should not be construed as a denial of the exigencies of human agency and self-actualization. I am not denying the human dimension in the construction of theistic talk. The work of Hopkins,[69] Beckford[70] and Coleman,[71] for example, have shown the sense in which theology is intrinsically meshed within the life experiences and cultures of human beings.

In effect, while God might be "other" and beyond finite reason, all talk about God is a form of human construction. So my decision to go beyond Boal, like that of Freire, is not a denial of theological implications or implicit theism of their respective works, but rather, is a desire to create an explicit context and framework for undertaking God-talk in light of the experience of the voiceless.

Secondly, in Boal's approach to participative theatre, there is an assumption that observers will enter into the dramatic aesthetic space,[72] in order to re-make the drama and influence the future trajectory of the narrative. I have to confess to not being a theatre specialist in the mould of Boal, so my critique of his approach may speak more of my lack of competence than any fault in his underlying method. In my experience, however, the alacrity with which marginalized and oppressed people—the voiceless in the present world order—might be enabled to enter into a drama, without any of the prerequisite attendant issues being addressed (as I have sought to do in the chapters preceding this one) seems extremely doubtful.

A more substantive critique of the "theater of the oppressed" rests with the disparities in power between the educationist/expert and the participants. In my previous work, I have attempted to make explicit the imbalances in power and disparities of esteem between those with whom one is working and that of the educator in any pedagogical process.[73] In both *Nobodies to Somebodies*[74] and *Acting in Solidarity*,[75] I have built into my ongoing methodologies for undertaking Practical theology an explicit recognition of the imbalances in power and esteem between myself and the people with whom I am undertaking this hoped-for process of theological reflection.

I feel that there is an unhelpful conceit in the notion that voiceless people can be invited into a process of remaking a drama without any explicit cognizance of the subtle and not so oblique socio-cultural constructs and systemic frameworks that might militate against such an involvement. I feel that the extensive preparatory work I have outlined in the previous chapters are an important means of attempting to create a hospitable space[76] for those who are voiceless, in which they might be enabled to undertake and construct their own theologies.

Contemporary Black Experiences

In some respects, the bridge between the secular, humanistic approach to performative action and the explicit theological model I am advocating can be found in the pioneering work of the Sistren Collective in Jamaica in the 1970s and 80s.[77]

The Sistren Collective was founded in 1977 in Jamaica, and was a coalition of largely working-class women drawn from a variety of women's voluntary organizations. Through a process of role-playing and workshops, a number of women were encouraged and enabled to "tell their stories." The narratives that emerged from this interactive, participative research project are contained in the book *Lionheart Gal*.[78]

While the testimonies and narratives are not necessary any more theological than that found in Boal's work, it is worth noting the extent to which the theistic and metaphysical are commonplace, constituent features of any discourse of Black Diasporan people. The work of such scholars as Hood,[79] Pinn,[80] Gossai and Murrell,[81] and Reddie[82] have shown the extent to which Black experiential discourse is usually redolent with religious/metaphysical sensibilities and concepts.[83] The ease with which metaphysical discourse was juxtaposed alongside seemingly elemental, socio-cultural realities reinforced in my own mind the ease with which I had been able to construct models of theological reflections from seemingly disparate and sometimes eclectic material.[84]

My analysis of the work of the Sistren Collective was to prove instructive in the development of a "process of dramatizing theologies." First, it is worth noting the importance of the vernacular in the narrative re-telling of these women. Honor Ford Smith writes:

> Those who are working class speak Patwah... This means that Patwah is written for performance, which is excellent, but what is not excellent is that it is not written for silent reflection or for purposes other than entertainment. Yet we all know that Jamaican people reflect all the time in their heads or conversations in Patwah... The language issue is a political issue because language is central to all power relations. It expresses the soul of a people. In our experience the development of Patwah expresses the refusal of a people to imitate a coloniser, the insistence on creation, their movement from obedience towards revolution... In *Lionheart Gal* I have tried to be as faithful as possible to each individual's use of language. However the stage of development of the written language constantly undercuts the richness of the oral version.[85]

As I have outlined in my writing of the sketch *The Wisdom of Solomon*,[86] Jamaican patois holds an important emotional and psycho-social and cultural resonance for Black people as the repository for notions of selfhood, identity and resistance.[87]

A number of scholars have responded to the pioneering work of Sistren in order to construct their own particular approaches to unearth the often submerged and subversive discourse of Black women. Marjorie Lewis, a Jamaican Womanist theologian, has reflected upon the pioneering work of the Sistren collective as she continues to develop a distinct and unique nomenclature for Black women in Jamaica and Britain (who share a common ancestry) termed "Nannyish t'eology."[88]

Drawing upon the themes of resistance, rebellion and subversion, all of which can be found in the narratives of the Jamaican women in the Sistren Collective, Lewis has constructed a Jamaican inspired notion of theology that is built upon the contextual experiences of Black women.[89] Lewis writes of her particular construction of theology:

I am of the view that the appropriate term is "nannyish t'eology," an expression couched in the Jamaican language, which clearly suggests its derivation from Nanny the icon and prototype. I offer this as the appropriate nomenclature for a contextualized Jamaican Womanist theology, because it embodies a consensus about the valued understanding of women's roles in Jamaican society.[90]

What has attracted me to Lewis's work is the interactive and performative element within her theological articulation and construction. While her work is not concerned with drama in its strictest sense, Lewis, nonetheless, has approached the development of "Nannyish t'eology" by means of extensive reference to the dramatic, performative qualities inherent within Jamaican tradition. Her work, drawing on the theories and practices of such women as Imani Tafari-Ama,[91] Carolyn Cooper[92] and Honor Ford Smith[93] has been a collaborative approach to unearthing the often silent voice of Jamaican women. In effect, this was a process of giving a voice to the voiceless.

Dianne Watts' work amongst African Caribbean mothers in Manchester, in the north-west of the UK, has also been influential in this study.[94] Her methodology for engaging with Black women of a variety of ages draws upon some of the literature cited by Lewis, in order to uncover some of the religious practices and traditions amongst African Caribbean women. Writing with reference to the submerged and concealed religious practices of African Caribbean women, Watts writes:

> The Jamaican belief in the hereafter is thus a mixture of Christian and African practices. At death and after three days, the soul that comes from God goes back to God. The personality soul returns to the land of the ancestors and may be reborn repeatedly in children in the lineage. The guardian and/or shadow soul usually remains with the family for nine days to ensure that all the funeral rites are completed.[95]

The participative methodology used by Watts for gaining access to the religious experiences of African Caribbean women, when fused with the approaches of the Sistren Collective and Lewis, assisted in developing an underlying methodology for a process of dramatizing theologies. These sources, coupled with the dramatic possibilities offered by Boal, when placed within the overarching framework of an action-reflection paradigm, have given rise to a consistent process for undertaking Black theological discourse with marginalized and oppressed people. In effect, these are the raw materials for what is a "process of dramatizing theologies."

Putting All This into a Theological Context

In this, the final section of this chapter, I want to outline the explicit theological considerations that have influenced this dramatic approach to articulating and doing theology. Working within an action-reflection framework, I have identified theories and practices that are explicitly dramatic (Boal), but not overly theological. Conversely, there have been approaches and ideas that have incorporated theological and religious themes, but the dramatic intent has either been hinted at or been more theoretical in its explication.

In this section, by way of a summation of this methodological discussion, I want to draw together the various threads for an inclusive way of doing theology from the bottom up—i.e. the development of an inclusive methodology for engaging with the voiceless. This final section is an investigation into the methodological meeting point for a theological and educational approach to performative action. In this respect, the work of Jose Irizarry and Lynne Westfield has been important.

Jose Irizarry is a religious educator who has undertaken research into the cultural foundational constituent in the theory and practice of religious education.[96] Irizarry begins by seeking to delineate the different ways of understanding the term "culture" within the context of a teaching and learning framework.[97] He argues that scholars need to attune themselves to the more complex nuances of culture and the fluid dynamics of relational positionality with regards to the self and others. Too often, the notion of culture is perceived in crude, static and reified terms.[98] Drawing on the work of Donald and Rattansi,[99] Tanner[100] and Wilkerson,[101] Irizarry outlines a method for uncovering the often hidden, tacit, taken-for-granted components that constitute the identity formation of the individual, particularly the self as religious educator, often working within the context of a faith community.

What has been instructive for this study has been Irizarry's approach to reflecting upon the cultural norms and values that exist within individuals and within the wider contexts of communities of faithful Christian practice. As I have attempted to construct a systematic, transferable methodology for undertaking a "process of dramatizing theologies," drawing on a plethora of sources, Irizarry's notion of the religious educator as "spec-actor" has proved hugely informative.

Irizarry is concerned that practical/pastoral theologians and scholars should be "spec-actors" (which in Boalian terms is to be both a performer within the dramatic encounter, as well as an observer, juxtaposed in the same self), who are able to "read" the cultural values and norms of the faith community in which they are immersed.[102]

The role of the spec-actor is to enable individuals and communities to reflect upon their own and collective agency. Then, through a process of performative action (in my case drama), they are enabled to transcend the finite limitation of the self. This means one has to go beyond the fixity of constructed selfhood, the identity of which is often imposed on individuals by the limitations of history, tradition and oppressive and coercive power. In effect, the inhibited and restricted selfhood of marginalized and oppressed peoples—in this study, largely Black people of the African Diaspora—is one that has been so denigrated and disparaged that it has denied them a voice in the present world order. Romney Moseley has termed this form of critical transformation a process of "becoming a self before God."[103] The role of the educator and theologian as a spec-actor can be summarized in the following words, where Irizarry writes:

> Boal's metaphor of spec-actor fits well the theological language of transcendence, as the capacity of the religious person to go beyond the limits imposed upon the self in order to move into a distinctive and sometimes unfamiliar "being." If the religious educator incorporates the idea of transcendence as a pedagogical imperative he will engage a process of acting out the limits of his own cultural identity. The intercultural religious educator introduces individual cultural selves to communal being that although sometimes unfamiliar signals the potential of the group to become a new "one," an alternative community that distinguishes itself from others—a glimpse of God's reign.[104]

The process of enabling individuals and communities to "act" out particular scenarios as a means of transforming the self and remaking their existential realities lies at the heart of the methodology of a "process of dramatizing theologies." Irizarry's notion of performative action as a reflexive and collaborative exercise in deconstructing, uncovering, remaking and ultimately transforming, enabled me to put a more explicit theological input into an eclectic framework that is based upon an action-reflection framework.

Assessing the Importance of Lynne Westfield to the Notion of Performative Action

Nancy Lynne Westfield is a religious educator at the theological school and the graduate school of Drew University in Madison, New Jersey. Westfield has become, in recent times, one of the most creative and eclectic of African American religious educators and Womanist scholars. Since discovering Westfield's work,[105] particularly her creative and eclectic methodologies for undertaking practical/pastoral work with African American women, I have been emboldened to develop my own creative work as a dramatist in order to undertake Black theological work.

What attracted me, initially, to Westfield's work was the reflexive nature of her approach to being a scholar. For Westfield, there is the determined desire to create an alternative framework and epistemology for her Womanist inspired approaches to religious education and Practical theology. Westfield writes:

I wanted to shape my work using the aesthetic as the subject of scholarship. I wanted to shape my work to be about ordinary African American women, but also did not want my work conveyed through the mainstream male voice that the scholarly guilds employ for communication. I understand that art, in and of itself, is an act of resistance, as act of humanness, an act of freedom born out of liberative activity, as well as born out of a personal experience of grace.[106]

Westfield's approach to doing theology with African American women has exerted a profound effect upon this study. In the first instance, Westfield provided the explicit African-centred component to my methodological odyssey to create a substantive educational framework and philosophical underpinning for my process of dramatizing theologies. While an action-reflection paradigm, coupled with the work of Freire, Boal and Irizarry, have been instructive in enabling me to develop a broad educational framework for this study, it was Westfield who provided the Black theological input into this methodological task.

Westfield's commitment to undertaking Womanist theology by means of a reflexive, participative and eclectic, creative methodology gave added impetus to the process of dramatizing theologies. Westfield writes:

My mode of writing and reasoning is a reflective narrative with other voices interwoven... As a womanist, I lean heavily upon personal narrative in order to relate black women's history and religious experience... My style is narrative in a poetic genre which emerges from a community deeply rooted in the language, imagery, rhythms of the King James version of the Bible.[107]

From my reading of Westfield, a number of methodological themes have emerged that have informed this work. First, Westfield utilizes poetry and creative, literary writing as a primary means of undertaking Black theological work with African American women. In 1995 she formed the "Dear Sisters' Literary Group."[108]

Westfield's utilization of poetry as a means of doing theology has been influenced by Womanist ethicist Emilie Townes, whose own writings is replete with poetic verse, written as a means of exploring Black theological concerns in an alternative construct.[109] Townes writes:

In my attempt to put pen to paper a spirituality that is lived, I sorted through these possibilities (work of poetic writers) for an entry point. In utter frustration, I turned to my own poetic voice to break the silence. Poetry came as a response to a sermon found in Toni Morrison's novel *Beloved*. The way had revealed itself! As I searched through other novels and consulted with friends, a methodology emerged that seemed true to the experience of Black women's spirituality and moved into a Womanist mode of seeking to push beyond what is the ordinary or the norm in Black life, to explore the possibilities.[110]

Second, in the midst of using poetry and literary readings from the repository of African American cultural heritage, Westfield wants to move from "pre-founded judgement of the import of our voices,"[111] where the scholar acts as an authorial expert in deciphering the content of Black theological speech, to a contemporaneous facilitator, enabling others to speak for themselves.[112]

In this respect, Westfield's approach is not unlike my own, in seeking to use drama as a participative medium in which the task of doing theology is a shared one between individuals. Westfield, drawing upon the important work of bell hooks,[113] argues for a process of doing theology that is interactive, participatory, dialogical,[114] and is rooted in the Freirian notion of seeing education as the practice of freedom.[115]

Third, Westfield's work is rooted within a Womanist theological paradigm and uses personal experience as the initial point of departure in the collaborative process of doing theology. Westfield has spoken of her own positionality as the underscoring of her scholarly work as an educator and theologian.[116] Observing a fellow Diasporan African educator and theologian being so unapologetic in framing her own experience as the initial point of departure in the pedagogical and theological task was hugely important for this study for it enabled me to break through the shackles of my own, hitherto, diffidence in departing from the conventional scholarly modes of operating.[117]

Finally, in methodological terms, Westfield's work has reinforced the importance of creating safe spaces in which this form of participative, interactive method for undertaking theological discourse can be undertaken. The literature pertaining to Black Diasporan religiosity is replete with references to the "concealed gatherings" of Black people.[118] In the previous chapter, when outlining the use of ethnography and participant observation as a methodological tool in which to gain access to the selfhood of the voiceless, I spoke of the importance of acknowledging the concealed and subversive nature of Black spirituality.

Whether in terms of signifying,[119] conjuration,[120] or cultural dissonance,[121] Black religio-cultural life is always heavily coded and often submerged. Consequently, in order to release the often subterranean authentic discourse of selfhood, so as to enable a more critically honest reflection upon the nature of self and God, it is essential that any form of participative theological reflection is undertaken in a "safe space." Namely, a space that is reflective of control by Black people, and in which African cultures, values and experiences are normative.[122] In many respects, this notion of safe space has been the central defining genius of the Black church in the African Diaspora.[123]

The survivalist ethic within Black people has been such that we have had good cause not to trust the blandishments of mainstream White controlled Christianity, but rather, have invested our trust in an immanent Jesus, who has been with us in all travails and hardships.[124]

Concealed gatherings are woven deep in the psyche of Diasporan African people. They hark back to a time when the very notion of Black self-determination and mutuality was not only an anathema to White authority, but was also an illegal activity. Black people, in response to the dehumanization of slavery, sought to create their own world—the need to create a place of safety for themselves.[125] Writing with reference to concealed gatherings, Westfield writes:

> The Dear Sisters' gatherings demonstrated a primary characteristic of concealed gatherings, i.e., the gatherings are laugh-fests. The gatherings are women laughing with each other rather than at each other. Women laugh about men, jobs, White people, neighbors, preachers, race, gender, pets, hairdressers, and wardrobes then and now.[126]

As defined in the previous chapter and amplified in this section of the study, a process of dramatizing theologies is predicated on the assumption that the educator and theologian is adept at creating safe spaces in which the voiceless can be enabled to work through substantive generative themes by means of an interactive, participative form of theological reflection.

Having Put All This Together, So What's Next?

Having developed an underlying theoretical educational framework for working with the voiceless in order to create a process of dramatizing theologies, I wanted to return to one of the groups, with whom I had worked previously, in order to assess this method for its efficacy and utility.

In an earlier section of this chapter, I outlined the process I developed to assist participants to reflect upon their identity and selfhood, arising from repeated performances of *The Wisdom of Solomon* and *Love is the Answer*.

In order to build upon this process, I identified a younger group of people with whom I could attempt to work in a collaborative manner. My decision to locate and work with a younger group of participants was prompted by a twin set of concerns. First, I was conscious that my work, hitherto, had been mainly with young adults. Yet my journeys around a number of inner-city and urban churches had alerted me to the preponderance of children in many of these churches, whose experiences of marginalization and disaffection were every bit as acute, in many respects even more so, than those of their older compatriots. Could my method for undertaking a process of dramatizing theologies transcend issues of age and maturation?

Second, by identifying with and working alongside a group of children, I was returning, if only briefly, to the roots of my scholarly work and ministry, for my initial research efforts in Practical theology had been with children and young people.[127]

In that initial work with children and young people, back in the late 1990s, my research efforts were directed at young people and children largely as a tactical device, in order to create more inclusive worshipping and learning communities of faith. I felt that if churches were able to genuinely appreciate and learn from those who were the youngest and most vulnerable members of their communities, then those ecclesial centres would be more adept at handling other related issues around diversity and inclusivity.[128]

Consequently, in order to test out my nascent methodology and to fulfil my previous covenant, to always want to assess the needs of children within the adult-orientated domain of the church, I agreed to meet with a group of children. This group consisted of six individuals, all Black, between the ages of nine and eleven. The gender balance was 50/50 males and females. Because of the age of the group, and in order to fulfil some of the "safeguarding"[129] issues that are now operative within many of the historic-mainline churches in the UK, I worked with another adult. She was an African Caribbean woman in her late thirties. The group met in what would otherwise have been an "After School Club" in the church.

Using the methodology outlined in the previous chapter, plus many of the insights described in this one, I invited the group to share with me some of the issues that affected them in their lives.

Working with a much younger group, it was decided that the barn dance exercise would benefit from being performed, rather operating purely as a metaphorical heuristic as described in Chapter 4. Quite naturally, the individuals in the group relished the opportunity to learn a few steps from a very rudimentary barn dance and then reflect upon the politics of the dance.

What emerged from our discussion was the clear sense that for many of these children issues of powerless, pressure and difference were clearly major factors in their lives. For many of them (five out of six), they were very much aware of living and existing in a global context, where issues of difference, power and wealth were very real concerns. It was interesting to note that all six of them had access to the Internet and were very computer literate.

In order to respond to the generative themes that had emerged from within the group, I wrote the following short, dramatic reading. Given the ages of the participants in the group, plus their developing levels of cognition and faith construction, the piece was relative short, requiring relatively little acting (it was a dramatic reading and not a conventional drama *per se.*) The full script of *Two Voices in the World* is reproduced in the following pages.

TWO VOICES IN THE WORLD

[*A dramatic reading for three voices.*]

No. 1: Two young children, united in their youth. They are living on opposite sides of the world. Night is coming. The children are dreaming.

No. 2: The night is here. Sleep is coming soon. I am looking at the stars. The stars are bright, but the sky is dark. I am alive. I can see the stars. I am a part of the world. I belong in this world, and the world belongs to me.

No. 3: The night is here. Sleep is coming soon. I am looking at the stars. The stars are bright, but the sky is dark. I am alive. I can see the stars. I am a part of the world. I belong in this world, and the world belongs to me.

No. 2: It is the dawn. The sun is rising and it is a new day. The sun is high. I can feel the sun on my skin. Then again, I'm not wearing many clothes, so the sun is melting my skin. My family cannot afford many clothes. This is a new day.

No. 3: It is the dawn. The sun is rising and it is a new day. There is no sun in the sky. The sun rarely comes around these parts these days. What with the pollution, the smog, acid rain and all that stuff, we're lucky if we see the sun at all. This is a new day.

No. 2: This is a day that has never been seen before. I have a lot to do before I can go to school. I have to feed all the animals on our farm. Then I have lots of other stuff to do. Then I go on to the streets to sell newspapers to car drivers on the main road, three miles from where I live. Then I go to school.

No. 3: This is a day that has never been seen before. I have to get ready to go to school. School is not as nice as it used to be. A really nasty thing happened at my school a few months ago. A big boy, a nasty looking boy, came into our school and began to do bad things to all the people. I don't see my best friend any more. He is dead. I don't like school much these days.

No. 1: I see all things. I love you both, for what you are, for who you are and where you are.

No. 2: School ends in the afternoon. The sun is lower than it was before, so it is not as hot. I have to go home and help my Dad on the farm. We have lots of things to do on our farm and there are not enough people to do all the things that need to be done. We can't afford anybody to do all the work, so I have to do my share of the chores.

No. 3: School ends in the afternoon. I have to wait for my Mum to come and collect me. My older sister could walk home from school all by herself when she was my age. My Mum would let her, and nothing bad ever happened to anyone. Now, since the bad things started to happen at my school, I have to be collected by people. I can't do anything by myself.

No. 2: In the early evening as darkness begins to fall, I have to go back on to the streets to sell newspapers again. I take my newspapers from the newspaper seller man. The papers are heavy. I take them to the main street and begin to wave them at the passers-by in their cars. Some people stop. Others drive on. When it is raining, I get soaked. I hate it when it's like this.

No. 3: I am at home when it gets dark. I am alone in my room. I play on my computer all night. My Mum is busy doing lots of stuff. I don't see my Dad much. Everyone I know is busy, so I have to spend a lot of my time on my own trying to do my own thing. I have a computer, so I play on that. I have lots of games, and I also surf the net. I don't go out much in the evening. I get bored sometimes.

No. 2: Christmas is coming soon. Our house doesn't have any decorations, as we can't afford anything like that. I like Christmas though. The whole of our family get together in the evening and we all begin to sing really old songs. I like to join in with the singing. Christmas is the best time of the year. I would like to get a present, but I've never ever had a present. Maybe one day. We will see.

No. 3: I like Christmas. I get to see my Dad. I also get lots of presents. I think I will get another computer, a bigger and better one than the one I have now. I also want some clothes and some trainers. A new watch and lots of other stuff as well. All my friends will get lots of presents as well. I would hate it if I got less presents than my friends. They would all laugh at me. I hope I get lots of presents. We will see.

No. 2: The night is here. Sleep is coming soon. I am looking at the stars. The stars are bright, but the sky is dark. I am alive. I can see the stars. I am a part of the world. I belong in this world, and the world belongs to me.

No. 3: The night is here. Sleep is coming soon. I am looking at the stars. The stars are bright, but the sky is dark. I am alive. I can see the stars. I am a part of the world. I belong in this world, and the world belongs to me.

No. 1: I see all things. I love you both, for what you are, for who you are and where you are. I came because I love you. One day, I hope that you will realize this for yourself.

No. 2: Goodnight world.

No. 3: Goodnight world.

The Theology at Play in *Two Voices in the World*

The two substantive theological themes running through *Two Voices in the World* are that of God's creation and the experience of being within that creation.

In terms of the first theme, I was conscious of writing for a younger age group, so I wanted to convey some of my initial thoughts arising from our conversations (following the barn dance exercise) in fairly direct, but, nonetheless, elusive images. In the drama, we see two characters with parallel lives, in vastly different contexts in the one world. Both are young, vulnerable and impressionable. They are young, but they are not naïve.

The development of Black theology, as I have intimated in this study, owes much to the groundbreaking work of James Cone[130] in particular, and that of the wider African American Christian community in general.[131] In many respects, the early years of this development witnessed a very American-centred form of discourse. Black theology became synonymous with the African American experience. By this, I mean it was very difficult for oppressed and marginalized Black people in other parts of the world to feel that Black theology spoke for or was even interested in them.

This myopic fault line has been addressed, in more recent times, by a number of theologians in North America and other parts of the world being in dialogue, seeking to untangle their differing and similar contextual experiences of being the voiceless, in a world of White hegemony.[132] The need to correlate the experiences of African Americans through recourse to Black theology with those of other marginalized and oppressed peoples by means of other theologies of liberation has become an important development in the last decade or so.[133]

North American Black theologians are beginning to connect their own contextual struggles with the travails and oppression of others in disparate parts of the world. Indeed, the works of such scholars as Dwight Hopkins[134] have begun to critique the extent to which the very nature of American capitalism and the pernicious effects of globalization are exerting an inequitable load upon the selfhood of the poor in other parts of the world. What are the links between American economic progress and development (including African Americans) and the continued exploitation of the poor in the global South?[135]

The sense that Black theology is a uniting construct in which the voice of all the marginalized and the oppressed is expressed, in a common humanity, is a common theme that runs through *Two Voices in the World*. The script, albeit in an implicit and non-didactic tone, invites the listener to reflect upon their part in a world that is divided sharply along economic and developmental lines. The drama outlines the ongoing experiences of both characters in a very personal and subjective manner.

When writing this piece for these children, it was my intention to juxtapose the subjective and personal with the objective and structural. Given that one of the central methods of Black theology is the use of subjective experience and narrative as a means of uncovering the larger macro structural systemic abuses that blight the lives of the poor and people of colour,[136] I used this approach to highlight the theological themes in the script. While this dramatic reading is *simply* a story about two children in different parts of the world, in the delineation of their individual narratives, a whole host of structural and systemic issues are highlighted. Why is one of the characters seemingly very poor and the other one much more affluent?[137] What are the roots of the violence and individualism that seem to stalk the contemporary experiences of those living in many affluent communities in the West?[138]

Two Voices in the World attempts to encapsulate some of the basic questions surrounding the disparity between rich and poor, Black and White, north and south and developed and underdeveloped. Yet, at the heart of the narrative is a seemingly transcendent figure that is in solidarity with the pain, the struggles and the disaffection of both children, who are seemingly alienated from an adult world, in which they are merely acolytes and ciphers, for whom and through whom things are done. This construct echoes the work and positionality of Jesus who instructs that the children should be brought to him and that nothing should prevent them from having a central place within the reign of God (Matt. 19:3–15).

The second theme at play in the drama is that of the oneness of God's creation. I do not intend to elaborate too much on this theme, as in many respects great attention is given to it in the final chapter, where I outline some of the practical dimensions of a "process of dramatizing theologies" for contemporary mission and ministry. In brief, however, it is worth noting the two characters have a sense that the world belongs to them. At the beginning and the end of the short piece, both characters repeat the mantra that "I belong to the world" and the "world belongs to me."

This seemingly simple aphorism remains a powerful central theme for Black theology and all theologies of liberation. The affirmation that one is a human being in the world and that such a world belongs as much to them as to any other category of person, although a simple statement, is nonetheless no less powerful for the fact that, for so many, this essential truth has long been denied them. The educational branch of Black theology, in terms of Black Christian education[139] and that of Black theology itself, both contain within them an explicit and implicit concern for those historic, structural forces and attitudes that have affected Black people and other people of colour. Scholars such as Robert Beckford[140] and Samuel Yeboah[141] have highlighted the dynamic and changeable nature of racism.

Black theology as a dynamic theistic response to the threat of non-being remains one of the central themes and concerns of this enterprise. Within *Two Voices in the World* both characters share the belief that they exist, that they are important and that they possess an innate self-worth.

James Cone's groundbreaking book *A Black Theology of Liberation* articulates the essential thrust for Black selfhood when he writes:

> There is more at stake in the struggle for survival than mere physical existence. You have to be *black*, with a knowledge of the history of this country, to know what America means to black persons. You also have to know what it means to be a non-person, a nothing, a person with no past, to know what black power is all about. Survival as a person means not only food and shelter, but also belonging to a community that remembers and understands the meaning of its past. Black consciousness is an attempt to recover a past deliberately destroyed by slave masters, an attempt to revive old symbols and create new ones.[142]

More recent work by the likes of Anthony Pinn[143] and Norman Gottwald[144] have shown the ways in which marginalized and oppressed peoples have gained sustenance, and an affirmation, for their innate selfhood by way of recovering the radical intent of religion, theology and the sacred scriptures. In terms of the former, Pinn writes:

> Black theology forged an ontological link between black people and the Divine that was expressed in the physical realm of blackness. What better way to forge liberation of a context of terror and dehumanization than to demand an understanding of liberation and justice as part of divine personality and character manifested in the faces of oppressed blacks?[145]

While not as explicit a rendering as has been articulated within the ranks of systematic theology or in biblical studies, the salient features of Black existential selfhood is, nevertheless, revealed within the brief pages of this text. As the piece was written primarily with young children in mind, its treatment of Black theological themes is perhaps more elusive than that found in some of the earlier pieces created within this study. Yet, the process of its construction and its relationship with a group of voiceless individuals remains consistent with the central thrust of what I have termed a "process of dramatizing theologies."

Further Reflections on *Two Voices in the World*

The final phase of working with these children was to access what impact this piece had exerted upon their consciousness. What had come into their thinking when given an opportunity to perform in and witness this piece? The group were asked to perform the reading on four occasions. By the fourth reading, given their ages, attention and concentration were beginning to wane. Despite the more limited engagement of this group (compared to their older compatriots), there remained, nevertheless, a fascinating encounter between myself and these young cohorts, when asked to reflect upon the dramatic reading.

The children asked a number of critical questions about the script. In response to questions such as "Who are the young children at the heart of the drama?" the group immediately thought that one was Black and the other White, or that one was definitely rich and from the North (or from round "here") and the other was poor and from the South? (they were from a long way away). Interestingly, none of this is stated in the script.

When I asked the group about the gender of the two characters, all of them assumed they were male. Again, this is not stated. All of the children had been exposed to a "World Faith" approach to non-confessional religious education in schools and had some sense of the religious and cultural practices and affiliations of people living in "far-away places." I wondered whether this form of awareness was engendered through an exposure to people of other cultures?[146]

The ability of the children to read their sense of understanding and engagement with the wider community and world into this text simply reinforced, to my mind, the ability of Black people to deconstruct and read their own experiences into any text, as a part of the hermeneutical process.[147]

Conclusion

My engagement with this group of children has highlighted the cross-generational possibilities of this approach to the articulation and doing of theology. Given the limited numbers on which this study has been constructed, I am somewhat loth to make too many generic appeals for its utility and efficacy. Within the context of a relatively small-scale piece of contextual theology, I remain confident for the dynamic, participative process that has emerged from the combination of practical inter-disciplinary theological methodologies juxtaposed with Black theological themes and content, held within the framework of drama.

This and the previous chapter have been an attempt to create a sustainable underlying methodology and philosophy of education for the development and articulation of a "process of dramatizing theologies." The process I have created (detailed in Chapters 4 and 5) is an attempt to create a consistent framework for the democratizing of theology. This is a desire to move beyond "talking for and about" the voiceless to a position of "doing theology" with and alongside them, in which their very presence is central to the process and the content of theological reflection. The substantive content of this emerging theology is, in many respects, not remarkably different from the traditional nomenclatures of "Black Theology" and "Womanist Theology" on which this study is based. The significant departure, however, is that it attempts to create a critical middle ground between the academy and the confessional faith communities that exist in many Black majority and Black-led churches across the many contours of the African Diaspora.

In the final chapter, I want to try and ground some of these emerging themes and ideas within a more practical domain, seeking to identify how a process of dramatizing theologies is incarnated within the everyday contexts in which Black, Womanist and Liberation theologies should be in evidence.

Chief amongst these concerns is the need to counter the ongoing, seemingly all-pervasive sin that is racism and its naturally concomitant White supremacy.[148] In the following chapter, I outline the theoretical framework and practical outworking for a new approach to unmasking, challenging and tackling the continuing terror and threat that is racism, which is no less present now than in previous epochs.

6   Practical Applications for a "Process of Dramatizing Theologies"

A Theology of Dramatic Engagement: An Anti-racist Application

In my previous book I recounted the narrative that gave rise to a newly developing theory and method for engaging in anti-oppressive and anti-racist practice by means of dramatic engagement.[1] I have termed this new concept a "theology of dramatic engagement." This concept first arose a number of years ago when, after prolonged reflection, I was able to give voice to and name an oppressive reality that had afflicted Black people living in Britain.[2] I coined this initial phenomenon a "theology of good intentions."[3] A "theology of good intentions" was my attempt to outline an approach to the seemingly rigid and unchanging response of White hegemony to the debilitating effects of racism upon Black people. Rather than attempt to deal with the systemic and structural underpinning that gives rise and fosters racial injustice, White power, both individual and corporate, is content to simply apologize and "say sorry" as if these words are infused with magic properties and are an end in themselves.[4] When first describing this phenomenon, I wrote:

> A "Theology of Good Intentions" is a way of responding to situations of injustice, in which the perpetrator fails to take full responsibility for their actions. It is a way of responding to the oppressed and powerless, by refusing to take the experiences or perspectives of these people seriously.[5]

The antidote to this pernicious phenomenon is based upon the dynamics and challenges of dramatic action—i.e. the format and methodology that lies at the heart of this book. The engagement of which I speak relates to the need to enter into the space and the experiences of the "other." It is the need to get beyond the rhetoric of polite conversation and instead deal with the messiness of the "other" through entering into a fictional space that has been created by a facilitator, be they a minister, or an educationist or a theologian, or all three.

In my previous work, I began to outline some aspects of a "theology of dramatic engagement" in more practical terms,[6] leading hopefully to renewed praxis. In this work, I want to return to this concept, but analyse it in terms of a "process of dramatizing theologies," and assess how this developing theory can enhance the subject selfhood of the marginalized and oppressed—voiceless people in the world.

In order to interrogate the workings of a "theology of dramatic engagement" I will reinterpret the central paradigm of this work which is *My God!?*.

Reinterpreting My God!?: Theoretical Reflections on a "Theology of Dramatic Engagement"

In using this term, what I want to suggest is that the primary way in which Christian understanding or action has developed is not usually through further in-depth study or thinking. Neither has been achieved by means of prolonged reflection and discussion. Although these elements are undoubtedly important, it is my belief that change occurs through active participation with others, especially those who are not like us.[7]

By returning to *My God!?* I believe we are presented with an interesting dramatic scenario, in which many of the hallmarks of a counter-hegemonic antidote to racial injustice are on display, and from which a workable praxis of resistance can be mounted.

I think the most basic and foundational points to be made about the sketch *My God!?* is that God stands at the centre of the whole dramatic episode. While the four characters play a major role in the drama it is God who is the central player. The other characters react to and take their philosophical and theological cues from the agency of the Divine. In short, it is God who is in control of things.

While this is a basic, dare one say, even contemptuously simple point, it is, nevertheless, an essential one and needs reiterating. I say this because in our so-called post-modern world in which there is a proliferation of philosophical and ideological frameworks by which one can attempt to interpret the world and human existence, the existence of religion and theistic belief remain important paradigms that still govern the thinking of many.

As I attempted to display in the latter part of Chapter 1, religion in general and Christianity in particular, remain important motivating forces for action in the world. This action can take many forms and many will argue as to the efficacy of religiously inspired activity but no one can doubt the potency of religion as a motivating force even in our so-called post-modern, post-religious epoch.

For Christians, the doctrine of creation, and the belief that we are created in the image of God should remain our initial point of departure in any attempt to talk about human identity and agency in the world. In effect, our conversation or discourse should always be *theistic*.[8] By making God the central defining "character" in the drama, the sketch forces all the four human players to define their identity and position in relationship to God. The subjectivity of the "human characters" in the sketch and their perspectives on truth and righteousness come into collision with the God figure who exists within human reality but who is not defined nor limited by the four men.

The relationship between God and the four men in the sketch echoes the various approaches of a number of theologians and educators who have approached the thorny question of racial injustice from within a Christian, theological paradigm. Whether addressing their concerns through the lens of Eucharistic theology[9] or Christian ethics,[10] religious scholars have mined Christian tradition in order to create a framework in which one can begin to challenge racism.

What I am advocating from my analysis of *My God!?* is for a paradigm that utilizes the intentional engagement of drama in order to create a framework in which people can explore their differences by inhabiting the fictional space of a character within a specific dramatic scenario.

In the sketch, the various characters are forced to test out their opposing views of God in the context of the other, with God as the "host." It is the initial attempt to contact God in and through prayer that initiates this dramatic encounter. A "theology of dramatic engagement" represents the challenge of moving from the relative comfort of one's subjectivity and inhabiting the space of the "other." Before I begin to outline some of the practical issues and insights that have arisen from the creative development of utilizing a "theology of dramatic engagement," I want to highlight some of the basic theological themes that are resonant in this concept.

Accepting God's Invitation

In emphasizing the essential theistic centred nature of the dramatic encounter in *My God!?* I have drawn upon a number of theological themes that I have addressed in my previous work, relating to what might be termed "body theology." The Pauline injunction that the body of Christ and the church that bears his name is one that is made up of many parts remains a symbol for a kind of unity that is complex and challenging at equal turns.[11]

I say complex and challenging because, as I asserted at an earlier juncture in this study, it is not a type of unity that is either built on a cosy or easy sense of homogeneity. Simple recourse to the Pauline text of Galatians 3:28 in the belief that this enables us to ignore or obliterate our differences is naive. This perspective has little cognizance of the real disparities in power and esteem in the world as many of us know it and experience it.[12] In a previous book, I argued that there was a radical inclusivity within the body politic of the Kingdom of God, when one interprets Jesus' parable of the banquet in Luke 14:7–14 in light of social-scientific thinking, drawing upon the concept of "re-defining the norm."[13]

I developed this concept as a way of speaking of a radical reversal of the usual societal, systemic norms that govern how institutions operate—namely, conferring power and authority on those whose experiences, education, ethnicity, gender and age all closely correlate with the essential template that govern who should be recognized and "invited to the party."[14] In effect, White middle-aged, middle-class Oxbridge[15] or Ivy League[16] educated men create institutional power (whether secular or religious, either in micro or macro terms) in their own image. I have even argued that Jesus is co-opted in the service of such hegemony, as he becomes the supreme symbol of White male power—Jesus in effect is identified as "one of them."[17]

Reading the analogy of the body, as invoked by the author of 1st Corinthians 12, through the lens of a "theology of dramatic engagement," is to commit ourselves to a form of corporate identity in which, at the invitation of God, we are challenged to occupy the same space as the "other" and work through our differences.

Clearly, I am aware of the inherent difficulties of trying to correlate early New Testament writings with my twenty-first century concept of dramatic engagement. I am sure that there are many New Testament scholars who may want to look away at this point, fearing the damage I am going to commit on this text by means of my own particular brand of "reader response" approach to interpreting this text.[18] And yet, in the service of being in critical solidarity with those who are the voiceless in our present world order, I refuse to be limited by the conventions of the biblical academy.

Drawing on the underlying themes of unity and diversity that are resonant within the Corinthians text, I am arguing that much of that vision and challenge is embedded within the dramatic context of *My God!?*. In the context of this sketch, the complexities and challenges of engaging with difference is clearly exemplified. The four male characters are invited into creative tension of the drama by God, whose appearance not only galvanizes the context, but also provides the very foundation for the basis of the drama as a whole.

Existing within the Same Paradigm

My interest in "body" theology has taken many forms. In the first instance, I wanted to explore how the notion of being non-visible (as opposed to being invisible) and labelled a "nobody" exerted profound negative effects upon Black young people and children living in Britain.[19] I argued that the development of a "Black Christian education of liberation," which unified

Black theology within a teaching and learning format, by means of trans-formative education, was the vehicle that would turn "nobodies into some-bodies." I was anxious that just as the seemingly insignificant and small organs of the body are treated with great respect by the other members, the marginalized and oppressed Black young people living in post-colonial Britain were equally deserving of special care and attention.

In my book *Acting in Solidarity* I returned to the body analogy in order to explore the challenges of collaborative ministry and partnership. Partnership is often invoked as a central theological theme and strategic modus operandi of the churches' ministry, but is either corrupted or simply ignored. In terms of the former, we are treated to a notion of partnership, which to borrow the wise words of a Methodist colleague, can be likened to that of the horse and the rider.[20] Theirs is a kind of partnership, but not of equals, nor is the work shared out equitably either. It does not take much imagination to work out which group can be likened to the rider and which is the horse!

Alternatively, the notion of partnership simply becomes one of empty rhetoric. We use the term because it appears to be the "politically correct" thing to do, but it is no more than an empty device to placate certain sensibilities, while leaving the status quo unchanged.[21]

I have returned to body theology because within the framework of a "theology of dramatic engagement" it offers a number of creative possibilities for enabling groups and communities to deal with contentious issues of difference and unity. Within the sketch, just as within the body analogy, the differences are not only invited, indeed created by God, but these realities have to be lived out within a common paradigm in which all exist.

The author of the text of 1st Corinthians is quite clear about the need of the different parts to co-exist in the one body. No one part can say that it does not need the particular "other." Leaving the body (and continuing to exist) is not an option.

In the sketch, it is interesting to note that the four male characters do not leave the drama. I have reflected upon this since first creating *My God!?* Why don't the four male characters walk out? I have sometimes speculated on what might have happened to the four male protagonists if I were to create a sequel? What would happen next? Would they leave? The challenge of remaining in the same paradigm is a very hard one.

As I demonstrated in the previous chapter, sharing the same space and interacting in that space is a crucial maxim of drama and theatre. Dramatic, performative action requires that we creatively engage with the "other" in a specified space in which the rules of engagement are constantly being defined and re-defined.[22]

The five characters in *My God!?* interact with one another. No one leaves the drama. Although God issues the challenge to the four male protagonists to reconsider their place in the drama when she says:

Then it looks like it's time you lot were leaving. I will not and, I repeat, will not be dictated to by you mere mortals. Either you accept me as I am and worship me accordingly, or you must reject me.

I would argue that this is still consistent with my understanding of God. "Free will" and human autonomy demands that God allows us the space to walk out and reject the whole scenario God has brought into being, but with freedom comes the realization that such a decision will spell the diminution of ourselves and the others we leave behind.

This challenge, as is sometimes stated in Jamaican speak, to "stay and burn and not cut and run," is one that poses hard questions for many Black theologians. The development of the Black Church in the US as a repository and incubator for the creation and development of Black theology came into being due to the decision of African Americans to leave the racialized ecclesial body of White America.[23]

Within the context of body theology and my working out of a "theology of dramatic engagement," am I criticizing this decision of African Americans to leave White American churches and form the now historic Black denominations in the US? Before answering this question, it is worth noting that within British influenced contexts, racism and White hegemony have not led to complete separation. Rather, difference and (in some cases) downright enmity have been contained by the use of parallel realities.[24] In effect, Black people and White people have separated into tribal territories, in which demographics and geography account for separation, but both remain housed within the one ecclesial body.

I think it would be profoundly unfair and an act of historical amnesia to suggest that African Americans were wrong to leave racist and discriminatory bodies in order to create safe, liberating spaces in which God's transformative presence might be experienced. As I have suggested in my earlier reflections on *My God!?* it is the power of White patriarchy that is challenged in the drama, not the powerless and voiceless presence of the oppressed. The latter is reflective of the experiences of African Americans in the eighteenth and nineteenth centuries, when the historic Black churches came into existence.[25] African Americans in the eighteenth and nineteenth centuries who founded the historic Black denominations and their churches did so, not out of any sense of arrogant paternalism, as displayed by the four male characters in the sketch (who want to dictate to God), but rather for the more legitimate cause of affirming their innate God-given selfhood.[26]

Despite the challenges of history and the nuances of differing contexts, the goal of existing and remaining within the same paradigm remains an important challenge for all Christian communities. The sketch highlights the very real challenges that are in evidence when attempts to exist within a dramatic format, whether figuratively (as I have defined it thus far) or in practical existential conditions (as I will describe it in a moment). The characters disagree (with violence nearly erupting), but they remain within the same paradigm, just as the author challenges the church in Corinth to realize this reality by invoking the analogy of the body and many parts.

Not Just Sharing Space but Engaging with the "Other"

One of the most enduring features of the "theology of good intentions" is the failure of White people with power to learn from the continuing slights, insults and racialized attitudes and behaviour that so often characterize their relationship with those who are marginalized and oppressed on the grounds of "race."[27] In short, people fail to learn from past mistakes or oversights, and continue to replicate the systemic and systematic abuses that have been practised on previous occasions. This failure is not one of genuine oversight, but is symptomatic of a racialized disregard for the subjectivity of Black people. I know it is not *de rigueur* to make comparisons between different models or examples of oppression, and it is certainly not my intention to enter into the spurious and potentially dangerous terrain of comparing differing examples of suffering. But it is interesting to note the extent to which White hegemony is assiduous in its attempts not to cause offence against Jewish people and risk the charge of anti-Semitism.

If such niceties and sensitivities were extended to Black people of African descent, I would not have felt compelled to develop this theory, in order to name the oppressive sin of "empty apologetic rhetoric." The most perfunctory display of sensitivity directed towards Black people, way back in 1998 at the annual British Methodist Conference in Scarborough, would have obviated the need to develop a "theology of good intentions."[28] This whole ongoing series of reflections was triggered, initially, by a crass and insensitive remark at this corporate British Methodist gathering, where the sufferings of Black people were trivialized.

So a "theology of dramatic engagement" (from this point onwards I will use the acronymn TDE) is not simply about co-existing with others within a theistically centred paradigm. This is a helpful start, but to my mind, represents a minimalist agenda. Rather, within the context of TDE, I want to assert the importance of going beyond co-existence towards inhabiting the space of the "other" by means of dramatic encountering. This process can be seen within the text of the sketch *My God!?*

In the sketch the different characters share the same dramatic paradigm with the God character at the centre of the drama. It might well be argued that the characters never seem to arrive at the point of actual engagement with one another. In theoretical terms that is true. The sketch ends at the point when the four male protagonists are confronted with the challenge laid down by God to engage with one another.

That engagement of which I speak emerges, however, in the continuing interaction of the individuals and groups who enter into the drama and bring the script to life through the dramatic encounter with the characters. As I have, hopefully, demonstrated in the previous chapter, entering into the dramatic possibilities of the drama and inhabiting the subjectivity of a character is central to the process of dramatizing theologies.

In this respect, the interaction of the players, and the new epistemologies that emerge from this involvement, represent the movement from text to reader (or in this case, player) that is so commonplace within the realms of Liberation theology.[29] In effect, the participants who act out the drama are enabled to go beyond the text, in and through the repeated enactment of the script and the follow-up plenary. This acting out of the script is essential, for a process of dramatizing theologies is built upon the dialectic interplay between the text and performance. *My God!?* as the central paradigm for outlining a process of dramatizing theologies, within which is housed TDE, is built upon the active involvement of ordinary voiceless people. In this respect, the text is but the starting point, and not the conclusive end in itself.

Within this practical form of Black Liberation theology sits TDE and the need for people to engage with one another. This engagement takes the form of people acting in character and then responding to the resulting discourse in order to clarify, describe and possibly re-define their own subjectivity and the selfhood of the "other." Using the method I have outlined in Chapters 3 and 4, TDE encourages people to enter into a mythical space created by the dramatist and incarnated in the drama, in order to reinterpret reality for its veracity and efficacy.

Taking the Characters and the Situation Seriously

In order for TDE to operate in a helpful manner it is imperative that participants are encouraged to take the dramatic context seriously. Taking the context seriously does not necessarily mean being serious or behaving in a fashion that precludes humour or laughter. Within African Caribbean and African American life, many of the truths of the Black experience have been most successfully mined within the context of stand-up and situation comedy. In terms of the former, comedians in the shape of Richard Prior, Chris Rock or Curtis Walker have operated pretty much in the mould of social satirists.

The humorous framework in which their insights are couched should not disguise the deeply critical nature of their analysis on a whole host of cultural, political and economic issues at play in the Black experience. Within Christian tradition, there has been a long tradition of critical and perceptive insights emerging from within a comic, sometimes absurdist perspective—the exponents of which are often termed as "holy fools."[30]

The dramatic sketches at the heart of this approach to theological reflection demand that participants are willing to enter into the "internal logic" of the sketch. By internal logic, I am referring to a process in which the participant takes seriously the perspective of the character they are playing, and imbue the role with a sense of seriousness. This mode of behaviour is not unlike that demanded of participants in Groome's[31] or Berryman's[32] respective pedagogical approaches to Practical theology. Internal logic is the sense that the world as defined by sketch, no matter how improbably or absurd is, in some sense, real and to be taken seriously.

The sense of asking participants to suspend their critical, realist judgements, in order to enter into the internal logic and dynamic of a piece of drama, was first attempted in my last study. The three pieces in the section entitled "Racial Justice/Black Theology" in *Acting in Solidarity*[33] differ in tone and treatment, but participants who were part of the research were encouraged to interact with the characters and with one another.

Acknowledging One's Positionality

Central to the workings of TDE is the sense that participants will be honest about their existential personhood prior to and during the drama. Who are they and what do they bring to the drama and the character they are playing? This approach to engaging with the "other" challenges individuals to move into a dialectical relationship with the "self," the character they are playing and the existential personhood of the "other." The relationship the individual subject constructs with other members of the drama is complicated by the dual identity adopted by their fellow performers, for each person has to engage with the fictional "other" as represented by the character that individual is playing, in addition to their existential self within the drama.

In many respects, the multiple positionality of each individual in the drama finds many echoes within a multiplicity of Diasporan religio-cultural contexts. Pinn has, for example, identified the many complex and codified ways in which African Americans engage with reality by analysing the varied rituals of "dress," "display" and the deployment of language.[34]

Within a British context, Tomlin[35] and Beckford[36] have observed the multiple positionality of African Caribbean peoples within religio-cultural settings. The inherent drama of Black life makes "us" ideal candidates for a methodology that calls for role-playing and the adoption of differing characters and multiple perspectives within a religio-dramatic format.[37]

Underlying TDE is the sense that each participant will ask themselves the most basic of existential questions. These include such concerns as (1) How am I different or similar to the character I am playing? (2) To what extent would I have handled this situation or scenario differently from the character I am playing? (3) How does this character relate to the others in the drama? (4) How could I (either one's existential self or that of the character they are playing) have handled this situation (in the drama) differently?

Participants are encouraged to reflect upon their role in the drama, utilizing an action-reflection model of critical thinking outlined in the previous chapter. The repeated enacting of the sketch is crucial, for it is in the repetition of the piece that nuances of meaning and new insights emerge. In addition to the philosophical necessities of repeated enaction of the drama, there is also the practical sense of "giving everyone a turn" in participating in the sketch.

The efficacy of a participative, dialogical, praxis-orientated approach to critical reflection has been demonstrated by Hope and Timmel.[38] These influential educators in Southern Africa have demonstrated how such a Freirian[39] inspired approach to critical reflection enables marginalized and oppressed peoples to become alive to the possibilities of re-creating their world.[40]

A "process of dramatizing theologies" provides the overarching framework for this particular approach to theological reflection. It is, for the most part, a resource and a method for marginalized and oppressed peoples. It should be noted, however, that TDE, which sits within this macro framework, is nevertheless a method for engaging with difference and "other" that has a wider applicability than the overall theory. TDE was created in order to overcome the pernicious effects of a "theology of good intentions" on the selfhood of Black people. As such, this concept is aimed primarily at those with power—essentially White hegemony.

Although the theory and practice of TDE has been used with voiceless people in Britain, the major thrust of its application has been developed with White people in mind.

Putting Theory into Practice—Using *My God!?* to Stimulate Reflection with the "Self" and with the "Other"

The following section has arisen from the piloting of *My God!?* with a group of White men and women. The group comprised twelve people. Five were ministers and seven were professional lay people all of whom were active in the church. All of the participants were chosen due to their experience in and commitment to issues pertaining to racial justice. I met with the group on two separate occasions in order to perform the sketch and then to reflect upon the process that had emerged from this participative exercise.

With the promise of strict anonymity (to the point of not naming the location in which these experiments were conducted), I asked the group to perform the sketch on six occasions. Individuals were given opportunities to play a range of different characters in the drama. The twelve participants (always in different permutations)[41] played out the drama and were then asked to reflect upon their involvement using the questions (purely indicative) I have outlined previously.

The main aim of the exercise was to enable the group and the individuals within it to reflect upon their individual agency and that of God. How did they see themselves in relation to God and to others?

Over many years as an educator, I have witnessed the ways in which biblical and theological issues become the point of departure and the foundational template for undertaking controversial discourse, whether in terms of "race," gender or sexuality. In using TDE with this group, I wanted to construct a mechanism that would enable participants to be more transparent about what informed their differing perspectives. What image of God or self did they possess and how did they inform their thinking of others, whether in terms of "race," gender or sexuality?

Having performed the sketch on a number of occasions, and facilitated group discussion on their involvement in the sketch, I asked the group to think about how the characters they had played related to God and to others in the sketch?

What Emerged from the Discussions— a Developing Practical Framework?

The following Bible study was used as a means of enabling the group and the individuals in it to reflect upon their individual identity and their relationship to others arising from the sketch. In creating this creative and practical framework, it was my hope to develop a process that would be a practical counterbalance to the theoretical considerations of TDE that have been discussed hitherto.

This study is concerned with creating an accessible and participatory means of carrying or detailing a liberative theology for the voiceless, in addition to developing a method for undertaking that discourse. It is not overly concerned with documenting the empirical outcomes of the various participants who have engaged with this approach to theological reflection.

Consequently, no real attempt was made to document what emerged from the group discussions.

My interest at this juncture is to share the practical resource that emerged from my interactions with the group, which gave way to the following reflections, which have been created in order to address the pernicious effects of a "theology of good intentions." The following framework, written in the form of a Bible study, was an attempt to synthesize the many issues that emerged from the group discussions, in order to create a practical resource that might have proved useful in other, differing contexts.

The decision to create this Bible study was, in part, a response to the reflections that emerged from the group, but was also informed by an engagement with the joint work of Ackroyd, Lewis-Cooper (née Lewis) and Muchopa.[42] In one of the early sections of their book, the authors stress that central to any learning process connected to issues of racial justice, participants must be prepared to explore their own identity and sense of self.[43]

The nature of difference, particularly the theological divides that arose from the sketch *My God!?*, became the basis for the following Bible study. The influence of Ackroyd *et al.* was juxtaposed with that of McFarland and his in-depth theological treatment of identity and difference.[44] Using aspects of McFarland's work as a dialogue partner in my attempts to address issues of difference and "other," I have attempted to develop a practical resource that will supplement the framework provided by the sketch *My God!?*, in order to give life to TDE.

Giving Life to TDE—The Bible Study that Arose from Repeated Performances of *My God!?*

- This Bible study is based upon John's Gospel, chapter 1: verses 35–51. Reference will also be made to the corresponding version of this story in Matthew's Gospel, chapter 16: verses 13–28, particularly verses 17–20.
- You, the leader/facilitator, hand every member of the group a piece of A4 paper. Ask each individual to turn their sheet horizontally, and then divide the paper into four sections by drawing three vertical lines across the paper. (Hopefully) they should have four equal rectangular boxes. Ask them to number these boxes from left to right: 1, 2, 3, 4. In the first box, ask each person to write the words *"Me."* In the second box, write the words *"My family."* In the third box write *"My friends."* In the fourth box write *"Jesus."*
- Ask each person to look at the first box. Each individual now attempts to do two things in this box. First, they should (in no more than four or five

lines) describe themselves as if they were talking to a stranger who knew nothing about them. Who are they? What is their age, where were they born, what are their hobbies, etc.? Below this description they add, *"What I think about me?"* Ask each person to then write a few words about what they think about themselves. What is the best thing about you? What don't you like? What are you good at? Not good at?

- In the second box, they continue in a similar vein from the first. Each person has to describe their family, as if they were talking to a complete stranger. Who is in their family? What is their family like? etc. Below this, they write *"What do my family think about me?"* How do they imagine their family sees them? (Some guesswork may be needed here.) Are they a popular member of the family? This bit is harder than the first box.

- In the third box they attempt to describe their friends—assuming, of course, that they have friends (leaders/facilitators need to be aware of this potentially painful issue). What are their friends like? Are their friends similar to themselves? If not, in what ways are they or their friends different? Below this, they write *"What do my friends think about me?"* How do their friends see them? Again, some guesswork may be needed here.

- In the final box, they have to describe Jesus. From what they have read, heard and possibly experienced, what is Jesus like, as if they were talking to a complete stranger? Below this, they write *"What does Jesus think about me?"* How do you think Jesus sees you? Do you think Jesus sees you differently than the others in the first three boxes? How might Jesus see you differently?

- Ask the groups to share the contents of their four boxes with each other. The different descriptions in the four boxes are a concise version of who we are, both in ourselves and in the eyes of others. The combination of how we see ourselves, and how other people who are a part of our lives view and see us, plays a major part in establishing our identity.

- What kind of person are they? If the members of the group know one another, how do they see each other?

- Ask each person to look at their first box again. What do they think of themselves? What do they think they are good at? What is the best thing about being them? What is the worst? Ask individuals to share what thoughts have occurred to them. To what extent has the person they have become been shaped by their family and friends? How easy would it be to become a new type of person? A person with completely new friends and hobbies? What about a new family?

- Our identity, the "who we are," is influenced by many things. How we see ourselves. How others see us. How we see them, etc. Think about the kind of things you are good at, or like doing. How did you know that you were good at doing them? (You may be good at sports, playing an instrument, playing computer games, making friends, doing school work and assignments, helping others, etc.).

- Look at John's Gospel, chapter 1: verses 35–51. In turns, read the passage. What happens to Simon, the brother of Andrew, when he meets Jesus? What does Jesus do? Jesus renames Andrew's brother, calling him Peter. How would you feel if you were suddenly given a new name?

- How many of you have "pet-names" or "nick-names"? Who gave you that name? Why? Often, names have a way of defining our character or shaping our identity. How many of you know someone called "Michael" and someone called "Mike" or "Mick"? People can be very particular about their names. Some people like having their name shortened, because it sounds less formal. It might even sound more trendy (compare Rob with Robert, or Sam with Samuel, for example).

- How do you think Simon felt having his name changed to Peter? Would you have complained? Why do you think Jesus changed Peter's name? A clue might be found in the alternative version of this story in Matthew's Gospel.

- Turn to Matthew chapter 16: verses 13–28. Read the passage. Look particularly at verses 17–20. What does Jesus say to Peter? In this passage Jesus asks his followers to respond to a question about his own identity. How are people seeing Jesus? According to the people, who are they saying Jesus is? Similar to the exercise you have just completed, this question is concerned with the identity of an individual. Just as you wrote down what you thought of yourself and how you felt others thought about you, Jesus is asking his followers about how others (and most probably themselves also) see him. What does Peter say?

- Jesus applauds Peter for his response. How does Jesus see Peter? What role or identity has Jesus in mind for Peter? What are the links between Jesus' calling of Peter in John's Gospel and this version in Matthew's?

- Ask the group to continue reading about Peter in the different Gospel passages, particularly the incident where he denies Jesus. Look also at Acts chapters 2, 3, 4, 5, 9, 10, 11 and 2–5, 9–12. See also, 1st and 2nd Peter. What becomes of Peter? What does he go on to achieve or accomplish?

- From what you may have already read or know about Peter, in what ways does he change? From our reading of the two passages Jesus sees certain qualities and characteristics in Peter. The name change would seem to indicate a new role and purpose Jesus had in mind for Peter— he is to be the rock on which the church will be built. Look at his actions and behaviour in some of the later passages that have been indicated. Jesus calls Peter and sees beyond the immediate aspects of his identity and the "who he is" (What is Peter's job before he is called?), in order to give him a new role and purpose. I am sure that Peter was as surprised at what he was asked and went on to do, as were the many people who might have known him in the "old days."

- Look at your sheet of paper. Think back to when you were younger. Were you the same person then, as you are now? What has changed? How have you changed? What things have led to the changes? What about your family and friends? What changes have occurred in that time?—Between then and now?

- Our identity, the "who we are," is never constant. Due to changing circumstances and events, we will change. Our hopes, expectations, likes, dislikes, hobbies, friends, even family, perhaps, may change. Look again at the four boxes on your sheet. *"What does Jesus think about me?"* Seeing how Peter made mistakes and did stupid things, and yet Jesus still saw the potential and the talents he possessed, how do you think Jesus sees you? What about the stupid or not so clever things you might (and will still) do?

- We believe that when we meet Jesus and we allow him to be active in our lives, we will be changed for the better. Our identity will change. Peter changed. Can you think of any other characters in the Gospels and the other books of the New Testament who are changed, through meeting or having an encounter with Jesus? (Some examples include the other disciples, Zacchaeus, Paul, etc.).

- Turn your sheet over. On the other side, write at the top of the page the words *"What I could be!"* Write down some of the changes you would like or think could happen to you. How could you be a better person? How could you better use the skills, talents and abilities you possess? In what ways could you become a nicer or more helpful person to your family, friends and others?

- Encourage the individuals in the group to date their sheet. Ask them to save the sheet. If they were to create another sheet in six months' time, what might be written on both sides (the first side with the four boxes and the second side with the question for the future) of the sheet? How, if at all, would your identity, the "who you are," have changed? Encourage individuals in the group to look at the life of Paul. What happens to him?

Concluding Thoughts on TDE—For Now?

A "theology of dramatic engagement" incorporates a number of strands in its approach to overcoming the liberal racist phenomenon of apologetic rhetoric. It involves the creative and critical engagement of participants within a dramatic format. In this work I have used the sketch *My God!?*, which is the central dramatic paradigm of this participative approach to Black theology, as a framework with which groups of people can engage in order to explore existential questions pertaining to identity and selfhood in relationship to a transcendent subject and others. It is an approach to countering racism that draws upon dramatic theory and performative action, in which individuals are challenged to act alongside others, in order to unmask the contours of their own selfhood.

Coupled with the theory and the dramatic format of the sketch is the resulting Bible study, which provides a practical, creative resource by which individuals can reflect upon their individual identity and its relationship to others.

This development in critical consciousness may provide the seeds for a transformative change in thinking, leading ultimately to changes in action and behaviour. Might this process be an effective antidote to the negativity of a "theology of good intentions"?

So, We're All in This Together, Then?

While this developing theory attempts to incorporate a more inclusive and participative process for articulating and doing theology, it remains none-theless rooted within the broader contours of Black theology. I have not sought to improve upon or substantially alter the basic foundations of Black and Womanist theology. Rather, I attempted to create a more sustainable process for making these disciplines accessible for non academics.

Unlike Jeff Astley's work on the import of theology that emerges from those who are below or beyond the academy,[45] this study has attempted to create a connection between the world of scholarship and the folk traditions of "ordinary people," going beyond mere theorizing, in order to create a practical mechanism for engaging with the voiceless.

Within the academy there has existed an ongoing discussion about the relative failure of Black theology to find a foothold within the contemporary life of the Black church and in ordinary Christian life. Scholars such as James Harris,[46] Dale Andrews,[47] Lynne Westfield,[48] Grant Shockley[49] and Yolanda Smith,[50] in addition to myself,[51] have all reflected on the disparity between Black theology as articulated in the academy and the practice in ordinary church contexts; and as a corollary, how this breach can be closed.

This approach to Black theological reflection is one that makes recourse to the ways of knowing, or the epistemological foundations of Black people of African descent. These are bound up in their ongoing experiences of struggle. By using drama as a theological method, one can enable marginal-ized and oppressed Black subjects to actualize many of the central themes

of Black Liberation theology, in order to remake their present consciousness, which in turn leads to renewed praxis.[52]

Working alongside marginalized people, through the medium of drama,
is nothing less than a process of critical advocacy. It is a way of assisting marginalized people to learn more about themselves and the world, through
the framework of religion. It is a process of being nurtured and educated
into such a world-view and being enabled to understand more about the
kind of faith that can sustain and empower. This, I believe, can be achieved
by means of drama, as an interactive and participative model for undertaking Black theological reflection in which marginalized and oppressed Black
people become the central agents in the learning process.

Possible Broader Applications?

Utilizing this inter-disciplinary method for undertaking Black theological research, which focused upon enabling ordinary marginalized and
oppressed peoples to be active participants in the research, has given
rise to a practical set of outcomes for the communities with whom the
research was undertaken. Many of the participants were empowered
to undertake their own theological reflections by means of interactive
drama. This emerging theology, in a dramatic form, is not only *for*, but
possibly of greater import, is *of* the voiceless.

It is *for* the voiceless, because it has been created, by means of drama,
to be a resource that will articulate something of the dynamic God-talk
of ordinary (Black) people. It is also *of* the voiceless, because the ongoing
interactive, action-reflection basis for undertaking this approach to theology offers the possibility[53] for ordinary people to exercise a measure
of control over the process, thereby enabling them to own the God-talk
that emerges.

I am not so naive as to believe that this process radically re-alters the
power relations between the professionally trained theologian and those
who are the non-specialist voiceless presence in the wider world. Johns
has critiqued the apparent anomalies and fissures in Paulo Freire's work,[54]
with and amongst the oppressed in Latin America.[55] Johns believes that his
democratic approach to education and knowledge production still carries
the inevitable stains of paternalism.[56]

In this method for doing theology with and alongside the voiceless, there
have been tensions, as I have tried to detail in Chapter 4, between the self-
conscious thinking of these individuals and the critical reflections on such
discourse by the professional scholar. There were occasions when I had to
engage and critique the perspectives offered by the groups. To what extent
was I guilty of overriding their concerns with my own?

And yet, despite these difficulties, I believe that an observational, participative action-reflection model for undertaking Black theological research is a potentially vital tool for the world of Pastoral/Practical theology. For those engaged with practical ministries that involve an ethical inter-human/ Divine encounter, action-reflection models represent an important means by which those "professionals" can reflect upon their practice.

Through this ongoing process of action and reflection, the creation of better practice may lead, as a corollary, to improved models for undertaking one's work. These improvements, if documented assiduously, may lead to important research findings and more effective paradigms for collaborative approaches to pastoral ministry.

As a contextual theologian I am loth to make generic pronouncement on the utility of this approach to undertaking theological reflections with individuals and groups.

In Chapter 4 I outlined some of the preliminary issues that were pressing concerns for any scholar attempting to undertake liberationist theological work with people who might be described as being the voiceless. In highlighting such concerns as "critical openness" and "self actualization" I wanted to bring to light some of the most pertinent issues at play in the marginalization and repressed selfhood of oppressed, voiceless people in Britain, if not the whole world.

For many people, the negation of their very selfhood has left them unable to conceive of a world in terms radically different from the one in which they often languish, and sometimes barely exist. In order that the voice of these repressed, alienated and marginalized peoples might be released, it is imperative that issues pertaining to critical openness, pedagogy and self-actualization are addressed. As I have tried to demonstrate in this study, what I am proposing is a form of Black theology that engages with other disciplines (principally social-science methodologies) in order to provide a holistic counter-hegemonic paradigm for empowering and liberating oppressed peoples.

And yet, as I outlined at an early juncture in Chapter 1 of this study, I am certainly not arguing that Black people represent the only oppressed and marginalized, voiceless people in the world. In directing my work at Black people, I am not making any claim to label Black people with the dubious honour of being the most "oppressed of the oppressed." Certainly, I agree with James Cone in the belief that the all-enveloping phenomenon that is racism makes particular demands upon Black people that are not replicated or reflected in the marginalization of the poor in the world.[57] As I have outlined previously, for Black people, particular for Black women, there are additional burdens imposed upon their selfhood, by virtue of the all-pervasive negativity that is associated with Blackness.[58]

Notwithstanding these very real differences in the unique nature of racism as a system of exploitation and oppression, I do not doubt that there are corresponding forms of oppression that are felt by other groups of marginalized people in the world.[59]

I would not be surprised if concerns such as critical openness, pedagogy and self-actualization were issues in parallel with justice and liberation movements across the world. I would welcome their engagement with this study and hope that within it they find helpful resources to assist them in their movement towards the quest for wholeness and authentic living.

Returning to the Beginning—Re-interpreting *The Calling* in Light of Black Theology

At the outset of this work I spoke about my formative developments as a so-called budding dramatist. I stated that the first piece I ever wrote was a relatively slight script entitled *The Calling*. I have already detailed the occasion that gave rise to its creation so there is little need to recount that narrative again. Rather, I want to return to *The Calling* because, in many ways, its very existence demonstrates the efficacy and the necessity for this creative process of dramatizing theologies.

When I first wrote this sketch I had no sense or inclination of the existence of Black theology. What prompted this piece was a sense of displacement and unease within the group of largely White liberal students at the University of Birmingham. As a Black working-class student, my immediate frames of reference were entirely different from those of my peers. My parents were Black working-class Jamaicans from the Caribbean, who had travelled to the UK in the late 1950s in search of a better life.[60]

In the many conversations of faith that ensued within the community of religiously minded students was the question of God's agency in human affairs. How could God be known? What was the nature of revelation? In the context of these discussions, I soon found that the Black religious context in which I had been nurtured had permitted me to assume certain "facts" as true. In the context of Black Caribbean social and cultural mores, the notion that God is not in the business of revealing God's own self to people, particularly those who are marginalized and oppressed, was a concept that was alien to me.

I lived in a context where God was spoken of in very literal, immanentist tones. God was as real as the air one breathed and the clothes one wore. I have spoken something of this dynamic in a previous piece of work.[61] In my previous discussions with Black elders in the West Midlands of the United Kingdom, I was struck at the ways in which these mature Christian people spoke of God in Christ in a very personal and affective manner. Jesus was their "best friend and confidante." He was the one who would not "chat your business."[62]

Black people have located within God the facility that exists through prayer, for a dynamic presence within their lives which is life enhancing and death defying.[63] Riggins Earl Jr. identifies Jesus within the context of African American thought as being intimately linked to their existential struggles.[64] Speaking of the experiential Christian religious experience of African Americans, Earl states:

> Every encounter with Jesus was predicated upon the theological and ethical presuppositions that he shares personally with them the salutatory gift of peace and the moral challenge of responsibility.[65]

I cannot remember the exact occasion that gave rise to this, my first ever piece of Christian drama, save for the fact that at some intuitive level it represented an attempt to counter the seemingly despairing White, Eurocentric liberalism of significant members of this University Methodist society. In the religious framework of the latter, God was often notable for God's absence within the context of human affairs. The language exchange in some of that discourse often viewed God as an absent landlord.

I do not wish to make the traditional and often compelling error of asserting a strong theism to all Black religious discourse. The work of Anthony Pinn, for example, has been notable in alerting us to the myopic nature of a good deal of Black religious discourse and the claims we often make for a seeming homogeneous Christian form of theism amongst Diasporan African people.[66]

In writing this sketch, it was not my intention to make any generic, grandiose claim for Black spirituality (indeed, none of the characters can be identified as being Black—more of which below); rather, this piece was my attempt to detail my own formative religious socialization within a Black African Caribbean context. In *The Calling* I was attempting to encapsulate what I had imbibed from my parents and the historic trajectory of faith that had first emerged in Africa and then metamorphosed as it migrated across the Atlantic, from the Caribbean to the UK.

THE CALLING

[*Enter STAN…walks centre stage.*]

STAN: [*To congregation*] What a week! What a traumatic experience. There I was, minding my own business, not saying a word, happy, outgoing; just going about my own business in my own sweet way. Then…it happened, God…called out to me. Without so much as a "how's your father," there God was. God calling me. And the funny thing was there were no angels, or flashing lights, or even a massive booming voice. There was just this presence. A feeling. All very eerie. "God wants me to serve him." What could I do? Well, I thought about it, considered it, mulled it over; and then I did the honourable and sensible thing... I ignored it. Closed God out of mind completely. Just my imagination I thought. I've been working too hard lately. I'll go and see the doctor tomorrow. He will know what to prescribe... But that presence! Seriously scary...

[*Enter JIM.*]

JIM: [*Greeting STAN*] Hi Stan... You look a bit down. Can't be that bad surely? You look like God has just spoken to you.

STAN: Well, as a matter of fact, seeing as you're asking... He has.

JIM: He has what?

STAN: God! He's spoken to me.

JIM: [*Trying not to laugh*] Come off it... Be serious. God! Spoken to you? I was only joking... [*Putting arm around STAN, patronisingly*]... Now you can tell me, I'm your friend. What's really wrong with you?

STAN: I'm telling you... He's spoken to me. God has spoken to me. God wants me to serve him.

JIM: [*Sceptical voice*] He does, does he?... Well well well...What kind of service... [*Looking Heavenward*]...does he want? Don't tell me, he wants you to lead the Methodists out of the West Midlands?

STAN: Be serious, you know God said nothing like that. I just know he wants me to serve him.

JIM: Sounds pretty peculiar if you ask me. I ask you, whoever heard of God calling people to do his work? Sure you haven't been overdoing the work at the office? You haven't been indulging in too many alcoholic, liquid lunches have you? Tried visiting a psychiatrist or a shrink or something?

STAN: [*Hurt*] If you're going to take that attitude, I'm leaving. Besides, God does call people. He called Samuel, didn't he?

JIM: Samuel who?

STAN: You know! That guy in the Bible, the Old Testament. They wrote a couple of books about him.

JIM: Ah yes... Well... That's different. God did call people in the past, but those were different days. No communications. God spoke to people then, but he used prophets and holy men… [*Looking at STAN*]… You're not a holy man. Trust me Stan, I know you, and we both know that you are no holy man. And why should God use you anyway, when he has all these wise and learned people all over the world to do his bidding? Some of these people have got degrees and stuff. God would choose them. No disrespect Stan, but not you.

STAN: Why not me?

JIM: God just wouldn't, that's all. I'd go to that shrink at the earliest opportunity, Stan.

[*Enter DIANE, running enthusiastically.*]

DIANE: [*Very excited*] Stan Stan, I've got some great news, brilliant news, superb news, wonderful news, I…

JIM: [*Interrupting DIANE*] Yeah, yeah; whatever. You think you've got news? You ain't heard nothing yet. Lover boy here… [*Pointing to STAN*]… This fruitcake thinks God's called him. Says he felt a presence. What a joke. I haven't had such a good laugh in ages.

DIANE: [*Subdued*] Funny you should say that… As a matter of fact… That's the good news I've got for Stan… [*Pious voice*]… I was sitting there reading the Good Book. "Thus spaketh the Lord in those days…"

JIM: [*Impatient*] Get on with it. What's the good news?

DIANE: [*Slightly upset*] As I was about to say… I was sitting there reading the Good Book and I heard this voice. Well, not exactly a voice…

JIM: Don't tell me, a presence.

DIANE: How did you guess? Has it happened to you? Have you felt this presence?

JIM: Don't be silly.

DIANE: Having read the Good Book, I then settled down for a good long prayer time, during which God told me to tell you, Stan, that he wants you to serve him as a lay preacher in the Church. Isn't that absolutely great?

JIM: You call that great? I call that a recipe for disaster.

STAN: I think I'm going to faint. I don't feel so well.

DIANE: Nonsense, you're highly favoured. God wants you.

JIM: But does Stan want God? If I were you Stan, I'd ignore him. Get him to pick on someone else. He'll soon leave you alone when he sees that you're not keen.

DIANE: He won't, you know. Look at Jonah. He was swallowed by the whale. God chased him everywhere until he obeyed. You can't ignore God or get away from him.

STAN: You sure know how to cheer a guy up, don't you? What am I going to do?

DIANE: Trust God, he will look after you... [*Pious voice*]... God never gives us more than we can bear. It says so in the Good Book.

JIM: [*Mimicking DIANE*] He never gives us more than we can bear... Ah shad-dup. That's easy for you to say, you haven't been called. Stan, I'd ask for a few more details before I'd consent to his schemes. A little bit of proof, a little insight into what to expect. That doesn't seem too unreasonable.

DIANE: You can't do that... Ask God questions? Test God! It's not right.

JIM: Says who? That Gideon guy did it. You're not the only one who knows the Bible and can quote from it. I know the story of Gideon; with the carpet and the dew... I would do that, Stan.

STAN: I'm confused... I don't know what to do.

DIANE: Trust the Lord. The Lord our God is Good.

JIM: [*Looking at DIANE angrily*] Will you stop quoting the Bible. We're talk-ing reality talk now; none of that old fashioned, out of date rubbish. Keep questioning, Stan. God simply doesn't call people anymore.

STAN: If only I could be sure.

DIANE: Forget about assurance. Just trust... Don't forget about faith.

JIM: Blind faith to an idiot.

DIANE: Don't listen to that cynic, Stan. God will never let you down. Put your faith in the Lord.

STAN: You know what I think...

[*JIM and DIANE walk off together slowly.*]

STAN: I suppose I had better trust him. God will look after me... Won't he?

THE END

Re-reading *The Calling* in Light of a "Process of Dramatizing Theologies"

Having outlined the central tenets of a "process of dramatizing theologies," I now want to re-read my first ever sketch in light of this newly developing method for doing and articulating theology. *The Calling* was written at a time when I still adhered to notions of "colour blind" theology and the concomitant neutral ways of reading texts, especially that of "Holy Scripture."[67]

On the basis of this particular form of hermeneutic (on which comment has been made in Chapter 2), I am struck, most forcibly, on re-reading *The Calling* in the absence of any form of cultural signifiers of contextual particularities within the sketch. All the characters are bland universal ciphers of the kind I have critiqued in a previous chapter.[68]

On re-reading this sketch, what has been instructive has been my reading of Stan, the central character in the drama. The drama opens with Stan trying to interpret the nature of his dramatic encounter with God. He is quite sure that he has encountered God but cannot put words to or give a rational account for that experience. Stan is troubled and disturbed.

My re-reading of Stan has been done through the interpretative lens of Black Liberation theology. Stan "knows what he knows." To make recourse to that old Caribbean aphorism I invoked in Chapter 1, "who feels it, knows it." Stan knows what he has felt, and although he cannot account for this experience in rational, cogent terms, he knows that this experience is real and is potentially transformative.

Within Black Liberation theology great emphasis is placed upon the human facility of experience as an initial point of departure in theological construction. Robert Beckford, in invoking the reggae superstar and "Third World" icon, Bob Marley, as a Black Liberation theologian, states that:

> "Real" knowledge for Marley must be validated by experience. Experience is a filter which enables us to find meaning in the world.[69]

The references to the centrality of experience in Black theological method are much too replete at this juncture to recount. Suffice it to say, however, that at an impressionistic, intuitive level, as a Black conservative Christian (going through a major process of shifting and changing faith), I was still able to draw upon a notion of Black experiential religiosity in my early scriptwriting.

Re-interpreting this piece in light of a "process of dramatizing theologies" is to see in Stan a prototypical Black religious believer. He uses his own experience in dialogue with Scripture to attempt to work through and work out the nature of his religious experience.

God who is on the Side of the Oppressed

In this Black theological re-reading, I have been struck by the tension that exists between Stan and Jim in the text. As the ethnicity of neither character is mentioned in the text my following assumptions tell you more about my preoccupations at this moment in time, as a Black religious scholar, than they necessarily reveal about the text itself. In the tension and incipient rancour between Jim and Stan, I clearly read the latter as Black and the former as White. Of course, it could quite easily be the case that neither is Black or both are. The kind of interchange that occurs between the two of them is not necessarily limited to the binary of a "Black" and "White" form of engagement. Conversations of this type could just as well happen within an intra Black religio-cultural setting; but the truth is, on the occasions when I have witnessed religious experiences being questioned, it has often been the case that it is White middle-class experience that is doing the critical interrogating.

In my previous publication I addressed some of these issues in a short dramatic piece entitled *In The Psychiatrist's Chair*.[70] In the reflections that accompany that piece I state that:

> On the many occasions I have used this sketch with groups I have been struck by the ways in which various individuals have noticed the many value judgements the psychiatrist makes when he is questioning Moses. The psychiatrist, a recognized authority figure, is clear about what God is not like. God for example cannot possibly be Argentinean nor can he be Black, but it is not unreasonable to suppose that God might be German.[71]

My assumptions in reading this piece are that Stan is a working-class Black man whose experience is being challenged by Jim, a professional, middle-class person. The research I undertook when writing *In The Psychiatrist's Chair* alerted me to the sense of discomfort and suspicion Black people feel when having to articulate their spirituality and religious sensibilities to liberal White people (particularly those with institutional power).

Jim is unconvinced about the possibility of God calling someone like Stan to ministry. For Jim, it is simply preposterous that Stan might be called by God. This form of discourse is not unusual in my experience. I have witnessed Black working-class people being "interrogated" for their use of religious language and facility to engage metaphysical concepts when articulating their spirituality. White corporate liberalism finds this form of discourse too "extreme" and not sufficiently "sensible" for their tastes. Jim has no problem in ridiculing and belittling Stan's experience. James Cone has analysed the multiple ways in which the White academy has sought to trivialize or marginalize the theology and experience of Black people.[72]

And yet, as I have stated previously, personal experience is a key source and norm for doing Black theology. Robert Beckford states that one of the defining characteristics of Black Christianity is the centrality of the experience of God. He writes:

> The Experience of God. This refers to an understanding of a living God involved in the affairs of Black people. God is therefore not a philosophical proposition but an experienced life-giving source. In the Black Church, faith is based on a living, breathing, walking and talking relationship with God. When Black Christians ask, "Do you know Jesus?" we seek an experiential answer.[73]

It is interesting to note that Diane, the third character in the drama, sides with Stan. Again, I have assumed that she is Black. Her frame of reference and method for doing theology (using a dialectical hermeneutic that juxtaposes personal experience and Scripture) are not dissimilar to Stan's. The two of them immediately join forces against Jim in a manner not unlike the discourse between the Black man and woman against their White adversaries in the opening sketch *We Know Best*.

In the final denouement Stan is resolved to follow his "gut experience" and trust in God in the working out of his call. He is aided in this process by Diane, whose strident wisdom echoes the God character in the central sketch *My God!?* (although it is worth noting that all three characters use the male pronoun to name God, in marked contrast to *My God!?*).

It is interesting to note that Diane proves to be the catalyst in this drama, moving the action onwards beyond the male impasse between Stan and Jim. The no-nonsense, common-sense wisdom of Diane (who I have interpreted as), a Black woman, challenges the White male superiority of Jim and brings comfort and support to Stan, the troubled and concerned Black man. In this respect, Diane represents the fortitude and strength of Black women as depicted by the likes of Rosetta Ross[74] and Cheryl Townsend Gilkes.[75]

A Democratizing of God's Agency

One of the factors with which Black and other marginalized and oppressed people have had to deal is the casual patrician arrogance that has asserted that God's agency and invitation to ministry is best effected, almost exclusively, through a particular class of persons. In Christian history and tradition this perspective has found form in the shape of patriarchal views that have privileged maleness and masculinity, often using Jesus' maleness as a form of theological justification. In using the central sketch in this study, *My God!?*, I have sought to challenge this view.

In terms of God's agency in human affairs, the gracious invitation to undertake God's ministry in Christ, preference has been given to educated, professional, White middle-class men. The claims of others, particularly if they were poor, of colour and limited in their formal education, were seen at best as "second best" and at worst, as lacking in any of the necessary qualities and skills required of representative status within the church.[76]

My re-reading of this sketch in light of the liberative praxis of Black spirituality has enabled me to reclaim Stan's actions as indicative of the tenacious enabling and transformative quality of Black faith. Stan, aided and abetted by Diane, is not sure of the meaning of his encounter with God save for the fact that God is with him and that constancy is beyond question.

Within the broader literature of Black theology this transformative inner quality of Black existential experience has been the locomotive fuel that has inspired the Black self to transcend the limitations placed upon it by White hegemony. Robert Beckford has spoken of the liberative facets of Black spirituality in his analysis of Black British Pentecostalism.[77] The claims to direct access to God by means of Divine knowledge through pneumatological experience can enable individuals and communities to transcend the traditional patrician inspired hierarchical divide as to the possession of knowledge and truth.[78] It has often been asserted that many Black people have prioritized the experience of God over and above notions of conceptual or cerebral knowledge about God.[79] In this respect, given that the process of gaining direct access to the transformative experience of God is open to all people, this form of knowledge production and epistemology can be seen as a democratization of ultimate truth—the truth of God.[80]

Clearly, there are numerous problems with this form of epistemological grounding. Recourse to pneumatological inspired concepts of knowledge can lead to conservative, spiritualized abstraction in the face of contemporary social ills,[81] or alternatively, to a form of top-down neo-conservative patriarchy that justifies itself by making claims to un-substantiated (and irrefutable) claims of Divine sanction in the name of God's own self.[82] In terms of the latter, the claims to Divine knowledge by means of God's revelation through the Holy Spirit can lead to unquantifiable claims for alleged progress and development that by their very nature can never be challenged.[83]

A counter response in defence of the immanent personalized spirituality to be found in much that is Black Christian faith expression can be made if one gives necessary cognizance to the connected, corporate nature of Black spirituality. In the context of Black spirituality, while the individual's experience of and relationship with God is rightly asserted and celebrated, it should also be noted that this dimension of religious experience is always authenticated within the context of the collective and corporate sense of religious identity, i.e. the individual is in a dialectical relationship with the collective and the corporate.[84] Dash, Jackson and Rasor, in their book *Hidden Wholeness*,[85] commenting upon the religious practices of African Americans within the institutional life of the Black church in the US, write:

> Beyond these quantitative indices of the strength of the black church, there are certain qualitative elements that are important... The source of these qualities is found in African and African American culture. They differ, obviously, from a European American perspective, the dominant worldview in the United States. Instead of a competitive individualism, a cooperative collectivism is encountered in the black church.[86]

Going Back in Order to Go Forwards

By returning to the first sketch I wrote, I have attempted to locate within my earliest work the nascent seeds for what was to become the process for dramatizing theologies. This participative approach to Black God-talk has attempted to draw upon a range of Black inspired theologies in order to create an interactive and dialogical means of engaging in constructive, critical and liberative Black theological conversation.

By returning to *The Calling* I have been able to re-connect with the vibrant spirituality of my parents, particularly my mother, which helped to shape the creation of this script in the first instance. The spirituality of my parents and their peers has been instrumental in my own formative development as a Christian and later as a Black theologian.[87] My counter response to the apparent aridity of much of the discourse of my White student peers was to draw upon the vibrant, life-affirming confidence of my parents' spirituality, which is reflective of broader pan-African traits,[88] in order to give life to the characters of Stan and Diane in *The Calling*.

By returning to this sketch I want to reassert that at the heart of this dramatic theological enterprise is the centrality of Black experience as a basic point of departure. It is the assertion of the claim that "who feels it, knows it." In asserting the existential claims to liberation and wholeness of marginalized and oppressed Black people, I am arguing for a deliberate, particularized and political reading of the nature, intent and agency of God.

In this, the final dramatic script in this study, there is the assumption that Stan's experience cannot be real. Can his discourse be trusted? Is what Black people say about God legitimate? Are Black people of any worth? These questions may seem somewhat pointed, and many will argue that they are perhaps somewhat outdated, for the extremes of Black negation and "absurd nothingness"[89] that so characterized our existence in the past are surely a relic of a bygone age?[90]

And yet, as we witness the countless suffering of Black people in Africa, starving in a world of extravagant plenty; as we witness the countless deaths of Black people in White-run police stations, and witness Black deaths in White-controlled State legislatures and see unsolved racist inspired crimes enacted on Black bodies; one is forced to ask, "how is any of this a relic of the past?" Black people continue to be the expendable, invisible after-thoughts of the capitalistic, globalized White-hegemonic world order.

In this text, drawing on the work of such luminaries as James Cone,[91] Jacquelyn Grant,[92] Delores Williams,[93] Robert Beckford,[94] Dwight Hopkins,[95] *et al.*, I have asserted once again that God is on the side of the oppressed. In the context of dramatizing theologies, God is on Stan's side in *The Calling*, just as God is not on the side of the four presumptuous and self-important men in *My God!?* God is with the troubled, confused individual in *Love is the Answer*. God is on the side of the vulnerable children in *Two Voices in the World*. God is equally alongside the Black couple fighting for dignity and self-respect in *We Know Best*, and is the one enabling and critiquing Solomon and empowering and affirming Sheba in *The Wisdom of Solomon*.

The themes in the sketches I have cited carry many central elemental features of Black and Womanist theologies. The substantive content of these pieces, plus the accompanying method for creating newer pieces in dialogue with those who are marginalized and oppressed, detail a new approach to the articulation and doing of Black Liberation theologies. This process of dramatizing theologies is a process that places voiceless people at the very heart of a participative process of Black God-talk.

Concluding Thoughts

I have returned to this sketch because in many ways it encapsulates the latent strength of Black spirituality—a habitual, almost blind, faith in God, which has been critiqued by the likes of Jones[96] and Pinn.[97] But notwithstanding their very real complaints, this work is an attempt to highlight the dynamic power of Black folk religion and bring it into greater conversation with Black and Womanist theologies. As such, it is a method, which in utilizing the experiences of the most marginalized and oppressed—Black voiceless people—is ultimately a resource for all humanity.

A process of dramatizing theologies is a participative approach to Black God-talk for all people; whether those without power or for individuals or groups who have too much of it for their own good. A democratizing of theology can only be good for all of us. This bottom-up process of liberative praxis can contribute to the revitalizing of the church and the broader work of God's reign in this world and in the world to come.

Appendix: Template for Assessing our Gifts and Graces

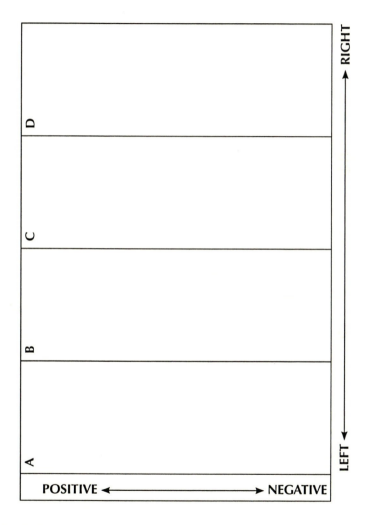

Diagram 1

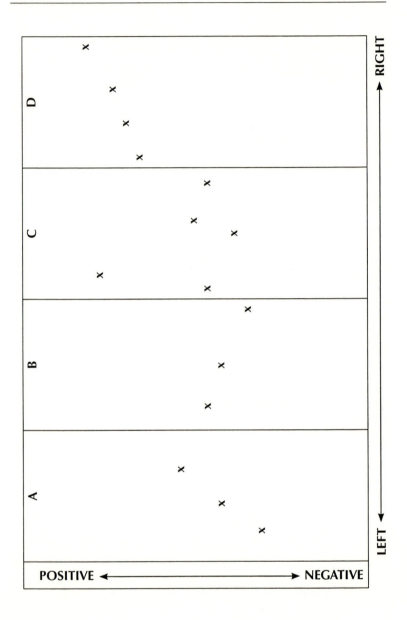

Diagram 2

Notes

Introduction
1. The use of drama in this book complements the use of letter-writing in the book edited by Philip R. Davies, *Yours Faithfully: Virtual Letters from the Bible* (London: Equinox, 2004). Both works are imaginative and interdisciplinary.
2. See examples of how role-playing and dramatic representation may be used in classrooms in the book edited by Mark Roncace and Patrick Gray, *Teaching the Bible: Practical Strategies for Classroom Instruction* (Atlanta: SBL, 2005).

Chapter 1
1. I will return to this sketch at the end of the final chapter.
2. See Anthony G. Reddie, *Nobodies to Somebodies: A Practical Theology for Education and Liberation* (Peterborough: Epworth Press, 2003). See also my earlier book *Growing into Hope: Christian Education in Multi-Ethnic Churches*— in two volumes: Vol. 1 is entitled *Believing and Expecting* and Vol. 2. is entitled *Liberation and Change* (Peterborough: Methodist Publishing House, 1998).
3. An alternative but complimentary approach can be found in my book *Faith, Stories and the Experience of Black Elders: Singing the Lord's Song in a Strange Land* (London: Jessica Kingsley, 2001). See also Anthony G. Reddie, "Forming Wisdom Through Cross-generational Connectedness," in *In Search of Wisdom: Faith Formation in the Black Church*, ed. Anne E. Streaty Wimberly and Evelyn L. Parker (Nashville, TN: Abingdon Press, 2002), 57–73.
4. See Reddie, *Nobodies to Somebodies*, 81–94.
5. See James H. Cone, *God of the Oppressed* (San Francisco: Harper, 1975) and James H. Cone, *A Black Theology of Liberation* (Maryknoll, NY: Orbis Books, 1990 [1970]); Gayraud S. Wilmore and James H. Cone, eds., *Black Theology: A Documentary History, 1966–1979* (Maryknoll, NY: Orbis Books, 1979) and James H. Cone and Gayraud S. Wilmore, eds., *Black Theology: A Documentary History, 1980–1992* (Maryknoll, NY: Orbis Books, 1993).
6. Dwight N. Hopkins, *(Introducing) Black Theology of Liberation* (Maryknoll, NY: Orbis Books, 1999) and *Down, Up and Over: Slave Religion and Black Theology* (Minneapolis: Fortress Press, 2000).
7. Robert Beckford, *Jesus is Dread* (London: Darton, Longman & Todd, 1998), *Dread and Pentecostal* (London: SPCK, 2000) and *God of the Rahtid: Redeeming Rage* (London: Darton, Longman & Todd, 2001).
8. See Albert Raboteau, *Slave Religion* (New York: Oxford University Press, 1978) and Eugene Genovese, *Roll Jordan Roll* (New York: Vintage Books, 1980). See also Hopkins, *Down, Up and Over*.
9. Some of my initial thinking can be found in *Nobodies to Somebodies*, 81–94.
10. See Anthony G. Reddie, *Acting in Solidarity: Reflections in Critical Christianity* (London: Darton, Longman & Todd, 2005).
11. See Reddie, *Nobodies to Somebodies*, 85–90. See also the work of Paulo

Freire, *Pedagogy of the Oppressed* (New York: Herder and Herder, 1993 [1970]) and Thomas Groome, *Sharing Faith: A Comprehensive Approach to Religious Education and Pastoral Ministries* (San Francisco: HarperSanFrancisco, 1991).

12. See Reddie, *Nobodies to Somebodies: A Comprehensive Approach to Religious Education and Pastoral Ministries* (San Francisco: HarperSanFrancisco, 1991), 120–31.

13. Ibid., 138.

14. Beckford, *God of the Rahtid*, 31–40.

15. See Anthony G. Reddie, "Introduction: In Memory of One Who Was Truly Unique," in *Legacy: Anthology in Memory of Jillian Brown*, ed. Anthony G. Reddie (Peterborough: Methodist Publishing House, 2000), ix.

16. Anthony G. Reddie, "Editorial," *Black Theology: An International Journal* 2.2 (July 2004): 135–38.

17. This phrase has been borrowed from the writings of many Womanist theologians who state that Black women suffer from double jeopardy (i.e. being Black and a woman) and often triple jeopardy (being Black, a woman and poor). For further information see Frances Beale, "Double Jeopardy: To be Black and Female," in *Black Theology: A Documentary History, 1966–1979*, ed. Gayraud S. Wilmore and James H. Cone (Maryknoll, NY: Orbis Books, 1979), 368–76. See also Theressa Hoover, "Black Women and Churches: Triple Jeopardy," in *Black Theology: A Documentary History, 1966–1979*, ed. Gayraud S. Wilmore and James H. Cone (Maryknoll, NY: Orbis Books, 1979), 377–88.

18. For a critique of the illusory nature of Black professional acceptability see Beckford, *God of the Rahtid*, 31–37.

19. See section entitled "A Problem Shared," in Reddie, *Acting in Solidarity*.

20. This group has since been renamed the BMLU—"Black Methodists for Liberation and Unity."

21. See section entitled "Complaints—Post Sketch Reflections," in Reddie, *Acting in Solidarity*.

22. Dale P. Andrews, *Practical Theology for Black Churches: Bridging Black Theology and African American Folk Religion* (Louisville, KY: Westminster/John Knox Press, 2002), 1–30.

23. Matthew 25:31–46.

24. See James H. Cone, *Black Theology and Black Power* (Maryknoll, NY: Orbis Books, 1989 [1969]) and *A Black Theology of Liberation*.

25. Beckford, *Jesus is Dread*.

26. Beckford, *Dread and Pentecostal*.

27. Beckford, *God of the Rahtid*.

28. Ibid., 1–10.

29. Ibid., 11–30.

30. Ibid., 8.

31. Ibid., 31–38.

32. See his autobiography entitled *Nigger* first published in 1963.

33. Beckford, *God of the Rahtid*, 40–47.

34. Ibid., 40–65.

35. See section entitled "So Why Christian Drama," in Reddie, *Acting in Solidarity*.

36. Beckford, *God of the Rahtid*, 31.

37. Reddie, "Editorial," 135.

38. Beckford, *God of the Rahtid*, 32.

39. Lee H. Butler, "Testimony as Hope and Care: African American Pastoral Care as Black Theology at Work," in *Living Stones in the Household of God: The Legacy and Future of Black Theology*, ed. Linda E. Thomas (Minneapolis: Fortress Press, 2003), 24–32.

40. Jeremiah Wright Jr., "Doing Black Theology in the Black Church," in *Living Stones in the Household of God*, ed. Linda E. Thomas, 13–23.

41. Linda E. Thomas, "Womanist Theology, Epistemology, and a New Anthropological Paradigm," in *Living Stones in the Household of God*, ed. Linda E. Thomas, 35–50.

42. See Dwight N. Hopkins and George L. Cummings, eds., *Cut Loose Your Stammering Tongue: Black Theology in the Slave Narrative* (Louisville, KY: Westminster/John Knox Press, 2nd edn, 2003); Will Coleman, *Tribal Talk: Black Theology, Hermeneutics, and African/American Ways of "Telling the Story"* (University Park, PN: Pennsylvania State University Press, 2000) and Hopkins, *Down, Up and Over*.

43. N. Lynne Westfield, "Towards a Womanist Approach to Pedagogy," *Religious Education* 98.4 (Fall 2003): 521–32 (520).

44. See Volume 1 of *Growing into Hope: Believing and Expecting*, 8. This training exercise was constructed (using data from the 1991 census) to assist predominantly White leaders who work with Black children to understand both the context in which Black people live in Britain, and the psychological and emotional affects of being a minority in a White-dominated country. Black people who predominantly live in inner-city areas have divided their existence in this country into areas of familiarity. Black children move interchangeably, from areas of great familiarity (where Black people although a minority are suddenly in the majority) to other situations where they become seemingly insignificant. This pattern has not changed appreciably since the post-war wave of mass African Caribbean migration to this country. This interchangeability of African Caribbean life, which is centred on differing contexts, has given rise to issues of cultural dissonance. This issue is dealt with in greater detail in one of my previous books. See Reddie, *Nobodies to Somebodies*.

45. See Robert E. Hood, *Must God Remain Greek?: Afro Cultures and God-talk* (Minneapolis: Fortress Press, 1990).

46. See Reddie, *Faith, Stories and the Experience of Black Elders*, 1–26.

47. Ken Leech, *Through Our Long Exile* (London: Darton, Longman & Todd, 2001), 87–135. See also his very influential *Struggle in Babylon* (London: Sheldon Press, 1988) and *The Eye of the Storm: Spiritual Resources for the Pursuit of Justice* (London: Darton, Longman & Todd, 1992).

48. Womanist theology can be seen as a related branch of Black theology. It is an approach to theology that begins with the experience of Black women and women of colour. Womanist theology utilizes the experience of Black women to challenge the tripartite ills of racism, sexism and classism. This discipline is influenced by (Black) feminist thought.

49. See Delores Williams, *Sisters in the Wilderness: The Challenge of Womanist God-Talk* (Maryknoll, NY: Orbis Books, 1993).

50. Winston James, "Migration, Racism and Identity," in *Inside Babylon*, ed. Winston James and Clive Harris (London: Verso, 1993). Also Ron Ramdin, *Reim-*

aging Britain: 500 Hundred Years of Black and Asian History (London: Pluto Press, 1999), 141–90 and 258–305.

51.   Paul Gilroy, *There Ain't No Black in the Union Jack* (London: Hutchinson, 1987). See also *The Black Atlantic: Modernity and Double Consciousness* (London: Verso, 1993).

52.   See Molefi Kete Asante, "Afrocentricity and Culture," in *African Culture: The Rhythms of Unity*, ed. Molefi Kete Asante and Kariamu Welsh Asante (New Jersey: First Africa World Press, 1990).

53.   See Eric Williams, *Capitalism and Slavery* (London: Andre Deutsch, 1983).

54.   Cornel West, *Race Matters* (Boston: Beacon Press, 1993), 11–15.

55.   Ella P. Mitchell, "Oral Tradition: Legacy of Faith for the Black Church," *Religious Education* 81.1 (Winter 1986): 99–102.

56.   Virginia Young, "Family and Childhood in a Southern Georgia Community," *American Anthropologist* 72 (1970): 269–88. Thomas Kochman, "Rapping in the Ghetto," in *Black Experience: Soul*, ed. Lee Rainwater (New Brunswick, NJ: Transaction Books, 1973), 51–76. Janice Hale, "A Comparative Study of the Racial Attitudes of Children who Attend a Pan-African and a Non-pan-African Preschool" (unpublished PhD dissertation, Georgia State University, 1974).

57.   See Jawanza Kunjufu, *Countering the Conspiracy to Destroy Black Boys* (Chicago: Afro-Am, 1982); *Countering the Conspiracy to Destroy Black Boys Vol. 2* (Chicago: Afro-Am, 1986); *Countering the Conspiracy to Destroy Black Boys Vol. 3* (Chicago: Afro-Am, 1990). Tony Sewell, *Black Masculinities and Schooling* (Stoke-on-Trent: Trentham Books, 1997).

58.   Sewell, *Black Masculinities and Schooling*. See also Cecile Wright, Debbie Weekes and Alex McGlaughan, eds., *"Race," Class and Gender in Exclusion from School* (London: Falmer Press, 2000).

59.   See Yvonne Channer, "The Youth and the Church: Impact of External Forces on Personal Beliefs," *Black Theology in Britain: A Journal of Contextual Praxis* 6 (2001): 9–24; Carver L. Anderson, "Where There is No Youth the Vision Will Perish," *Black Theology in Britain: A Journal of Contextual Praxis* 6 (2001): 25–39 and Kate Coleman, "Black to the Future: Re-Evangelizing Black Youth," *Black Theology in Britain: A Journal of Contextual Praxis* 6 (2001): 41–51. See also Janet Johnson, "Unity and the Regeneration of Black Youth," *Black Theology in Britain: A Journal of Contextual Praxis* 4 (2000): 66–83.

60.   Jack L. Seymour, "The Clue to Christian Religious Education: Uniting Theology and Education, 1950 to the Present," *Religious Education* 99.3 (Summer 2004): 272–86.

61.   Ibid., 275.

62.   See Paulo Freire, *Pedagogy of the Oppressed* (New York: Herder and Herder, 1993 [1970]). Also *Education for Critical Consciousness* (New York: Continuum, 1990 [1973]) and *A Pedagogy of Hope: Relieving Pedagogy of the Oppressed* (New York: Continuum, 1999).

63.   My initial reflections on the work and legacy of Paulo Freire are contained in my previous book entitled *Nobodies to Somebodies, op. cit.*

64.   See Reddie, *Nobodies to Somebodies*, 81–84.

65.   Freire, *Pedagogy of the Oppressed*.

66.   Gustavo Gutteriez, *A Theology of Liberation* (Maryknoll, NY: Orbis Books, 1973).

67. www.vms.utexas.edu/~possible/freire

68. Freire, *Education for Critical Consciousness*, 18–20.

69. Allen J. Moore, "A Social Theory of Religious Education," in *Religious Education as Social Transformation*, ed. Allen J. Moore (Birmingham, AL: Religious Education Press, 1989), 27.

70. John Westerhoff III, "Formation, Education, Instruction," *Religious Education* 82.4 (Fall, 1987): 578–91 (581).

71. John L. Elias, "Paulo Freire: Religious Educator," *Religious Education* 71.4 (January–February, 1976): 40–56 (48).

72. Paulo Freire, "Know, Practice and Teach the Gospels," *Religious Education* 79.4 (Fall, 1984): 547–48.

73. Freire, *Pedagogy of the Oppressed*, 33.

74. Freire, *Education for Critical Consciousness*, 3–58.

75. Westerhoff, "Formation, Education, Instruction," 583–84.

76. Cheryl Bridges Johns, *Pentecostal Formation: A Pedagogy among the Oppressed* (Sheffield: Sheffield Academic Press, 1998), 111–40.

77. Ibid., 62–110.

78. Ibid., 93.

79. See Beckford, *Dread and Pentecostal*, 95–121.

80. Stephen Carter, "The Black Church and Religious Freedom," in *Black Faith and Public Talk: Critical Essays on James H. Cone's Black Theology and Black Power*, ed. Dwight N. Hopkins (Maryknoll, NY: Orbis Books, 1999), 20–28 (20).

81. Ibid., 26.

82. See Bhikhu Parekh, *Rethinking Multiculturalism: Cultural Diversity and Political Theory* (Basingstoke: Macmillan Press, 2000).

Chapter 2

1. Reddie, *Nobodies to Somebodies*, 68–70.

2. See www.yourdictionary.com.

3. See www.yourdictionary.com.

4. James Michael Lee, "Religious Education and Theology," in *Theological Perspectives on Christian Formation: A Reader on Theology and Christian Education*, ed. Jeff Astley, Leslie J. Francis and Colin Crowder (Grand Rapids, MI: Eerdmans, 1996), 43–66.

5. Paul H. Hirst, "Christian Education: A Contradiction in Terms?", in *Critical Perspectives on Christian Education*, ed. Jeff Astley and Leslie J. Francis (Leominster: Gracewings, 1994), 305–313.

6. John M. Hull, "Christian Theology and Educational Theory: Can There be Connections?," in *Critical Perspectives on Christian Education*, ed. Jeff Astley and Leslie J. Francis, 314–30.

7. Jeff Astley, "Aims and Approaches in Christian Education," in *Learning in the Way: Research and Reflection on Adult Christian Education*, ed. Jeff Astley (Leominster: Gravewings, 2000), 1–32. See also *The Philosophy of Christian Religious Education* (Birmingham, AL: Religious Education Press, 1994) by the same author.

8. See David Willows, *Divine Knowledge: A Kierkegaardian Perspective on Christian Education* (Aldershot: Ashgate, 2001).

9. Reddie, *Nobodies to Somebodies*, 74–94.

10. See Gordon Lamont and Ronni Lamont, *Drama Toolkit: Sketches and Guidelines for Exploring the Bible through Drama* (Swindon: The Bible Society, 1989), 1–22.

11. See Michael Perry, *The Dramatised Bible* (London: Marshall Pickering, 1989).

12. Ibid., ix.

13. See Reddie, *Acting in Solidarity*, section entitled "Biblical Re-telling."

14. See Nigel Forde, *Theatrecraft* (Bromley, Kent: MARC Europe, 1989). See also Maraget Love, *Let's Dramatise* (Nutfield, Surrey: National Christian Education Council [NCEC], 1968); Derek Haylock, *Plays on the Word* (London: National Society/Church House Publishing, 1993); Dave Hopwood, *Acting Up* (London: National Society/Church House Publishing, 1995); Dave Hopwood, *Playing Up* (London: National Society/Church House Publishing, 1998) and Dave Hopwood, *Curtain Up* (London: National Society/Church House Publishing, 2000).

15. Cited in Roger Grainger, *Presenting Drama in Church* (London: Epworth Press, 1985), 7.

16. Paul Burbridge and Murray Watts, *Time to Act* (London: Hodder & Stoughton, 1979).

17. Paul Burbridge and Murray Watts, *Lighting Sketches* (London: Hodder & Stoughton, 1981).

18. Paul Burbridge and Murray Watts, *Red Letter Days* (London: Hodder & Stoughton, 1986).

19. For the majority of my time while a member of Birmingham University Methodist Society (Meth. Soc.), I was a part of a Christian drama group called *Rise 'n' Shine*. *Rise 'n' Shine* existed from 1987 to 1991 and performed at the annual Greenbelt Christian Arts Festival for a number of years, winning a prize in the Fringe in 1991. The core members of the group were Charles (Chas) Bayfield, Rupert Kaye and Anthony Reddie.

20. Burbridge and Watts, *Time to Act*, 112.

21. Ibid., 112.

22. Ibid., 12.

23. Ibid.

24. O. B. Hardison Jr., *Christian Rite and Christian Drama in the Middle Ages* (Baltimore: The Johns Hopkins University Press, 1965), 35–79.

25. Ibid., 39.

26. Ibid., 39.

27. For a very brief discussion on this matter, see Anthony Reddie, "Bearing Witness to the Light," *Roots Worship: Worship and Learning for the Whole Church* 5 (May/June 2003): 2–3.

28. Debra Dean Murphy, "Worship as Catechesis: Knowledge, Desire, and Christian Formation," *Theology Today* 58.3 (October 2001): 321–32.

29. Robert K. Martin, "Education and the Liturgical Life of the Church," *Religious Education* 98.1 (Winter 2003): 43–64.

30. Rosemary Woolf, *The English Mystery Plays* (London: Routledge and Kegan Paul, 1972), 3.

31. Ibid., 4.

32. Ibid., 25–54.

33. Ibid., 55.

34. Ibid., 105–269.

35. Ibid., 85.

36. Claire Sponsler, *Drama and Resistance: Bodies, Goods, and Theatricality in Late Medieval England* (Minneapolis: University of Minneapolis Press, 1997).

37. Ibid., 75–103.

38. See *Yiimimangaliso: The Mysteries*—first performed at the Joseph Stone Theatre, Cape Town, South Africa, May 2001. Birmingham production at the Hippodrome, Tuesday 11—Saturday 15 February 2003.

39. See Chapter 1 and my assessment of the structural historical forces that rendered Black people a voiceless presence in the "New World Order."

40. I would contend that although carnival is no longer the socio-cultural and political signifier of yesteryear, it remains a potent symbol of Black resistance. This resistance is manifested simply in the manner in which Black people insist upon celebrating their complex subjectivity in dance and drama, despite the strictures of the Metropolitan police and the White middle-class gentrified context of Notting Hill.

41. Errol Hill, *The Trinidad Carnival* (London: New Beacon Books, 1997), 6–11.

42. Gerard Aching, *Masking and Power: Carnival and Popular Culture in the Caribbean* (Minneapolis: University of Minnesota Press, 2002), 1–47.

43. See Peter van Koningsbruggen, *Trinidad Carnival: A Quest for National Identity* (London: Macmillan Education, 1997).

44. This is a form of codified role playing, which involves costumes, music and dance. See www.bacchanaljamaica.com. Junkuno is a traditional seasonal folk celebration that takes place around Christmas time, which involves costumes, role play, music, mime and puppetry. Junkunu can be perceived as a folk-orientated form of morality play for children and younger people in a manner not dissimilar to "Punch and Judy."

45. See Hood, *Must God Remain Greek*, 43–51 and Anthony B. Pinn, *Varieties of African American Religious Experience* (Minneapolis: Fortress Press, 1998), 14–34.

46. Beckford, *God of the Rahtid*, 48–58 and 96–112. See also Anthony B. Pinn, ed., *Noise and Spirit: The Religious Sensibilities of Rap Music* (New York: New York University Press, 2003).

47. See John Cowley, *Carnival, Canboulay and Calypso: Traditions in the Making* (Cambridge: Cambridge University Press, 1996).

48. See Carolyn Cooper, *Noises in the Blood: Orality, Gender and Vulgar Body of Jamaican Popular Culture* (Durham, NC: Duke University Press, 1995).

49. See Hemchand Gossai and Nathaniel S. Murrell, eds., *Religion, Culture and Tradition in the Caribbean* (London: Macmillan, 2000).

50. Daniel J. N. Middleton, "Riddim Wise and Scripture Smart: Interview and Interpretation with Ras Benjamin Zephaniah," in *Religion, Culture and Tradition in the Caribbean*, ed. Hemchand Gossai and Nathaniel S. Murrel (London: Macmillan, 2000), 257–70.

51. Ibid., 259.

52. Beckford, *Dread and Pentecostal*, 176–82.

53. Dale P. Andrews, *Practical Theology for Black Churches: Bridging Black Theology and African American Folk Religion* (Louisville, KY: John Knox Press, 2002), 16–23.

54. See Anthony B. Pinn, *Terror and Triumph: The Nature of Black Religion* (Minneapolis: Fortress Press, 2003).

55. Ibid., 139–73.

56. Carol Tomlin, *Black Language Style in Sacred and Secular Contexts* (Brooklyn, NY: Caribbean Diaspora Press, 1999), 125–66.

57. Joel Edwards, ed., *Let's Praise Him Again: An African Caribbean Perspective on Worship* (Eastbourne: Kingsway Publications, 1992).

58. Gerard S. Sloyan, "Symbols of God's Presence to the Church—Verbal and Nonverbal," *Theology Today* 58.3 (October 2001): 312–18.

59. See Rupert E. Davies, *Methodism* (Peterborough: Epworth Press, 1985), 150–84.

60. Sloyan, "Symbols of God's Presence to the Church," 304–20.

61. John Westerhoff III, *Living the Faith Community* (San Francisco: Harper and Row, 1985). See also John Westerhoff III and William Willimon, *Liturgy and Learning Through the Life Cycle* (New York: Seabury Press, 1980).

62. E. Byron Anderson, "Liturgical Catechesis: Congregational Practice as Formation," *Religious Education* 92.3 (Summer 1997): 349–62.

63. See also Murphy, "Worship as Catechesis," 321–32 and James Michael Lee, *The Content of Religious Instruction* (Birmingham, AL: Religious Education Press, 1985), 196–276.

64. Helen Allan Archibald, "Originating Visions and Visionaries of the REA," *Religious Education* 98.4 (Fall 2003): 415–25.

65. Allen J. Moore, "One Hundred Years of the Religious Education Association," *Religious Education* 98.4 (Fall 2003): 426–36.

66. John Sutcliffe, ed., *Tuesday's Child: A Reader for Christian Educators* (Birmingham, UK: Christian Education Publications, 2001), 11–27.

67. Carina Robins, *Drama for God: A Handbook of Christian Drama* (Ibadan, Nigeria: Daystar Press, 1977), 4–6.

68. See www.murderinthecathedral.fslife.co.uk for further details.

69. Sutcliffe, ed., *Tuesday's Child*, 46–71.

70. See Ronald Goldman, *Readiness for Religion* (London: Routledge and Kegan Paul, 1965).

71. Ibid., 3–39.

72. Ibid., 8.

73. Elizabeth Lane, *A Pageant of Bible Plays* (Nutfield, Surrey: National Christian Education Council, 1965).

74. Ibid., 7.

75. Love, *Let's Dramatise*.

76. Ibid., 7.

77. The notion of "generic themes" comes from Thomas Groome and his methodological approach to Christian religious education and Practical theology he terms "shared praxis." See Thomas Groome, *Christian Religious Education: Sharing Our Story and Vision* (San Francisco: Jossey-Bass, 1999 [1980]); *Sharing Faith*.

78. The Christian drama scripts I have looked at include the following: Burbridge and Watts, *Time to Act*; Burbridge and Watts, *Lighting Sketches*; Burbridge and Watts, *Red Letter Days*; Lamont and Lamont, *Drama Toolkit*; Haylock, *Plays on the Word*; Derek Haylock, *Plays for all Seasons* (London: National Society/Church House Publishing, 1997); Dave Hopwood, *A Fistful*

of Sketches (London: National Society/Church House Publishing, 1996); Hopwood, *Acting Up*; Hopwood, *Playing Up*; Dave Hopwood, *Curtain Up* (London: National Society/Church House Publishing, 2000); Stephen Deal, *Short Change* (Leicester: Nimbus Press, 2002); John L. Bell and Graham Maule, *Jesus and Peter* (Glasgow: Wild Goose Publications, 1999); Bell and Maule, *Just Acting* (London: Christian Aid, 2002). See also The Unity Theatre Company (http://www.wsz.com/unity/Christian Drama Emporium).

79. See Beckford, *Jesus is Dread*, 1–60.

80. Beckford, *Dread and Pentecostal*, 67–130. See also Anne H. Pinn and Anthony B. Pinn, *(Fortress Introduction to) Black Church History* (Minneapolis: Fortress Press, 2002).

81. See Vincent L. Wimbush, *The Bible and African Americans* (Minneapolis: Fortress Press, 2003) and Peter T. Nash, *Reading Race, Reading the Bible* (Minneapolis: Fortress Press, 2003).

82. See Pinn, *Terror and Triumph*.

83. See Philip F. Esler, *Galatians* (London: Routledge, 1998).

84. See Tissa Balasuriya, *The Eucharist and Human Liberation* (London: SCM Press, 1979).

85. Inderjit S. Bhogal, *A Table for All* (Sheffield: Penistone Publications, 2000), 11–34.

86. A noted exception within these pieces under investigation are the works of Bell and Maule (see their "Jesus and Peter" series of sketches) and the Christian Aid material.

87. See Tissa Balasuriya, "Liberation of the Affluent," *Black Theology: An International Journal* 1.1 (November, 2002): 83–113.

88. See Cone, *God of the Oppressed*.

89. See Wilmore and Cone, *Black Theology: A Documentary History*. I. *1966–1979*.

90. See Hopkins, *Down, Up and Over* and Hopkins and Cummings, eds., *Cut Loose Your Stammering Tongue*.

91. W. E. B. Dubois, *The Souls of Black Folk* (New York: Bantam Books, 1989), 3.

92. See Reddie, *Nobodies to Somebodies*, 68–70 and 142–46.

93. Chinua Achebe, *Things Fall Apart* (London: David Campbell, 1992).

94. Jacqueline Battalora, "Whiteness: The Workings of an Ideology in American Society and Culture," in *Gender, Ethnicity and Religion: Views from the Other Side*, ed. Rosemary Radford Ruether (Minneapolis: Fortress Press, 2002), 3–23.

95. See Robert Beckford, *God and the Gangs* (London: Darton, Longman & Todd, 2004), 72–81. See also Robert Beckford, *Jesus Dub: Faith, Culture and Social Change* (London: Routledge, 2005).

96. Nancy Lynne Westfield, "Teaching for Globalized Consciousness: Black Professor, White Student and Shame," *Black Theology: An International Journal* 2.1 (January 2004): 73–83.

97. See R. S. Sugirtharajah, ed., *Voices from the Margins* (London: SPCK, 1995), and R. S. Sugirtharajah, *Postcolonial Criticism and Biblical Interpretation* (Oxford: Oxford University Press, 2002). See also Leela Gandi, *Postcolonial Theory* (Edinburgh: Edinburgh University Press, 1998).

98. See Dennis Jacobsen, *Doing Justice: Congregations and Community Orga-*

nizing (Minneapolis: Fortress Press, 2001). See also Norma Cook Everist, ed., *The Difficult but Indispensable Church* (Minneapolis: Fortress Press, 2002), 179–90.

99.   See Callum Davidson, *The Death of Christian Britain: Understanding Secularisation 1800–2000* (London: Routledge, 2001). See also Grace Davie, *Religion in Britain since 1945: Believing without Belonging* (Oxford: Basil Blackwell, 1994).

100.   Clive Marsh, *Christianity in a Post-Atheist Age* (London: SCM Press, 2002).

101.   Gordon Lynch, *After Religion: "Generation X" and the Search for Meaning* (London: Darton, Longman & Todd, 2002).

102.   Alan Richardson and John Bowden, eds., *A New Dictionary of Christian Theology* (London: SCM Press, 1999), 31–34.

103.   Mervin Willshaw, "Apologetics—a Discipline whose Time has Come," in *Coming of Age: Challenges and Opportunities in the 21st Century*, ed. Stuart J. Burgess (York: Stuart J. Burgess, 1999), 72–77.

104.   Emmanuel Y. Lartey, *In Living Colour* (London: Cassell, 1997), 9–14.

105.   Jim Wallis, "The Call to Conversion," in *Urban Theology: A Reader*, ed. Michael Northcott (London: Cassell, 1998), 302–309.

106.   Inderjit S. Bhogal, "Citizenship," in *Legacy: Anthology in Memory of Jillian Brown*, ed. Anthony G. Reddie (Peterborough: Methodist Publishing House, 2000), 137–41.

107.   Cone, *A Black Theology of Liberation*, 6.

108.   James H. Cone, *Risks of Faith: The Emergence of a Black Theology of Liberation, 1968–1998* (Boston: Beacon Press, 1999), 3–12.

109.   See Gay L. Byron, *Symbolic Blackness and Ethnic Difference in Early Christian Literature* (New York: Routledge, 2002).

110.   See Nash, *Reading Race, Reading the Bible*.

111.   See Peter J. Parris, *The Social Teaching of the Black Churches* (Philadelphia: Fortress Press, 1985) and Andrews, *Practical Theology for Black Churches*.

112.   Reddie, *Nobodies to Somebodies*, 29–36.

113.   See Isaac Julien, "Black Is, Black Ain't: Notes on De-Essentializing Black Identities," in *Black Popular Culture*, ed. Gina Dent (Seattle: Bay Press, 1992), 255–63.

114.   See Tomlin, *Black Language Style in Sacred and Secular Contexts*. See also Lerleen Willis, "All Things to All Men? Or What has Language to Do with Gender and Resistance in the Black Majority Church in Britain," *Black Theology in Britain* 4.2 (May 2002): 195–213.

115.   Sewell, *Black Masculinities and Schooling*, 75–139.

116.   Robert S. Beckford, "Theology in the Age of Crack: Crack Age, Prosperity Doctrine and 'Being There'," *Black Theology in Britain: A Journal of Contextual Praxis* 4.1 (November 2001): 9–24.

117.   Beckford, *Dread and Pentecostal*, 204.

118.   Pinn and Pinn, *Black Church History*, 103–122.

119.   See Cone, *A Black Theology of Liberation*, 110–28. See also Jacquelyn Grant, *White Women's Christ and Black Women's Jesus* (Atlanta: Scholars Press, 1989), 194–222.

120.   Cone, *God of the Oppressed*, 134.

121.   See Mokgethi Motlhabi, "The Problem of Ethical Method in Black Theology," *Black Theology: An International Journal* 2.1 (January 2004): 57–72. Motlhabi

assesses the ethical method of five Black theologians, including James Cone. He is of the opinion that Cone's work represents the most consistent ethical method for articulating a sustainable praxis for Black theology.

122.   James H. Evans Jr., *We Have Been Believers: An African American Systematic Theology* (Minneapolis: Fortress Press, 1992), 77–83.

123.   See Anita Jackson Robinson, *Catching Both Sides of the Wind: Conversations with Five Black Pastors* (London: The British Council of Churches, 1985).

124.   Cone, *God of the Oppressed*.

125.   Beckford, *Dread and Pentecostal*.

126.   Reddie, *Growing into Hope*, 2 vols., and *Nobodies to Somebodies*.

127.   Mary Daly, *Beyond God the Father* (London: The Women's Press, 1995).

Chapter 3

1.   See Reddie, *Faith, Stories and the Experience of Black Elders*, 15.

2.   J. Deotis Roberts, *Black Religion, Black Theology: The Collected Essays of J. Deotis Roberts*, ed. David E. Goatley (Harrisburg, PA: Trinity Press International, 2003), 73–86.

3.   Peter J. Paris, *The Spirituality of African Peoples* (Minneapolis: Fortress Press, 1995), 27–50.

4.   Vincent L. Wimbush, *African Americans and the Bible: Sacred Texts and Social Contexts* (New York: Continuum, 2000).

5.   Paris, *The Spirituality of African Peoples*, 43.

6.   Kortright Davis, *Emancipation Still Comin': Explorations in Caribbean Emancipatory Theology* (Maryknoll, NY: Orbis Books, 1990), 77–78.

7.   Balasuriya, "Liberation of the Affluent," 83–113.

8.   Noel L. Erskine, *Decolonizing Theology* (Maryknoll, NY: Orbis Books, 1981).

9.   Hopkins, *Down, Up, and Over*, 13–50.

10.   See Eldridge Cleaver, *Soul On Ice* (New York: Laurel, 1992). See also Huew P. Newton, *Seize The Time: The Story of the Black Panther Party* (London: Hutchinson, 1970), and Angela Y. Davis, *An Autobiography* (London: Women's Press, 1990).

11.   Some of the reflections from that period are documented in Anthony G. Reddie, "Open to Learning and Nurturing," in *Open All Hours?!* (London: Thames North Synod, The United Reformed Church, 2002), 5.08–5.10.

12.   Into this category I must cite Dr Emmanuel Y. Lartey, Professor of Pastoral Theology and Care at Columbia Theological Seminary, The Revd Inderjit Bhogal, a Methodist minister in the British Methodist Church and Dr Robert Beckford of the University of Birmingham.

13.   Alice Walker, *The Color Purple* (London: Women's Press, 1983) and *In Search of our Mothers' Gardens: Womanist Prose* (London: Women's Press, 1984).

14.   Grant, *White Women's Christ and Black Women's Jesus*.

15.   See Williams, *Sisters in the Wilderness*. See also Kelly Brown Douglas, *The Black Christ* (Maryknoll, NY: Orbis Books, 1994); Emile Townes, *Womanist Justice, Womanist Hope* (Atlanta, GA: Scholars Press, 1993); Renita J. Weems, *Just a Sister Away: A Womanist Vision of Women's Relationships in the Bible* (Philadelphia: Innisfree Press, 1988); Katie G. Cannon, *Black Womanist Ethics* (Atlanta, GA: Scholars Press, 1988).

16. Demetrius K. Williams, "The Bible and Models of Liberation in the African American Experience," in *Yet With a Steady Beat: Contemporary U.S. Afrocentric Biblical Interpretation*, ed. Randall C. Bailey (Atlanta: Society for Biblical Literature, 2003), 33–59. See also Beckford, *Dread and Pentecostal*, 192–94.

17. Horace O. Russell, "Understandings and Interpretations of Scripture in Eighteenth and Nineteenth Century Jamaica," in *Religion, Culture and Tradition in the Caribbean*, ed. Hemchand Gossai and Nathaniel Samuel Murrell (London: Macmillan Press, 2000), 95–117.

18. Vincent Harding, "Religion and Resistance Among Antebellum Slaves, 1800–1860," in *African American Religion: Interpretive Essays in History and Culture*, ed. Timothy E. Fulop and Albert J. Raboteau (New York: Routledge, 1997), 107–130.

19. Joseph Washington, *Black Religion* (Boston: Beacon Press, 1964).

20. Ibid., 33.

21. Pinn, *Terror and Triumph*, 157–79.

22. Paris, *The Spirituality of African Peoples*, 27–49.

23. Ibid., 36.

24. William R. Jones, *Is God a White Racist?* (Boston: Beacon Press, 1973).

25. Ibid., 4–24.

26. William R. Jones, "Is Faith in God Necessary for a Just Society? Insights from Liberation Theology," in *The Search For Faith and Justice*, ed. Gene G. James (New York: Paragon, 1987), 92.

27. Anthony B. Pinn, *Why Lord?: Suffering and Evil in Black Theology* (New York: Continuum, 1995).

28. Frederick L. Ware, *Methodologies of Black Theology* (Cleveland, OH: Pilgrim Press, 2002), 66–114.

29. Pinn, *Why Lord?*, 139–58.

30. Cone, *God of the Oppressed*, 194.

31. Cone, *A Black Theology of Liberation*, 61.

32. Hopkins, *(Introducing) Black Theology of Liberation*, 18–29.

33. See Reddie, *Faith, Stories and the Experience of Black Elders*, 74–76.

34. Andrews, *Practical Theology for Black Churches*, 17.

35. Three out of the four male protagonists would *appear* to be White—or to put it another way, only one is identified as not being White.

36. Deotis Roberts, *Black Religion, Black Theology*, 31–49.

37. Ibid., 34–35.

38. Nathaniel S. Murrell, "Dangerous Memories, Underdevelopment, and the Bible in Colonial Caribbean Experience," in *Religion, Culture and Tradition in the Caribbean*, ed. Hemchand Gossai and Nathaniel Samuel Murrell (London: Macmillan Press, 2000), 9–35.

39. Bob Dylan, "With God On Our Side" from *The Times They Are a-Changing* (Columbia Records, 1964).

40. Walter Mosley, *What Next?: A Memoir Toward World Peace* (London: Serpent's Tail, 2003).

41. See Cornel West, *Democracy Matters: Winning the Fight Against Imperialism* (New York: The Penguin Press, 2004).

42. Walker, *In Search of our Mothers' Gardens*.

43. Ibid., xi.

44. See Marjorie Lewis, "Diaspora Dialogue: Womanist Theology in Engagement with Aspects of the Black British and Jamaican Experience," *Black Theology: An International Journal* 2.1 (January 2004): 85–109. In this piece, Lewis utilizes Womanist perspectives in order to create a new designation for Black women in Britain and Jamaica, namely, "Nannyish t'eology."

45. Stephanie Y. Mitchell, *Introducing Womanist Theology* (Maryknoll, NY: Orbis Books, 2002), 3–24.

46. Grant, *White Women's Christ and Black Women's Jesus*.

47. Ibid., 9–61.

48. See Sallie McFague, *Models of God* (Philadelphia: Fortress Press, 1987). See also Sallie McFague, *Metaphorical Theology: Models of God in Religious Language* (Philadelphia: Fortress Press, 1985), and Daly, *Beyond God the Father*.

49. McFague, *Metaphorical Theology*, 22–23.

50. Grant, *White Women's Christ and Black Women's Jesus*, 195–230.

51. Ibid.

52. Williams, *Sisters in the Wilderness*.

53. Linda E. Thomas, ed., *Living Stones in the Household of God: The Legacy and Future of Black Theology* (Minneapolis: Fortress Press, 2003).

54. See Reddie, *Faith, Stories and the Experience of Black Elders*.

55. Mitchell, *Introducing Womanist Theology*, 19.

56. See Lorraine Dixon, "Are Vashti and Esther our Sistas?," in *Legacy: Anthology in Memory of Jillian Brown*, ed. Anthony G. Reddie (Peterborough: Methodist Publishing House, 2000), 97–108.

57. Ibid., 100.

58. Williams, *Sisters in the Wilderness*.

59. Kelly D. Brown Douglas, "Womanist Theology: What is its Relationship to Black Theology?," in *Black Theology: A Documentary History. II. 1980–1992*, ed. James H. Cone and Gayraud S. Wilmore (Maryknoll, NY: Orbis Books, 1993), 291.

60. See Freire, *Pedagogy of the Oppressed*.

61. See Elaine F. Foster, "Women and the Inverted Pyramid of the Black Churches in Britain," in *Refusing Holy Orders: Women and Fundamentalism in Britain*, ed. G. Saghal and N. Yuval-Davis (London: Virago, 1992).

62. Dwight N. Hopkins, *Head and Heart: Black Theology, Past, Present and Future* (New York: Palgrave/Macmillan, 2002), 89–105.

63. Ibid., 104–105.

64. I will describe the methodological issues of this approach to theology in Chapter 5.

65. JoAnne Marie Terrell, *Power in the Blood?: The Cross in the Experience of African American Experience* (Maryknoll, NY: Orbis Books, 1998), 99–125.

66. Cone, *A Black Theology of Liberation*, 110.

67. See Beckford, *Jesus is Dread*.

68. J. Deotis Roberts, *Africentric Christianity: A Theological Appraisal for Ministry* (Valley Forge, PA: Judson Press, 2000), 61–64.

69. James H. Cone, "Black Theology and Third World Theologies," in *Black Theology: A Documentary History. II. 1980–1992*, ed. James H. Cone and Gayraud S. Wilmore (Maryknoll, NY: Orbis Books, 1993), 388–98.

70. Hopkins, *Head and Heart*, 112.

71.   I continue to attend Moseley Road Methodist Church, in the Moseley Road and Sparkhill circuit of the Birmingham District, in the UK. Moseley Road is a Black majority church in which most of the members are first and second generation people of African Caribbean descent. The church was founded in the mid nineteenth century and became a Black majority setting in the early 1980s.

72.   This is a means of indicating one's disgust or indignation towards a particular person or situation.

73.   Cain Hope Felder, ed., *Stony the Road We Trod: African American Biblical Interpretation* (Minneapolis: Fortress Press, 1991).

74.   Randall C. Bailey, "Africans in Old Testament Poetry and Narratives," in *Stony the Road We Trod: African American Biblical Interpretation*, ed. Cain Hope Felder (Minneapolis: Fortress Press, 1991), 167.

75.   Randall C. Bailey, " 'Is That Any Name for a Nice Hebrew Boy?': Exodus 2:1-10: The De-Africanization of an Israelite Hero," in *The Recovery of Black Presence: An Interdisciplinary Exploration*, ed. Randall C. Bailey and Jacquelyn Grant (Nashville, TN: Abingdon Press, 1995), 25–36.

76.   Randall C. Bailey, ed., *Yet With A Steady Beat: Contemporary Afrocentric Biblical Interpretation* (Atlanta: Society for Biblical Literature, 2003).

77.   Deotis Roberts, *Africentric Christianity*, 42–56.

78.   The Bible Society of the West Indies has recently produced a series of audio-cassette recordings of dramatic readings of well-known biblical narratives in Jamaican patois, entitled "De Krismos Stori." See www.jis.gov.jm/foreign_affairs.

79.   Cone, *A Black Theology of Liberation*, 117–20.

80.   Hopkins, *(Introducing) Black Theology of Liberation*, 65–86.

81.   As excellent example of this overarching approach can be found in Cain Hope Felder, ed., *The Original African Heritage Study Bible* (Nashville, TN: The James C. Winston Publishing Company, 1993).

82.   See Kwesi Owusu, ed., *Black British Culture and Society: A Text Reader* (London: Routledge, 2000).

83.   Reddie, *Nobodies to Somebodies*, 25–26.

84.   See Brown Douglas, *The Black Christ*.

85.   Beckford, "Theology in the Age of Crack," 9–24.

86.   Beckford, *God of the Rahtid*, 40–47. See also Beckford, *God and the Gangs*.

87.   See Anne S. Wimberly, *Soul Stories: African American Christian Education* (Nashville, TN: Abingdon Press, 1996).

88.   See Reddie, *Growing into Hope*, vols. 1 and 2.

89.   Hope Felder, ed., *The Original African Heritage Study Bible*, 1375–1581.

90.   Deotis Roberts, *Africentric Christianity*, 61–67.

91.   A BBC four-part series entitled "Black Ambition" detailed the progress of a handful of Black British young people at Cambridge University (BBC2, January/ February 2004). It is interesting to note the ideological and philosophical assumptions behind this programme. "Black Ambition," in highlighting the fact that Black British people can excel within post-colonial Britain, simply reminds us that most Black British are unable or prevented from doing so. One could not imagine a programme called "White (middle-class) Ambition" because this is the normative constituency that makes up Oxbridge.

92.   It is interesting to note the number of prominent Black people who have been elevated to "penultimate" or "nearly there" positions of power in White

majority political settings. One can cite Andrew Young, Colin Powell and Condeleezza Rice as examples in the US. In the UK one can highlight Paul Boeteng.

93. Hope Felder, ed., *The Original African Heritage Study Bible*, 688–710.

94. See Reddie, *Nobodies to Somebodies*, 132–40.

95. See Anthony G. Reddie, ed., *Legacy: Anthology in Memory of Jillian Brown* (Peterborough: Methodist Publishing House, 2000), 50–52, 70–73.

96. See Katie G. Cannon, *Katie's Canon: Womanism and the Soul of the Black Community* (New York: Continuum, 1995). See also Cheryl Townsend Gilkes, *If it Wasn't for the Women* (Maryknoll, NY: Orbis Books, 2001) and Rosetta E. Ross, *Witnessing and Testifying: Black Women, Religion, and Civil Rights* (Minneapolis: Fortress Press, 2003).

97. See Ross, *Witnessing and Testifying*.

98. See Anthony G. Reddie, "Pentecost—Dreams and Visions [A Black Theological Reading]" (Birmingham: International Bible Reading Association, 2001), 27–42. This work led indirectly to this much more systematic and overarching method and substantive content of Black theology in this text.

99. Bex means extremely angry in Jamaican patois.

100. See also some of the pieces in Reddie, *Acting in Solidarity*.

101. Dubois, *The Souls of Black Folk*, 3.

102. Pinn, *Terror and Triumph*, 82–107.

103. Dubois, *The Souls of Black Folk*, xxxi.

104. Ibid., 3.

105. Doreen Morrison, "Resisting Racism—By Celebrating 'Our' Blackness," *Black Theology: An International Journal* 1.2 (May 2003): 203–223.

106. Fred Smith, "A Prophetic Christian Education for Black Boys: Overcoming Violence," *Black Theology: An International Journal* 1.2 (May 2003): 175–87.

107. Joseph V. Crockett, *Teaching Scripture: From an African American Perspective* (Nashville, TN: Discipleship Resources, 1990), 15–26.

108. See Edward P. Wimberly, *Relational Refugees: Alienation and Reincorporation in African American Churches and Communities* (Nashville, TN: Abingdon Press, 2000).

109. See Edward P. Wimberly, *Claiming God, Reclaiming Dignity: African American Pastoral Care* (Nashville, TN: Abingdon Press, 2003).

110. Beckford, *God of the Rahtid*, 37.

111. See Cone, *Risks of Faith*.

112. See Townes, *Womanist Justice, Womanist Hope*.

113. See Weems, *Just a Sister Away*.

114. See Josiah U. Young III, *Dogged Strength Within the Veil: Africana Spirituality and the Mysterious Love of God* (Harrisburg, PA: Trinity Press International, 2003).

115. See Beckford, *Jesus Dub*.

Chapter 4

1. Joe Aldred's trilogy of books, *Preaching with Power* (London: Cassells, 1998), *Sisters with Power* (London: Continuum, 2000) and *Praying with Power* (London: Continuum, 2000), have been important texts in articulating Black religiosity and faith in Britain, from mainly Black British theologians.

2. See Molefi K. Asanta and Kariamu W. Asante, ed., *African Culture: The Rhythms of Unity* (Trenton, NJ: Africa World Press, 1990).

3. Lartey, *In Living Colour*, 9–14.

4. Ibid., 12.

5. Victor Anderson, *Beyond Ontological Blackness: An Essay on African American Cultural Religions and Cultural Criticism* (New York: Continuum, 1995), 86–117.

6. See Reddie, *Faith, Stories, and the Experience of Black Elders*.

7. Laurie Green, *Urban Ministry and the Kingdom of God* (London: SPCK, 2003), 4–17.

8. Kenneth Leech, *Through Our Long Exile* (London: Darton, Longman & Todd, 2001), 17–93.

9. See John Vincent, *Hope from the City* (Peterborough: Epworth Press, 2000).

10. See John M. Hull, "Critical Openness in Christian Nurture," in *Critical Perspectives on Christian Education*, ed. Jeff Astley and Leslie J. Francis (Leominster: Gracewings, 1994), 251–75.

11. Grant Shockley, "From Emancipation to Transformation to Consummation: A Black Perspective," in *Does The Church Really Want Religious Education?*, ed. Marlene Mayr (Birmingham, AL: Religious Education Press, 1988), 221–48.

12. Jeff Astley, ed., *Learning in the Way: Research and Reflections on Adult Christian Education* (Leominster: Gracewings, 2000), viii.

13. Shockley, "From Emancipation to Transformation to Consummation," 221–48.

14. Harold Dean Trulear, "African American Religious Education," in Barbara Wilkerson, ed., *Multicultural Religious Education* (Birmingham, AL: Religious Education Press, 1997), 178–82.

15. Beckford, *God and the Gangs*, 85–90.

16. Hull, "Critical Openness in Christian Nurture," 251–75.

17. Lee, "Religious Education and Theology," 45–68.

18. Aspects of this particular approach to Christian nurture and development within a Black church context can be seen in George L. Champion, Sr., *Christian Education for the African American Church* (Riviera Beach, FL: Port Printing Company, 1990) and Lora-Ellen McKinney, *Christian Education in the African American Church* (Valley Forge, PA: Judson Press, 2003).

19. Jeff Astley, "Dimensions of Christian Education," in *Learning in the Way*, ed. Jeff Astley (Leominster: Gracewings, 2000), 33–71.

20. See Groome, *Sharing Faith*. See also N. Lynne Westfield, *Dear Sisters: A Womanist Practice of Hospitality* (Cleveland, OH: The Pilgrim Press, 2001). It is also worth noting Anne Hope and Sally Timmel, *Training for Transformation: A Handbook for Community Workers*, 4 vols. (Gweru, Zimbabwe: Mambo Press, 1999).

21. James Fowler, *Stages of Faith* (San Francisco: HarperSanFrancisco, 1995).

22. K. E. Nipkow and Friedrich Schweitzer, eds., *Stages of Faith and Religious Development: Implications for Church, Education and Society* (London: SCM Press, 1992).

23. Westerhoff, *Living the Faith Community*.

24. See my *Nobodies to Somebodies*, 47–48 for a brief overview of the work and legacy of Grant Shockley.

25. Wimberly, *Soul Stories* and Anne E. Streaty Wimberly and Evelyn L. Parker, eds., *In Search of Wisdom: Faith Formation in the Black Church* (Nashville: Abingdon Press, 2002).

26. See Philip Richter and Leslie Francis, *Gone But Not Forgotten* (London: Darton, Longman & Todd, 1998).

27. Parekh, *Rethinking Multiculturalism*, 23–31.

28. See Lee, *The Content of Religious Instruction*.

29. Jeff Astley, "Growing into Christ: The Psychology and Politics of Christian Maturity," in *The Contours of Christian Education*, ed. Jeff Astley and David Day (Great Wakering, Essex: McCrimmons, 1992), 317.

30. Pinn, ed., *Noise and Spirit*.

31. Michael Eric Dyson, *Between God and Gangsta Rap* (New York: Oxford University Press, 1996).

32. See Beckford, *God of the Rahtid*.

33. Linda E. Thomas, "Womanist Theology, Epistemology, and a New Anthropological Paradigm," 37–50. See also pp. 107–115.

34. See M. Bulmer, *The Chicago School of Sociology* (Chicago: University of Chicago Press, 1984).

35. See W. F. Whyte, *Learning from the Field: A Guide from Experience* (with the collaboration of Kathleen Whyte) (London: SAGE, 1984).

36. See M. Hammersley, "What's Wrong with Ethnography? The Myth of Theoretical Description," *Sociology* 24.4 (1990): 597–615; *What's Wrong with Ethnography? Methodological Explorations* (London: Routledge, 1992); *Social Research: Philosophy, Politics and Practice* (London: SAGE, 1993); M. Hammersley and P. Atkinson, *Ethnography: Principles in Practice* (London: Routledge, 1983).

37. B. Glaser and A. Strauss, *The Discovery of Grounded Theory* (Chicago: Aldine, 1967).

38. Ken Pryce, *Endless Pressure: A Study of West Indian Life Styles in Bristol* (Bristol: Bristol Classical Press, 1986).

39. A. Bryman, *Doing Research in Organisations* (London: Routledge, 1988).

40. D. Silverman, *Qualitative Methodology and Sociology* (Aldershot: Gower, 1985).

41. Tony May, *Social Research: Issues, Methods and Process* (Buckingham: Open University Press, 1997), 134.

42. This phrase denotes a philosophical and theoretical approach to ethnography that stresses the desirability of studying a social situation in its "natural state" without any undue influence being exerted upon that situation by the researcher.

43. L. Stanley and S. Wise, *Breaking Out Again: Feminist Ontology and Epistemology* (London: Routledge and Kegan Paul, 1993), 161.

44. See Clifford Geertz, *The Interpretation of Cultures* (New York: Basic Books, 1973); *Local Knowledge* (New York: Basic Books, 1983); *Works and Lives: The Anthropologist as Author* (Cambridge: Polity Press, 1988).

45. Robert Jackson, *Religious Education: An Interpretive Approach* (London: Hodder & Stoughton, 1997), 30–48.

46. Ibid., 41–45.

47. Robert Jackson and Eleanor Nesbitt, *Hindu Children in Britain* (Stoke on Trent: Trentham Books, 1993).

48. Ibid., 20.

49. Ibid., 20.

50. Geertz, *Local Knowledge*, 57–58.

51. See Peter Weller, ed., *Religions in the UK: A Multi-Faith Directory* (Derby: University of Derby in association with the Inter Faith Network for the United Kingdom, 1997), 234. See also G. Baumann, *Contesting Culture: Discourses of Identity in Multi-Ethnic London* (Cambridge: Cambridge University Press, 1996), 122.

52. Dhadeka Sashedi Raj, "Shifting Culture in the Global Terrain: Culture Identity Construction among Hindu Punjabis in London" (unpublished PhD thesis, University of Cambridge, 1997).

53. Lubna Nazir Chaudhry, "Researching 'My People,' Researching Myself: Fragments of a Reflexive Tale," *Qualitative Studies in Education* 10.4 (1997): 441–53.

54. Ibid., 443.

55. See Michael Eric Dyson, *Reflecting Black: African-American Cultural Criticism* (Minneapolis: University of Minneapolis Press, 1993), 221–330 for a good example of this kind of work. See also Beckford, *Jesus is Dread*.

56. See my doctoral thesis "The Christian Education of African Caribbean Children in Birmingham: Creating a New Paradigm through Developing Better Praxis" (unpublished PhD thesis, University of Birmingham, 2000).

57. See http://www.windbags.freeserve.co.uk for a brief description and analysis of barn dances.

58. Due to poor recording quality and other methodological flaws, material from groups two and three were not utilized to any great extent in this work. I was later able to re-do some of this qualitative work, which has been used subsequently in a later piece of work. See Chapter 6 in Anthony G. Reddie, *Black Theology in Transatlantic Dialogue: Inside Looking Out, Outside Looking In* (New York: Palgrave, forthcoming, 2006).

59. This was not a controlled, scientific piece of research (the group was not created to be a representation of a larger population in survey terms), so the responses should not be taken as empirical evidence.

60. See Reddie, *Nobodies to Somebodies*, 152–54. See also Anthony G. Reddie, "Pentecost—Dreams and Visions (A Black Theological Reading)," in *Discovering Christ: Ascension and Pentecost*, ed. Maureen Edwards (Birmingham, UK: International Bible Reading Association, 2001), 27–42.

61. See Jerome W. Berryman, *Godly Play: An Imaginative Approach to Religious Education* (Minneapolis: Augsburg, 1991).

62. Westfield, *Dear Sisters*.

63. See Janice Hale-Benson, *Black Children: Their Roots, Culture, and Learning Styles* (Baltimore: The Johns Hopkins University Press, 1986).

64. Hale-Benson, *Black Children*, 21–44.

65. See Dwight N. Hopkins, "Black Theology on Theological Education," in *Black Faith and Public Talk*, ed. Dwight N. Hopkins (Maryknoll, NY: Orbis Books, 1999), 41–52.

66. Beckford, *God of the Rahtid*, 12.

67. A Jamaican patois spelling of the word 'ugly'.

68. See Robert Beckford, *Dread and Pentecostal* (London: SPCK, 2000), 198–204, where Beckford outlines a number of linked, yet contrasting Christological positions of Black theologians.

69. James H. Cone, *God of the Oppressed* (New York: Seabury Press, 1975), 115–37.

70. See E. P. Sanders, *Jesus and Judaism* (London: SCM Press, 1985) and Geza Vermes, *Jesus in his Jewish Context* (Minneapolis: Fortress Press, 2003).

71. See Ware, *Methodologies of Black Theology*, 115–44.

72. Theophus H. Smith, *Conjuring Culture: Biblical Formations of Black America* (New York: Oxford University Press, 1994), 4–6.

73. Smith, *Conjuring Culture*, 4–6.

74. Ware, *Methodologies of Black Theology*, 135.

75. Albert J. Raboteau, *Slave Religion* (New York: Oxford University Press, 1978).

76. Robert E. Hood, *Must God Remain Greek: Afro-cultures and God-Talk* (Minneapolis: Fortress Press, 1990).

77. Bridges Johns, *Pentecostal Formation*, 62–137.

78. Beckford, *Dread and Pentecostal*, 168–82.

79. Paris, *The Spiritualities of African Peoples*, 27–57.

80. Brigid M. Sackey, "Spiritual Deliverance as a Form of Health Delivery: A Case Study of the Solid Rock Chapel International," *Black Theology in Britain: A Journal of Contextual Praxis* 4.2 (May 2002): 150–71.

81. Reddie, *Faith, Stories and the Experience of Black Elders*, 106.

82. Christine Callender, *Education for Empowerment: The Practice and Philosophies of Black Teachers* (Stoke on Trent: Trentham Books, 1997), 65–95.

83. See Pinn, *Terror and Triumph* and Patricia Hill Collins, *Black Feminist Thought: Knowledge, Consciousness and the Politics of Empowerment* (London: Routledge, 1990) as excellent examples for the kind of work I have in mind.

84. Reddie, *Nobodies to Somebodies*, 97–99.

85. Ibid., 97–98.

86. See Reddie, *Faith, Stories and the Experience of Black Elders*, 108–10, and *Nobodies to Somebodies*, 122–25.

87. An excellent example of this method can be found in Juan Luis Segundo, *The Liberation of Theology* (Maryknoll, NY: Orbis Books, 1976).

88. See Harry H. Singleton, III, *Black Theology and Ideology: Deideological Dimensions in the Theology of James H. Cone* (Collegeville, MN: The Liturgical Press, 2002).

89. See Beckford, *God and the Gangs*.

90. Ibid., 85–111.

91. Ibid., 105–111.

92. Ibid., 106.

93. Ibid., 106.

94. Jillian Brown, "A Sermon," in Anthony G. Reddie, *Legacy: Anthology in Memory of Jillian Brown* (Peterborough: The Methodist Publishing House, 2000), 39–44.

95. Robert Beckford, "Prophet of Dub: Dub as a Heuristic for Theological Reflection," *Black Theology: An International Journal* 1.1 (November 2002): 79–82.

96. See Nicola M. Slee, *Women's Faith Development: Patterns and Processes*

(Aldershot: Ashgate, 2004). Slee outlines the basic modes of Apophatic faith, concluding that this is one of the preferred ways of speaking of and relating to God that is characteristic of women's faith development.

97. See Barbara Bush, *Slave Women in Caribbean Society 1650–1880* (Indianapolis: Indiana University Press, 1990).

98. See R. Burton, *Afro-Creole: Power, Opposition and Play in the Caribbean* (New York and London: Cornell University Press, 1997).

99. See Horace Campbell, *Rasta and Resistance: From Marcus Garvey to Walter Rodney* (London: Hansib Press, 1985).

100. Stella Dadzie, "Searching for the Invisible Woman: Slavery and Resistance in Jamaica," *Race and Class* 32.2 (1990): 21–38.

101. R. Hart, *Blacks in Rebellion* (Kingston, Jamaica: Institute of Social and Economic Research, 1985).

102. Sewell, *Black Masculinities and Schooling*.

103. Anderson, *Beyond Ontological Blackness*.

104. Ibid., 118–32.

105. Ibid., 132–58.

Chapter 5

1. This issue will be discussed at a later point in this chapter.

2. Reddie, *Acting in Solidarity*.

3. John Elliot, *Action Research for Educational Change* (Milton Keynes: Open University Press, 1991), 69.

4. Luis Cotton and Lawrence Minion, *Research Methods in Education* (London: Routledge, 1989), 186–202.

5. W. Carr and S. Kemmis, *Becoming Critical: Education, Knowledge and Action Research* (London: Falmer Press, 1986), 162.

6. See K. Lewin, "Action Research and Minority Problems," *Journal of Social Issues* 2 (1946): 3–12.

7. Khalid Irshad and Jean Imrie, "Improving Attainment Through Action Research: An Introduction to Hillingdon's Raising Achievement Project," *Multicultural Teaching* 15.2 (Spring 1997): 16.

8. Lawrence Stenhouse, "The Teacher as Researcher," in *An Introduction to Curriculum Research and Development*, ed. Lawrence Stenhouse (London: Heinemann, 1975).

9. Jean McNiff, Pamela Jean Lomax and Jack Whitehead, *You and Your Action Research Project* (London: Routledge, 1996), 8.

10. Christine O'Hanlon, "Reflection and Action in Research: Is There a Moral Responsibility to Act?," *Educational Action Research* 2.2 (1994): 281–88.

11. Elliot, *Action Research for Educational Change*, 9.

12. See Elliot, *Action Research for Educational Change*, for a helpful discussion on the dialectic between the improvement of practice and the production of knowledge. What is the epistemology of educational practice within the action research paradigm?

13. McNiff *et al.*, *You and Your Action Research Project*, 8.

14. In the area of action research, when speaking of particular settings, one is most usually highlighting an educational context.

15. Freire, *Pedagogy of the Oppressed*, 68.

16. McNiff *et al.*, *You and Your Action Research Project*, 8.

17. Herbert Altrichter, Peter Posch and Bridget Somekh, *Teachers Investigating their Work* (London: Routledge, 1993), 102.

18. Ibid., 103.

19. Elliot, *Action Research for Educational Change*, 51.

20. McNiff *et al.*, *You and Your Action Research Project*, 20.

21. See Laurie Green, *Let's Do Theology: A Pastoral Cycle Resource Book* (London: Morbray, 1990).

22. See John Ballard and John Pritchard, *Practical Theology in Action: Christian Thinking in the Service of Church and Society* (London: SPCK, 1996). See also James Woodward and Stephen Pattison, eds., *The Blackwell Reader in Pastoral and Practical Theology* (Oxford: Blackwell, 2000), and David Willows and John Swinton, eds., *Spiritual Dimensions of Pastoral Care: Practical Theology in a Multidisciplinary Context* (London: Jessica Kingsley, 2000).

23. See Elliot, *Action Research for Educational Change*; Altrichter *et al.*, *Teachers Investigating their Work*; Carr and Kemmis, *Becoming Critical*; R. Winter, *Action-Research and the Nature of Social Enquiry: Professional Innovation and Educational Work* (Averbury, Aldershot: Falmer Press, 1987); McNiff *et al.*, *You and Your Action Research Project*.

24. Many have argued that any research that attempts to take the autonomy and input of others seriously will, as a corollary, become contradictory as human beings are such by their very nature.

25. Morwenna Griffiths, "Action Research: Grassroots Practice or Management Tool?" in *Managing Staff Development in Schools: An Action Research Approach*, ed. P. Lomax (Clevedon: Multi-Lingual Matters, 1999), 43.

26. See Niccolo Machiavelli, *The Prince* (trans. W. K. Marriot and Dominic Baker-Smith; New York: Random House, 1992).

27. Postcolonial scholars such as Musa Dube have argued for a de-colonizing of the biblical text in order to both show up and undermine the exploitative, imperialistic tensions that often reside within many biblical narratives. For an interesting explication of this approach see Musa W. Dube, *Postcolonial Feminist Interpretation of the Bible* (Missouri: Chalice Press, 2000).

28. See section entitled "Assessing the Work and 'Ministry' of Paulo Freire" in Chapter 1.

29. See Jon Sobrino, *Jesus the Liberator: A Historical-theological Reading of Jesus of Nazareth* (Tunbridge Wells: Burns and Oates, 1993).

30. See Leonardo and Clodovis Boff, *Introducing Liberation Theology* (Tunbridge Wells: Burns and Oates, 1998).

31. See Gustavo Gutierrez, *A Theology of Liberation* (Maryknoll, NY: Orbis Books, 1973).

32. See Freire, *Pedagogy of the Oppressed*. Also *Education for Critical Consciousness* and *A Pedagogy of Hope*.

33. Bridges Johns, *Pentecostal Formation*, 24–45.

34. Ibid., 41–42.

35. See Freire, *Education for Critical Consciousness*, 41–58.

36. Bridges Johns, *Pentecostal Formation*, 42.

37. Ibid., 42.

38. Ibid., 42.

39. Theophus H. Smith, *Conjuring Culture*, 4–6.

40. See Hood, *Must God Remain Greek?*

41. See Reddie, *Faith, Stories and the Experience of Black Elders.*

42. Ibid., 15.

43. Ibid., 105–106.

44. See section entitled "Listening and Critiquing the Voices of the Voiceless" in Chapter 4.

45. See Groome, *Sharing Faith* and *Christian Religious Education.*

46. See Daniel S. Schipani, *Religious Education Encounters Liberation Theology* (Birmingham, AL: Religious Education Press, 1988).

47. Hope and Timmel, *Training for Transformation.*

48. See Reddie, *Growing into Hope*, 2 vols. See also Reddie, *Nobodies to Somebodies.*

49. See Augusto Boal, *Theater of the Oppressed* (London: Pluto Press, 2000). See also www.unomaha.edu/~pto/augusto.htm for further biographical details on Boal.

50. www.unomaha.edu/~pto/augusto.htm.

51. Boal, *Theater of the Oppressed.*

52. Ibid., 1–50.

53. See Max Harris, *The Dialogical Theatre* (New York: St. Martin's Press, 1993), 3–64.

54. See Jane Milling and Graham Ley, *Modern Theories of Performance* (Basingstoke and New York: Palgrave, 2001), 117–32.

55. See David A. Schlossman, *Actors and Activists: Politics, Performance, and Exchange Among Social Worlds* (New York and London: Routledge, 2002), 25–119.

56. www.unomaha.edu/~pto/augusto.htm

57. Boal, *Theater of the Oppressed*, 83–95.

58. Pinn, *Terror and Triumph*, 157–79.

59. Boal, *Theater of the Oppressed*, 90, original emphasis.

60. See Augusto Boal, *Games for Actors and Non-Actors* (London: Routledge, 1992), *Rainbow of Desire* (London and New York: Routledge, 1995) and *Legislative Theatre* (London and New York: Routledge, 1998).

61. Boal, *Theater of the Oppressed*, 126–30.

62. Boal, *Games for Actors and Non-Actors.*

63. Ibid., 210–23.

64. Boal, *Rainbow of Desire*, 18–27.

65. Boal, *Games for Actors and Non-Actors*, 6.

66. See Groome, *Sharing Faith.* See also Groome, *Christian Religious Education.*

67. Groome, *Sharing Faith*, 156.

68. See Pinn, *Terror and Triumph.* See also Beckford, *God of the Rahtid.*

69. See Hopkins, *Down, Up and Over.*

70. See Beckford, *Jesus is Dread.*

71. See Will Coleman, *Tribal Talk* (Pennsylvania: Pennsylvania Sate University Press, 2000).

72. Boal, *Rainbow of Desire*, 16–39.

73. See Reddie, *Faith, Stories and the Experience of Black Elders*, 116–26.

74. Reddie, *Nobodies to Somebodies*, 132–40.

75. See Reddie, *Acting in Solidarity*.

76. See *Unfinished Business: Children and the Churches*—Consultative Group on Ministry among Children (London: CCBI Publications, 1996), 58–60 for a brief discussion on the notion of church as a hospitable space for those who are weak and vulnerable, thinking, in this particular context, of children.

77. See Sistren (with Honor Ford Smith), *Lionheart Gal: Life Stories of Jamaican Women* (London: The Women's Press, 1986).

78. Ibid., xiii–xxxi.

79. Hood, *Must God Remain Greek?*, 43–51.

80. Pinn, *Varieties of African American Religious Experience*, 14–34.

81. Gossai and Murrell, eds., *Religion, Culture and Tradition in the Caribbean*.

82. See Reddie, *Faith, Stories and the Experience of Black Elders*, 63–76.

83. See also Paris, *The Spirituality of African Peoples*.

84. See Chapter 2 and the development of sketches *The New Arrival* and *Style and Fashion*.

85. *Lionheart Gal*, xxviii–xxix.

86. See Chapter 3 for the development of this piece and substantive Black theological themes contained within the drama.

87. See Tomlin, *Black Language Style in Sacred and Secular Contexts*. See also Willis, "All Things to All Men?," 195–213.

88. Lewis, "Diaspora Dialogue," 85–109.

89. Ibid., 100–109.

90. Ibid., 100.

91. Imani Tafari-Ama, "Rastawoman as Rebel: Case Studies in Jamaica," in *Chanting Down Babylon: The Rastafari Reader*, ed. N. S. Murrell, W. D. Spencer and A. A. McFarlane (Philadelphia: Temple University Press, 1998), 89–106.

92. Cooper, *Noises in the Blood*.

93. Honor Ford Smith, *Ring Ding in a Tight Corner: A Case Study of Funding and Organizational Democracy in Sistren, 1977–1988* (Toronto: The Women's Program, 1989).

94. See Diane Watt, "Traditional Religious Practices Amongst African Caribbean Mothers and Community OtherMothers," *Black Theology: An International Journal* 2.2 (July 2004): 195–212.

95. Ibid., 207.

96. See Jose R. Irizarry, "The Religious Educator as Cultural Spec-actor: Researching Self in Intercultural Pedagogy," *Religious Education* 98.3 (Summer 2003): 365–81.

97. Ibid., 365–68.

98. Ibid., 365–68.

99. See J. Donald and A. Rattansi, *"Race," Culture and Difference* (London: SAGE, 1992).

100. Kathryn Tanner, *Theories of Culture: A New Agenda for Theology* (Minneapolis: Fortress Press, 1997).

101. Barbara Wilkerson, ed., *Multicultural Religious Education* (Birmingham, AL: Religious Education Press, 1997).

102. Irizarry, "The Religious Educator," 370–75.

103. Romney M. Moseley, *Becoming a Self Before God: Critical Transformations* (Nashville: Abingdon Press, 1991).

104. Irizarry, "The Religious Educator," 374.

105. See Westfield, *Dear Sisters*.

106. Ibid., 22.

107. Ibid., 5.

108. Ibid., 40–77.

109. See Emilie Townes, *In a Blaze of Glory* (Nashville, TN: Abingdon Press, 1995).

110. Ibid., 11.

111. Westfield, "Towards a Womanist Approach to Pedagogy," 528.

112. Ibid., 528.

113. See bell hooks, *Teaching to Transgress* (New York: Routledge, 1994).

114. Westfield, "Towards a Womanist Approach to Pedagogy," 528–31.

115. See Freire, *Education for Critical Consciousness*, 41–58.

116. N. Lynne Westfield, "Kitchen Table Banter," *Religious Education* 96.3 (Summer 2001): 423–29.

117. A good example of this can be seen in my previous book *Acting in Solidarity*.

118. Westfield, *Dear Sisters*, 64–77.

119. Beckford, *God of the Rahtid*, 12.

120. See Theophus H. Smith, *Conjuring Culture*.

121. Reddie, *Nobodies to Somebodies*, 97–98.

122. See Beckford, *Jesus is Dread*, 25–60.

123. See Peter J. Paris, *The Social Teachings of the Black Churches* (Philadelphia: Fortress Press, 1985).

124. James H. Cone, *For My People* (Maryknoll, NY: Orbis Books, 1984), 206–207.

125. See Eugene Genovese, *Roll Jordan Roll* (New York: Vintage Books, 1980).

126. Westfield, *Dear Sisters*, 65.

127. See Reddie, *Growing into Hope*.

128. See Reddie, *Nobodies to Somebodies*, 141–53.

129. Safeguarding is a concept and a developing code of practice that seeks to protect minors and those who work with them from potential or accusations of sexual (or other forms) of abuse. Many of the member churches of the ecumenical forum "Churches Together in Britain and Ireland" (CTBI) are signatures to this developing policy to protect children and young people. Those who work with children and young people have to sign declarations and submit themselves to police checks before they can undertake their work (whether paid or voluntary). A major tenet of this procedure is that no one adult should be working alone with a group of children or young people.

130. See Cone, *Black Theology and Black Power*.

131. See Wilmore and Cone, eds., *Black Theology: A Documentary History, 1966–1979*, 1–33. See also pp. 67–111.

132. See Dwight N. Hopkins, ed., *Black Theology: USA and South Africa* (Maryknoll, NY: Orbis Books, 1989). See also Simon Maimela and Dwight N. Hopkins, eds., *We are One Voice: Essays on Black Theology in the USA and South Africa* (Braamfontein, South Africa: Skotaville, 1989).

133. See Cone, "Black Theology and Third World Theologies," and J. Deotis Roberts, "Common Themes: Black Theology and Minjung Theology," in James H. Cone and Gayraud S. Wilmore, eds., *Black Theology: A Documentary History*. II. *1980–1992* (Maryknoll, NY: Orbis Books, 1993), 388–98 and 405–409 respectively.

134. Hopkins, *Heart and Head*, 127–54.

135. See Balasuriya, "Liberation of the Affluent," 83–113.

136. See Beckford, *God and the Gangs*, 29–40 and Hopkins, *(Introducing) Black Theology of Liberation*, 44–45.

137. See Itumeleng J. Mosala, *Biblical Hermeneutics and Black Theology in South Africa* (Grand Rapids: Eerdmans, 1989).

138. See Cornel West, "Black Theology and Human Identity," in *Black Faith and Public Talk: Critical Essays on James Cone's Black Theology and Black Power*, ed. Dwight N. Hopkins (Maryknoll, NY: Orbis Books, 1999), 11–19.

139. In a previous paper I have described Black Christian education as the "practical" or "applied" wing of Black Liberation theology. See Anthony G. Reddie, "God-Talk and Black Empowerment," *The Epworth Review* 30.4 (October 2003): 53–62 and *Nobodies to Somebodies*.

140. Beckford, *Dread and Pentecostal*, 67–94.

141. Samuel K. Yeboah, *The Ideology of Racism* (London: Hansib, 1988).

142. Cone, *A Black Theology of Liberation*, 14.

143. See Pinn, *Terror and Triumph*.

144. Norman Gottwald, "The Role of Biblical Politics in Contextual Theologies," in *Reading the Bible in the Global Village: Cape Town* (Atlanta: Society for Biblical Literature, 2002), 111–23.

145. Pinn, *Terror and Triumph*, 104.

146. I have made this exploratory link in a previous piece of research. See Reddie, *Faith, Stories and the Experience of Black Elders*, 77–82.

147. Beckford, *God and the Gangs*, 85–104.

148. See James H. Cone, "Theology's Great Sin: Silence in the Face of White Supremacy," *Black Theology: An International Journal* 2.2 (July 2004): 139–52.

Chapter 6

1. See section "Racial Justice/Black Theology," in Reddie, *Acting in Solidarity*.

2. I suspect that this phenomenon affects Black people in all parts of the world, but as I am a contextual theologian, Britain is my immediate sphere of operations.

3. See Reddie, *Nobodies to Somebodies*, 153–72.

4. Ibid., 153–54.

5. Ibid.

6. The section entitled "Racial Justice/Black Theology" includes three pieces —two short dramas and a dramatic exercise, all written by me—in order to give expression to my understanding of this concept, a *theology of dramatic engagement*. These three pieces, plus the other 12 in *Acting in Solidarity*, are more practically oriented materials for the exploration of a vision/version of Christianity that is self-critical and inclusive.

7.   Some of my initial thinking has been inspired by Jose Irizarry. See Irizarry, "The Religious Educator," 365–81.

8.   See Vernon White, *Identity* (London: SCM Press, 2002) for an interesting exploration of identity within a theological framework.

9.   Tee Garlington, "The Eucharist and Racism," in *Ending Racism in the Church*, ed. Susan E. Davies and Sister Paul Teresa Hennesee, SA (Cleveland, OH: The Pilgrim Press, 1998), 74–80.

10.   E. Hammond Oglesby, *O Lord, Move This Mountain: Racism and Christian Ethics* (St. Louis: Chalice Press, 1998).

11.   See 1st Corinthians 12:12–31.

12.   See section entitled "Dealing with the Reality of Difference" in Chapter 2.

13.   Reddie, *Nobodies to Somebodies*, 132–40.

14.   Ibid., 132–40.

15.   This term denotes the conflation of the two oldest universities in the UK, namely Oxford and Cambridge. Hence the term Oxbridge.

16.   This term is one that is used to denote the eight universities in the United States that are generally considered to be pre-eminent seats of learning in higher education. The universities are: Brown, Columbia, Cornell, Dartmouth, Harvard, Pennsylvania, Princeton, and Yale.

17.   Reddie, *Nobodies to Somebodies*, 136.

18.   Robert Beckford argues that "reader-response" approaches to hermeneutics are valid strategies for marginalized and oppressed peoples to excavate liberative themes from within biblical texts. See Beckford, *God and the Gangs*, 96–100.

19.   Reddie, *Nobodies to Somebodies*, 7–11.

20.   Although I cannot attest to the provenance of this aphorism, it came to my attention via Mr. Naboth Muchopa, the Connexional (national) Secretary for Racial Justice in the Methodist Church in Britain.

21.   See section entitled "Ministry of the Whole People of God in the World," in Reddie, *Acting in Solidarity*.

22.   See Irizarry, "The Religious Educator," 365–81. See also Clark C. Apt, *Serious Games* (New York: Viking Press, 1970).

23.   See Pinn and Pinn, *Black Church History*.

24.   Black Methodists, Anglicans and those in the Baptist and Reformed traditions in the UK have not left to form separate churches, but have attempted to create their own self-identified spaces within the corporate whole. A similar strategy has been used by Black members of White-dominated churches in Southern Africa. In the British context see Heather Walton, *A Tree God Planted: Black People in British Methodism* (London: Ethnic Minorities in Methodism Working Group, The Methodist Church, 1984) and John Wilkinson, *Church in Black and White: The Black Tradition in Mainstream Churches in England* (Edinburgh: Saint Andrew Press, 1993). In terms of the latter see Jean Knighton-Fitt, *Beyond Fear* (Cape Town: Pretext Publishers, 2003).

25.   See Henry H. Mitchell, *Black Church Beginnings* (Grand Rapids, MI: Eerdmans, 2004).

26.   Pinn, *Terror and Triumph*, 81–156.

27.   Reddie, *Nobodies to Somebodies*, 158.

28.   See Anthony G. Reddie, "A Theology of Good Intentions," in *Coming of Age: Challenges and Opportunities in the 21st Century*, ed. Stuart J. Burgess (York: Stuart Burgess, 1999), 89–94.

29.   Beckford, *God and the Gangs*, 96–114.

30.   See J. Saward, *Perfect Fools* (Oxford: Oxford University Press, 1990). See also H. Lewin, ed., *A Community of Clowns* (Geneva: WCC, 1987).

31.   See Groome, *Sharing Faith* and *Christian Religious Education*.

32.   Jerome W. Berryman, *Godly Play: An Imaginative Approach to Religious Education* (Minneapolis: Augsburg, 1995 [1st edn in 1991 by HarperSanFrancisco]).

33.   See the following pieces: "Stakeholding" (which in actual fact is a dramatic exercise, not a sketch), "The Quest for Racial Justice" and "Black Voices," in Reddie, *Acting in Solidarity*.

34.   See Pinn, *Terror and Triumph*.

35.   See Tomlin, *Black Language Style in Sacred and Secular Contexts*.

36.   See Beckford, *God of the Rahtid*, 11–18.

37.   Gossai and Murrell offer an interesting insight into the creative, dramatic religious sensibilities of the diverse range of peoples in the Caribbean. I am interested, particularly, in the cultural repertoire of Black people of African descent, whose capacity to move between and within seemingly contradictory and exclusive religio-cultural codes speaks of a fluidity and hybridity, which lends itself to this form and method for undertaking theological reflection. See Gossai and Murrell, eds., *Religion, Culture and Tradition in the Caribbean*.

38.   Hope and Timmell, *Training for Transformation*.

39.   See Chapter 1 for my brief assessment of the legacy of influence of Paulo Freire upon this approach and method for doing theology with marginalized and oppressed peoples.

40.   Freire, *Education for Critical Consciousness*, 41–58.

41.   The five people who acted in each performance of the sketch were always changed.

42.   See Sandra Ackroyd, Marjorie Lewis-Cooper and Naboth Muchopa, *Strangers No More: Transformation Through Racial Justice* (London: The Methodist Church, 2001) for an analysis of the different forms in which racism is manifested. See also Naboth Muchopa, *Making a Positive Difference* (London: The Methodist Church, 2001).

43.   See Ackroyd *et al.*, *Strangers No More*, 8–11.

44.   See Ian A. McFarland, *Difference and Identity: A Theological Anthropology* (Cleveland, OH: The Pilgrim Press, 2001).

45.   See Jeff Astley, *Ordinary Theology: Looking, Listening and Learning in Theology* (Aldershot: Ashgate, 2002).

46.   James H. Harris, "The Black Church and Black Theology: Theory and Practice," in *Black Theology: A Documentary History*. II. *1980–1992*, ed. James H. Cone and Gayraud S. Wilmore (Maryknoll, NY: Orbis Books, 1993), 85–93.

47.   Andrews, *Practical Theology for Black Churches*.

48.   Westfield, *Dear Sisters*.

49.   See Charles R. Foster and Fred Smith, *Black Religious Experience: Conversations on Double Consciousness and the Work of Grant Shockley* (Nashville, TN: Abingdon Press, 2004).

50. See Yolanda Y. Smith, *Reclaiming the Spirituals: New Possibilities for Africa American Christian Education* (Cleveland, OH: The Pilgrim Press, 2004).

51. See section entitled "Racial Justice/Black Theology" in Reddie, *Acting in Solidarity*. This represented my first attempt to use drama as an accessible means for articulating and doing Black theology.

52. See Freire, *Education for Critical Consciousness*.

53. As I have outlined in this chapter, this method is by no means fool-proof. The educator and theologian must never become complicit in the tempting deceit of believing that they are completely relinquishing power (thereby becoming powerless) to those who are the voiceless.

54. Paulo Freire's work has been an enormous influence on this study. See reference to his work and legacy in Chapter 1.

55. Bridges Johns, *Pentecostal Formation*, 24–61.

56. Ibid., 56–61.

57. Singleton, III, *Black Theology and Ideology*, 105–111.

58. See Frances Beale, "Double Jeopardy: To be Black and Female," and Theressa Hoover, "Black Women and the Churches: Triple Jeopardy," in *Black Theology: A Documentary History, 1966–1979*, ed. Gayraud S. Wilmore and James H. Cone (Maryknoll, NY: Orbis Books, 1979), 368–76 and 377–88 respectively.

59. See Ann-Cathrin Jarl, *In Justice: Women and Global Economics* (Minneapolis: Fortress Press, 2003), 115–34.

60. I have detailed aspects of my formative experiences in a previous piece of work. See Anthony G. Reddie, "Unbroken Thread of Experience," in *Family and All That Stuff*, ed. Joan King (Birmingham: National Christian Education Council [NCEC], 1998), 153–60.

61. See Reddie, *Faith, Stories and the Experience of Black Elders*, 39–46.

62. A Caribbean colloquialism for "not telling your private stories/experiences to other people."

63. Paris, *The Spirituality of African Peoples*, 27–45.

64. Riggins R. Earl Jr., *Dark Salutations: Ritual, God, and Greetings in the African American Community* (Harrisburg, PA: Trinity Press International, 2001), 1–16.

65. Ibid., 2.

66. See Pinn, *Varieties of African American Religious Experience*, 154–85. See also Anthony B. Pinn, " 'Handlin' My Business': Exploring Rap's Humanist Sensibilities," in *Noise and Spirit: The Religious and Spiritual Sensibilities of Rap Music*, ed. Anthony B. Pinn (New York and London: New York University Press, 2003), 85–106.

67. See Anthony G. Reddie, " 'Pentecost'—Dreams and Visions [A Black Theological Reading of Pentecost]," in *Discovering Christ: Ascension and Pentecost*, ed. Maureen Edwards (International Bible Reading Association, March 2001), 33.

68. See Chapter 2 and section entitled "Problematic Sameness."

69. Beckford, *Jesus is Dread*, 118.

70. See section 1 entitled "Biblical Re-telling" for the sketch "In The Psychiatrist's Chair." Reddie, *Acting in Solidarity*.

71. Reddie, *Acting in Solidarity*, 20.

72. Cone, "Theology's Great Sin," 143.

73. Beckford, *Dread and Pentecostal*, 40.

74. Ross, *Witnessing and Testifying*.
75. Gilkes, *If It Wasn't for the Women*.
76. Hopkins, *Down, Up, and Over*, 51–106.
77. See Beckford, *Dread and Pentecostal*.
78. Ibid., 168–76.
79. Beckford, *God and the Gangs*, 31–32.
80. Ibid., 17–19.
81. Beckford, *Dread and Pentecostal*, 174–76.
82. See Foster, "Women and the Inverted Pyramid."
83. Lee, "Religious Education and Theology," 45–68.
84. Carlyle Fielding Stewart, III, *Black Spirituality and Black Consciousness* (Trenton, NJ: Africa World Press, 1999), 27–98.
85. Michael I. N. Dash, Jonathan Jackson and Stephen C. Rasor, *Hidden Wholeness* (Cleveland, OH: United Church Press, 1997).
86. Ibid., 85.
87. See Anthony G. Reddie, "Inter-Generational Conversations and Prayer," in *Praying with Power*, ed. Joe Aldred (London: Continuum, 2000), 102–118.
88. Young, *Dogged Strength Within the Veil*, 91–109.
89. See Anthony G. Reddie, "Jazz Musicians of the Word," *The College of Preachers—The Journal* (January 2004): 21–28.
90. This claim was made to me by a participant at a one-day workshop in Black Theology I led in the latter part of 2003.
91. See Cone, *For My People*.
92. See Grant, *White Women's Christ and Black Women's Jesus*.
93. See Williams, *Sisters in the Wilderness*.
94. See Beckford, *Jesus is Dread*.
95. See Hopkins, *Down, Up, and Over*.
96. Jones, *Is God a White Racist?*
97. Pinn, *Why Lord?*

Bibliography

Achebe, Chinua. *Things Fall Apart*. London: David Campbell, 1992.

Aching, Gerard. *Masking and Power: Carnival and Popular Culture in the Caribbean*. Minneapolis: University of Minnesota Press, 2002.

Ackroyd, Sandra, Marjorie Lewis-Cooper and Naboth Muchopa, *Strangers No More: Transformation Through Racial Justice*. London: The Methodist Church, 2001.

Aldred, Joe. *Preaching with Power*. London: Cassells, 1998.

—*Praying with Power*. London: Continuum, 2000.

—*Sisters with Power*. London: Continuum, 2000.

Altrichter, Herbert, Peter Posch and Bridget Somekh. *Teachers Investigating their Work*. London: Routledge, 1993.

Anderson, Carver L. "Where There is No Youth the Vision Will Perish." *Black Theology in Britain: A Journal of Contextual Praxis* 6 (2001): 25–39.

Anderson, E. Byron. "Liturgical Catechesis: Congregational Practice as Formation." *Religious Education* 92.3 (Summer 1997): 349–62.

Anderson, Victor. *Beyond Ontological Blackness: An Essay on African American Cultural Religious and Cultural Criticism*. New York: Continuum, 1995.

Andrews, Dale P. *Practical Theology for Black Churches: Bridging Black Theology and African American Folk Religion*. Louisville, KY: Westminster/John Knox Press, 2002.

Apt, Clark C. *Serious Games*. New York: Viking Press, 1970.

Archibald, Helen. "Originating Visions and Visionaries of the REA." *Religious Education* 98.4 (Fall 2003): 414–25.

Asante, Molefi Kete. "Afrocentricity and Culture." In *African Culture: The Rhythms of Unity*, ed. Molefi Kete Asante and Kariamu Welsh Asante. New Jersey: First Africa World Press, 1990.

Asante, Molefi K., and Kariamu W. Asante, ed. *African Culture: The Rhythms of Unity*. Trenton, NJ: Africa World Press, 1990.

Astley, Jeff. "Growing into Christ: The Psychology and Politics of Christian Maturity." In *The Contours of Christian Education*, ed. Jeff Astley and David Day. Great Wakering, Essex: McCrimmons, 1992.

—*The Philosophy of Christian Religious Education*. Birmingham, AL: Religious Education Press, 1994.

—"Aims and Approaches in Christian Education." In *Learning in the Way: Research and Reflection on Adult Christian Education*, ed. Jeff Astley. Leominster: Gracewings, 2000.

—"Dimensions of Christian Education." In *Learning in the Way: Research and Reflection on Adult Christian Education*, ed. Jeff Astley. Leominster: Gracewings, 2000.

—*Ordinary Theology: Looking, Listening and Learning in Theology*. Aldershot: Ashgate, 2002.

Astley, Jeff, ed. *Learning in the Way: Research and Reflection on Adult Christian Education*. Leominster: Gracewings, 2000.

Bailey, Randall C. "Africans in Old Testament Poetry and Narratives." In *Stony the Road We Trod: African American Biblical Interpretation*, ed. Cain Hope Felder. Minneapolis: Fortress Press, 1991.

—" 'Is That Any Name for a Nice Hebrew Boy?': Exodus 2:1-10: The De-Africanization of an Israelite Hero." In *The Recovery of Black Presence: An Interdisciplinary Exploration*, ed. Randall C. Bailey and Jacquelyn Grant. Nashville, TN: Abingdon Press, 1995.

Bailey, Randall C., ed. *Yet With A Steady Beat: Contemporary Afrocentric Biblical Interpretation*. Atlanta: Society for Biblical Literature, 2003.

Balasuriya, Tissa. *The Eucharist and Human Liberation*. London: SCM Press, 1979.

—"Liberation of the Affluent." *Black Theology: An International Journal* 1.1 (November 2002): 83–113.

Ballard, John, and John Pritchard. *Practical Theology in Action: Christian Thinking in the Service of Church and Society*. London: SPCK, 1996.

Battalora, Jacqueline. "Whiteness: The Workings of an Ideology in American Society and Culture." In *Gender, Ethnicity and Religion: Views from the Other Side*, ed. Rosemary Radford Ruether. Minneapolis: Fortress Press, 2002.

Baumann, G. *Contesting Culture: Discourses of Identity in Multi-Ethnic London*. Cambridge: Cambridge University Press, 1996.

Beale, Frances. "Double Jeopardy: To be Black and Female." In *Black Theology: A Documentary History, 1966–1979*, ed. Gayraud S. Wilmore and James H. Cone. Maryknoll, NY: Orbis Books, 1979.

Beckford, Robert, S. *Jesus is Dread*. London: Darton, Longman & Todd, 1998.

—*Dread and Pentecostal: A Political Theology for the Black Church in Britain*. London: SPCK, 2000.

—*God of the Rahtid: Redeeming Rage*. London: Darton, Longman & Todd, 2001.

—"Theology in the Age of Crack: Crack Age, Prosperity Doctrine and 'Being There'." *Black Theology in Britain: A Journal of Contextual Praxis* 4.1 (November 2001): 9–24.

—"Prophet of Dub: Dub as a Heuristic for Theological Reflection." *Black Theology: An International Journal* 1.1 (November 2002): 79–82.

Beckford, Robert. *God and the Gangs*. London: Darton, Longman & Todd, 2004.

—*Jesus Dub: Faith, Culture and Social Change*. London: Routledge, 2006.

Bell, John L., and Graham Maule. *Jesus and Peter*. Glasgow: Wild Goose Publications, 1999.

—*Just Acting*. London: Christian Aid, 2002.

Berryman, Jerome W. *Godly Play: An Imaginative Approach to Religious Education*. Minneapolis: Augsburg, 1995 (1st edn in 1991 by HarperSanFrancisco).

Bhogal, Inderjit S. "Citizenship." In *Legacy: Anthology in Memory of Jillian Brown*, ed. Anthony G. Reddie. Peterborough: Methodist Publishing House, 2000.

—*A Table for All*. Sheffield: Penistone Publications, 2000.

Boal, Augusto. *Games for Actors and Non-Actors*. London: Routledge, 1992.

—*Rainbow of Desire*. London and New York: Routledge, 1995.

—*Legislative Theatre*. London and New York: Routledge, 1998.

—*Theater of the Oppressed*. London: Pluto Press, 2000.

Boff, Leonardo, and Clodovis Boff. *Introducing Liberation Theology*. Tunbridge Wells: Burns and Oates, 1998.

Brown, Jillian. "A Sermon." In Anthony G. Reddie, *Legacy: Anthology in Memory of Jillian Brown*. Peterborough: The Methodist Publishing House, 2000.

Brown Douglas, Kelly D. "Womanist Theology: What is its Relationship to Black Theology?." In *Black Theology: A Documentary History*. II. *1980–1992*, ed. James H. Cone and Gayraud S. Wilmore. Maryknoll, NY: Orbis Books, 1993.

—*The Black Christ*. Maryknoll, NY: Orbis Books, 1994.

Bryman, A. *Doing Research in Organisations*. London: Routledge, 1988.

Bulmer, M. *The Chicago School of Sociology*. Chicago: University of Chicago Press, 1984.

Burbridge, Paul, and Murray Watts. *Time to Act*. London: Hodder & Stoughton, 1979.

—*Lighting Sketches*. London: Hodder & Stoughton, 1981.

—*Red Letter Days*. London: Hodder & Stoughton, 1986.

Burton, R. *Afro-Creole: Power, Opposition and Play in the Caribbean*. New York and London: Cornell University Press, 1997.

Bush, Barbara. *Slave Women in Caribbean Society 1650–1880*. Indianapolis: Indiana University Press, 1990.

Butler, Lee H. "Testimony as Hope and Care: African American Pastoral Care as Black Theology at Work." In *Living Stones in the Household of God: The Legacy and Future of Black Theology*, ed. Linda E. Thomas. Minneapolis: Fortress Press, 2003.

Byron, Gay L. *Symbolic Blackness and Ethnic Difference in Early Christian Literature*. New York: Routledge, 2002.

Callender, Christine. *Education for Empowerment: The Practice and Philosophies of Black Teachers*. Stoke on Trent: Trentham Books, 1997.

Campbell, Horace. *Rasta and Resistance: From Marcus Garvey to Walter Rodney*. London: Hansib Press, 1985.

Cannon, Katie G. *Black Womanist Ethics*. Atlanta, GA: Scholars Press, 1988.

—*Katie's Canon: Womanism and the Soul of the Black Community*. New York: Continuum, 1995.

Carr, W., and S. Kemmis. *Becoming Critical: Education, Knowledge and Action Research*. London: Falmer Press, 1986.

Carter, Stephen. "The Black Church and Religious Freedom." In *Black Faith and Public Talk: Critical Essays on James H. Cone's Black Theology and Black Power*, ed. Dwight N. Hopkins. Maryknoll, NY: Orbis Books, 1999.

Champion, George L. Sr. *Christian Education for the African American Church*. Riviera Beach, FL: Port Printing Company, 1990.

Channer, Yvonne. "The Youth and the Church: Impact of External Forces on Personal Beliefs." *Black Theology in Britain: A Journal of Contextual Praxis* 6 (2001): 9–24.

Chaudhry, Lubna Nazir. "Researching 'My People,' Researching Myself: Fragments of a Reflexive Tale." *Qualitative Studies in Education* 10.4 (1997): 441–53.

Cleaver, Eldridge. *Soul On Ice*. New York: Laurel, 1992.

Coleman, Kate. "Black to the Future: Re-Evangelizing Black Youth." *Black Theology in Britain: A Journal of Contextual Praxis* 6 (2001): 41–51.

Coleman, Will. *Tribal Talk: Black Theology, Hermeneutics, and African/American Ways of "Telling the Story"*. University Park, PN: Pennsylvania State University Press, 2000.

Collins, Patricia Hill. *Black Feminist Thought: Knowledge, Consciousness and the Politics of Empowerment*. London: Routledge, 1990.

Cone, James H. *God of the Oppressed*. New York: Seabury Press, 1975.

—*For My People*. Maryknoll, NY: Orbis Books, 1984.

—*Black Theology and Black Power*. Maryknoll, NY: Orbis Books, 1989 [1969].

—*A Black Theology of Liberation*. Maryknoll, NY: Orbis Books, 1990 [1970].

—"Black Theology and Third World Theologies." In *Black Theology: A Documentary History*. II. *1980–1992*, ed. James H. Cone and Gayraud S. Wilmore. Maryknoll, NY: Orbis Books, 1993.

—*Risks of Faith: The Emergence of a Black Theology of Liberation, 1968–1998*. Boston: Beacon Press, 1999.

—"Theology's Great Sin: Silence in the Face of White Supremacy." *Black Theology: An International Journal* 2.2 (July 2004): 139–52.

Cone, James H., and Gayraud S. Wilmore. *Black Theology: A Documentary History*. II. *1980–1992*. Maryknoll, NY: Orbis Books, 1993.

Cooper, Carolyn. *Noises in the Blood: Orality, Gender and Vulgar Body of Jamaican Popular Culture*. Durham, NC: Duke University Press, 1995.

Cotton, Luis, and Lawrence Minion. *Research Methods in Education*. London: Routledge, 1989.

Cowley, John. *Carnival, Canboulay and Calypso: Traditions in the Making*. Cambridge: Cambridge University Press, 1996.

Crockett, Joseph V. *Teaching Scripture: From an African American Perspective*. Nashville, TN: Discipleship Resources, 1990.

Dadzie, Stella. "Searching for the Invisible Woman: Slavery and Resistance in Jamaica." *Race and Class* 32.2 (1990): 21–38.

Daly, Mary. *Beyond God the Father*. London: The Women's Press, 1995 [1986].

Dash, Michael I. N., Jonathan Jackson and Stephen C. Rasor. *Hidden Wholeness*. Cleveland, OH: United Church Press, 1997.

Davidson, Callum. *The Death of Christian Britain: Understanding Secularisation 1800–2000*. London: Routledge, 2001.

Davie, Grace. *Religion in Britain since 1945: Believing without Belonging*. Oxford: Basil Blackwell, 1994.

Davies, Rupert E. *Methodism*. Peterborough: Epworth Press, 1985.

Davis, Angela Y. *An Autobiography*. London: Women's Press, 1990.

Davis, Kortright, *Emancipation Still Comin': Explorations in Caribbean Emancipatory Theology*. Maryknoll, NY: Orbis Books, 1990.

Deal, Stephen. *Short Change*. Leicester: Nimbus Press, 2002.

Dixon, Lorraine, "Are Vashti and Esther our Sistas?." In *Legacy: Anthology in Memory of Jillian Brown*, ed. Anthony G. Reddie. Peterborough: Methodist Publishing House, 2000.

Donald, J., and A. Rattansi. *"Race," Culture and Difference*. London: SAGE, 1992.

Douglas, Kelly Brown. *The Black Christ*. Maryknoll, NY: Orbis Books, 1994.

Dube, Musa W. *Postcolonial Feminist Interpretation of the Bible*. Missouri: Chalice Press, 2000.

Dubois, W. E. B. *The Souls of Black Folk*. New York: Bantam Books, 1989.

Dyson, Michael Eric. *Reflecting Black: African-American Cultural Criticism*. Minneapolis: University of Minneapolis Press, 1993.

—*Between God and Gangsta Rap*. New York: Oxford University Press, 1996.

Earl Jr., Riggins R. *Dark Salutations: Ritual, God, and Greetings in the African American Community*. Harrisburg, PA: Trinity Press International, 2001.

Edwards, Joel, ed. *Let's Praise Him Again: An African Caribbean Perspective on Worship*. Eastbourne: Kingsway Publications, 1992.

Elias, John L. "Paulo Freire: Religious Educator." *Religious Education* 71.4 (January–February, 1976): 40–56.

Elliot, John. *Action Research for Educational Change*. Milton Keynes: Open University Press, 1991.

Erskine, Noel L. *Decolonizing Theology*. Maryknoll, NY: Orbis Books, 1981.

Esler, Philip F. *Galatians*. London: Routledge, 1998.

Evans Jr., James H. *We Have Been Believers: An African American Systematic Theology*. Minneapolis: Fortress Press, 1992.

Everist, Norma Cook, ed. *The Difficult but Indispensable Church*. Minneapolis: Fortress Press, 2002.

Felder, Cain Hope, ed. *Stony the Road We Trod: African American Biblical Interpretation*. Minneapolis: Fortress Press, 1991.

—*The Original African Heritage Study Bible*. Nashville, TN: The James C. Winston Publishing Company, 1993.

Forde, Nigel. *Theatrecraft*. Bromley, Kent: MARC Europe, 1989.

Foster, Charles R., and Fred Smith. *Black Religious Experience: Conversations on Double Consciousness and the Work of Grant Shockley*. Nashville, TN: Abingdon Press, 2004.

Foster, Elaine. "Women and the Inverted Pyramid of the Black Churches in Britain." In *Refusing Holy Orders: Women and Fundamentalism in Britain*, ed. G. Saghal and N. Yuval-Davis. London: Virago, 1992.

Fowler, James. *Stages of Faith*. San Francisco: HarperSanFrancisco 1995.

Freire, Paulo. "Know, Practice and Teach the Gospels." *Religious Education* 79.4 (Fall, 1984).

—*Education for Critical Consciousness*. New York: Continuum, 1990 [1973].

—*Pedagogy of the Oppressed*. New York: Herder and Herder, 1993 [1970].

—*A Pedagogy of Hope: Relieving Pedagogy of the Oppressed*. New York: Continuum, 1999.

Gandi, Leela. *Postcolonial Theory*. Edinburgh: Edinburgh University Press, 1998.

Garlington, Tee. "The Eucharist and Racism." In *Ending Racism in the Church*, ed. Susan E. Davies and Sister Paul Teresa Hennesee, SA. Cleveland, OH: The Pilgrim Press, 1998.

Geertz, Clifford. *The Interpretation of Cultures*. New York: Basic Books, 1973.

—*Local Knowledge*. New York: Basic Books, 1983.

—*Works and Lives: The Anthropologist as Author*. Cambridge: Polity Press, 1988.

Genovese, Eugene. *Roll Jordan Roll*. New York: Vintage Books, 1980.

Gilkes, Cheryl Townsend. *If It Wasn't for the Women*. Maryknoll, NY: Orbis Books, 2001.

Gilroy, Paul. *There Ain't No Black in the Union Jack*. London: Hutchinson, 1987.

—*The Black Atlantic: Modernity and Double Consciousness*. London: Verso, 1993.

Glaser, B., and A. Strauss. *The Discovery of Grounded Theory*. Chicago: Aldine, 1967.

Goldman, Ronald. *Readiness for Religion*. London: Routledge and Kegan Paul, 1965.

Gossai, Hemchand, and Nathaniel S. Murrel, eds. *Religion, Culture and Tradition in the Caribbean.* London: Macmillan, 2000.

Gottwald, Norman. "The Role of Biblical Politics in Contextual Theologies." In *Reading the Bible in the Global Village: Cape Town.* Atlanta: Society for Biblical Literature, 2002.

Grainger, Roger. *Presenting Drama in Church.* London: Epworth Press, 1985.

Grant, Jacquelyn. *White Women's Christ and Black Women's Jesus.* Atlanta: Scholars Press, 1989.

Green, Laurie. *Let's Do Theology: A Pastoral Cycle Resource Book.* London: Morbray, 1990.

—*Urban Ministry and the Kingdom of God.* London: SPCK, 2003.

Griffiths, Morwenna. "Action Research: Grassroots Practice or Management Tool?" In *Managing Staff Development in Schools: An Action Research Approach*, ed. P. Lomax. Clevedon: Multi-Lingual Matters, 1999.

Groome, Thomas. *Christian Religious Education: Sharing Our Story and Vision.* San Francisco: Jossey-Bass, 1999 [1980].

—*Sharing Faith: A Comprehensive Approach to Religious Education and Pastoral Ministries.* San Francisco: HarperSanFrancisco, 1991.

Gutierrez, Gustavo. *A Theology of Liberation.* Maryknoll, NY: Orbis Books, 1973.

Hale, Janice. "A Comparative Study of the Racial Attitudes of Children who Attend a Pan-African and a Non-pan-African Preschool." Unpublished PhD dissertation, Georgia State University, 1974.

Hale-Benson, Janice. *Black Children: Their Roots, Culture, and Learning Styles.* Baltimore: The Johns Hopkins University Press, 1986.

Hammersley, M. "What's Wrong with Ethnography? The Myth of Theoretical Description." *Sociology* 24.4 (1990): 597–615.

—*What's Wrong with Ethnography? Methodological Explorations.* London: Routledge, 1992.

—*Social Research: Philosophy, Politics and Practice.* London: SAGE, 1993.

Hammersley, M., and P. Atkinson. *Ethnography: Principles in Practice.* London: Routledge, 1983.

Harding, Vincent. "Religion and Resistance Among Antebellum Slaves, 1800–1860." In *African American Religion: Interpretive Essays in History and Culture*, ed. Timothy E. Fulop and Albert J. Raboteau. New York: Routledge, 1997.

Hardison Jr., O. B. *Christian Rite and Christian Drama in the Middle Ages.* Baltimore: The Johns Hopkins University Press, 1965.

Harris, James H. "The Black Church and Black Theology: Theory and Practice." In *Black Theology: A Documentary History.* II. *1980–1992*, ed. James H. Cone and Gayraud S. Wilmore. Maryknoll, NY: Orbis Books, 1993.

Harris, Max. *The Dialogical Theatre.* New York: St. Martin's Press, 1993.

Hart, R. *Blacks in Rebellion.* Kingston, Jamaica: Institute of Social and Economic Research, 1985.

Haylock, Derek. *Plays on the Word.* London: National Society/Church House Publishing, 1993.

—*Plays for all Seasons.* London: National Society/Church House Publishing, 1997.

Hill, Errol. *The Trinidad Carnival.* London: New Beacon Books, 1997.

Hirst, Paul H. "Christian Education: A Contradiction in Terms?" In *Critical Perspec-*

tives on Christian Education, ed. Jeff Astley and Leslie J. Francis. Leominster: Gracewings, 1994.

Hood, Robert E. *Must God Remain Greek?: Afro Cultures and God-Talk*. Minneapolis: Fortress Press, 1990.

hooks, bell. *Teaching to Transgress*. New York: Routledge, 1994.

Hoover, Theressa. "Black Women and the Churches: Triple Jeopardy." In *Black Theology: A Documentary History, 1966–1979*, ed. James H. Cone and Gayraud S. Wilmore. Maryknoll, NY: Orbis Books, 1979.

Hope, Anne, and Sally Timmel. *Training for Transformation: A Handbook for Community Workers*, 4 vols.. Gweru, Zimbabwe: Mambo Press, 1999.

Hopkins, Dwight N. *(Introducing) Black Theology of Liberation*. Maryknoll, NY: Orbis Books, 1999.

—"Black Theology on Theological Education." In *Black Faith and Public Talk*, ed. Dwight N. Hopkins. Maryknoll, NY: Orbis Books, 1999.

—*Down, Up and Over: Slave Religion and Black Theology*. Minneapolis: Fortress Press, 2000.

—*Head and Heart: Black Theology, Past, Present and Future*. New York: Palgrave/Macmillan, 2002.

Hopkins, Dwight N., ed. *Black Theology: USA and South Africa*. Maryknoll, NY: Orbis Books, 1989.

Hopkins, Dwight N., and George L. Cummings, eds. *Cut Loose Your Stammering Tongue: Black Theology in the Slave Narrative*. Louisville, KY: Westminster/John Knox Press, 2nd edn, 2003.

Hopwood, Dave. *Acting Up*. London: National Society/Church House Publishing, 1995.

—*A Fistful of Sketches*. London: National Society/Church House Publishing, 1996.

—*Playing Up*. London: National Society/Church House Publishing, 1998.

—*Curtain Up*. London: National Society/Church House Publishing, 2000.

Hull, John M. "Christian Theology and Educational Theory: Can There be Connections?" In *Critical Perspectives on Christian Education*, ed. Jeff Astley and Leslie J. Francis. Basingstoke: Gracewings, 1994.

—"Critical Openness in Christian Nurture." In *Critical Perspectives on Christian Education*, ed. Jeff Astley and Leslie J. Francis. Basingstoke: Gracewings, 1994.

Irizarry, Jose R. "The Religious Educator as Cultural Spec-actor: Researching Self in Intercultural Pedagogy." *Religious Education* 98.3 (Summer 2003): 365–81.

Irshad, Khalid, and Jean Imrie. "Improving Attainment Through Action Research: An Introduction to Hillingdon's Raising Achievement Project." *Multicultural Teaching* 15.2 (Spring 1997).

Jackson, Robert, *Religious Education: An Interpretive Approach*. London: Hodder & Stoughton, 1997.

Jackson, Robert, and Eleanor Nesbitt. *Hindu Children in Britain*. Stoke on Trent: Trentham Books, 1993.

Jacobsen, Dennis. *Doing Justice: Congregations and Community Organizing*. Minneapolis: Fortress Press, 2001.

James, Winston. "Migration, Racism and Identity." In *Inside Babylon*, ed. Winston James and Clive Harris. London: Verso, 1993.

Jarl, Ann-Cathrin. *In Justice: Women and Global Economics*. Minneapolis: Fortress Press, 2003.

Johns, Cheryl Bridges. *Pentecostal Formation: A Pedagogy Among the Oppressed*. Sheffield: Sheffield Academic Press, 1998.

Johnson, Janet. "Unity and the Regeneration of Black Youth." *Black Theology in Britain: A Journal of Contextual Praxis* 4 (2000): 66–83.

Jones, William R. *Is God a White Racist?* Boston: Beacon Press, 1973.

—"Is Faith in God Necessary for a Just Society? Insights from Liberation Theology." In *The Search For Faith and Justice*, ed. Gene G. James. New York: Paragon, 1987.

Julien, Isaac. "Black Is, Black Ain't: Notes on De-Essentializing Black Identities." In *Black Popular Culture*, ed. Gina Dent. Seattle: Bay Press, 1992.

Knighton-Fitt, Jean. *Beyond Fear*. Cape Town: Pretext Publishers, 2003.

Kochman, Thomas. "Rapping in the Ghetto." In *Black Experience: Soul*, ed. Lee Rainwater. New Brunswick, NJ: Transaction Books, 1973.

Kunjufu, Jawanza. *Countering the Conspiracy to Destroy Black Boys*. Chicago: Afro-Am, 1982.

—*Countering the Conspiracy to Destroy Black Boys Vol. 2*. Chicago: Afro-Am, 1986.

—*Countering the Conspiracy to Destroy Black Boys Vol. 3*. Chicago: Afro-Am, 1990.

Lamont, Gordon, and Ronni Lamont. *Drama Toolkit: Sketches and Guidelines for Exploring the Bible through Drama*. Swindon: The Bible Society, 1989.

Lane, Elizabeth. *A Pageant of Bible Plays*. Nutfield, Surrey: National Christian Education Council, 1965.

Lartey, Emmanuel Y. *In Living Colour: An Intercultural Approach to Pastoral Care and Counselling*. London: Cassell, 1997.

Lee, James Michael. *The Content of Religious Instruction*. Birmingham, AL: Religious Education Press, 1985.

—"Religious Education and Theology." In *Theological Perspectives on Christian Formation: A Reader on Theology and Christian Education*, ed. Jeff Astley, Leslie J. Francis and Colin Crowder. Grand Rapids, MI: Eerdmans, 1996.

Leech, Kenneth. *Struggle in Babylon*. London: Sheldon Press, 1988.

—*The Eye of the Storm: Spiritual Resources for the Pursuit of Justice*. London: Darton, Longman & Todd, 1992.

—*Through Our Long Exile*. London: Darton, Longman & Todd, 2001.

Lewin, H., ed. *A Community of Clowns*. Geneva: WCC, 1987.

Lewin, K. "Action Research and Minority Problems." *Journal of Social Issues* 2 (1946): 3–12.

Lewis, Marjorie. "Diaspora Dialogue: Womanist Theology in Engagement with Aspects of the Black British and Jamaican Experience." *Black Theology: An International Journal* 2.1 (January 2004): 85–109.

Love, Margaret. *Let's Dramatise*. Nutfield, Surrey: National Christian Education Council, 1968.

Lynch, Gordon. *After Religion: "Generation X" and the Search for Meaning*. London: Darton, Longman & Todd, 2002.

Machiavelli, Niccolo. *The Prince*. Trans. W. K. Marriot and Dominic Baker-Smith. New York: Random House, 1992.

Maimela, Simon, and Dwight N. Hopkins, eds. *We are One Voice: Essays on Black Theology in the USA and South Africa*. Braamfontein, South Africa: Skotaville, 1989.

Marsh, Clive. *Christianity in a Post-Atheist Age*. London: SCM Press, 2002.

Martin, Robert K. "Education and the Liturgical Life of the Church." *Religious Education* 98.1 (Winter 2003): 43–64.

May, Tony. *Social Research: Issues, Methods and Process*. Buckingham: Open University Press, 1997.

McFague, Sallie. *Metaphorical Theology: Models of God in Religious Language*. Philadelphia: Fortress Press, 1985.

—*Models of God*. Philadelphia: Fortress Press, 1987.

McFarland, Ian A. *Difference and Identity: A Theological Anthropology*. Cleveland, OH: The Pilgrim Press, 2001.

McKinney, Lora-Ellen. *Christian Education in the African American Church*. Valley Forge, PA: Judson Press, 2003.

McNiff, Jean, Pamela Jean Lomax and Jack Whitehead. *You and Your Action Research Project*. London: Routledge, 1996.

Middleton, Daniel J. N. "Riddim Wise and Scripture Smart: Interview and Interpretation with Ras Benjamin Zephaniah." In *Religion, Culture and Tradition in the Caribbean*, ed. Hemchand Gossai and Nathaniel S. Murrel. London: Macmillan, 2000.

Milling, Jane, and Graham Ley. *Modern Theories of Performance*. Basingstoke and New York: Palgrave, 2001.

Milwood, Robinson. "In Conversation." In *Catching Both Sides of the Wind: Conversations with Five Black Pastors*, ed. Anita Jackson. London: The British Council of Churches, 1985.

Mitchell, Ella P. "Oral Tradition: Legacy of Faith for the Black Church." *Religious Education* 81.1 (Winter 1986): 99–102.

Mitchell, Henry H. *Black Church Beginnings*. Grand Rapids, MI: Eerdmans, 2004.

Mitchell, Stephanie Y. *Introducing Womanist Theology*. Maryknoll, NY: Orbis Books, 2002.

Moore, Allen J. "A Social Theory of Religious Education." In *Religious Education as Social Transformation*, ed. Allen J. Moore. Birmingham, AL: Religious Education Press, 1989.

—"One Hundred Years of the Religious Education Association." *Religious Education* 98.4 (Fall 2003): 426–36.

Morrison, Doreen. "Resisting Racism—By Celebrating 'Our' Blackness." *Black Theology: An International Journal* 1.2 (May 2003): 203–223.

Mosala, Itumeleng J. *Biblical Hermeneutics and Black Theology in South Africa*. Grand Rapids: Eerdmans, 1989.

Moseley, Romney M. *Becoming a Self Before God: Critical Transformations*. Nashville: Abingdon Press, 1991.

Mosley, Walter. *What Next?: A Memoir Toward World Peace*. London: Serpent's Tail, 2003.

Motlhabi, Mokgethi. "The Problem of Ethical Method in Black Theology." *Black Theology: An International Journal* 2.1 (January 2004): 57–72.

Muchopa, Naboth. *Making a Positive Difference*. London: The Methodist Church, 2001.

Murphy, Debra Dean. "Worship as Catechesis: Knowledge, Desire, and Christian Formation." *Theology Today* 58.3 (October 2001): 321–32.

Murrell, Nathaniel S. "Dangerous Memories, Underdevelopment, and the Bible in Colonial Caribbean Experience." In *Religion, Culture and Tradition in the Caribbean*, ed. Hemchand Gossai and Nathaniel Samuel Murrell. London: Macmillan Press, 2000.

Nash, Peter T. *Reading Race, Reading the Bible*. Minneapolis: Fortress Press, 2003.

Newton, Huew P. *Seize The Time: The Story of the Black Panther Party*. London: Hutchinson, 1970.

Nipkow, K. E., and Friedrich Schweitzer, eds. *Stages of Faith and Religious Development: Implications for Church, Education and Society*. London: SCM Press, 1992.

O'Hanlon, Christine. "Reflection and Action in Research: Is There a Moral Responsibility to Act?" *Educational Action Research* 2.2 (1994): 281–88.

Oglesby, E. Hammond. *O Lord, Move This Mountain: Racism and Christian Ethics*. St. Louis: Chalice Press, 1998.

Owusu, Kwesi, ed. *Black British Culture and Society: A Text Reader*. London: Routledge, 2000.

Parekh, Bhikhu. *Rethinking Multiculturalism: Cultural Diversity and Political Theory*. Basingstoke: Macmillan, 2000.

Paris, Peter J. *The Social Teachings of the Black Churches*. Philadelphia: Fortress Press, 1985.

—*The Spiritualities of African Peoples: The Search for a Common Moral Discourse*. Minneapolis: Fortress Press, 1995.

Perry, Michael. *The Dramatised Bible*. London: Marshall Pickering, 1989.

Pinn, Anne H., and Anthony B. Pinn. *(Fortress Introduction to) Black Church History*. Minneapolis: Fortress Press, 2002.

Pinn, Anthony B. *Why Lord?: Suffering and Evil in Black Theology*. New York: Continuum, 1995.

—*Varieties of African American Religious Experience*. Minneapolis: Fortress Press, 1998.

—"'Handlin' My Business': Exploring Rap's Humanist Sensibilities." In *Noise and Spirit: The Religious and Spiritual Sensibilities of Rap Music*, ed. Anthony B. Pinn. New York and London: New York University Press, 2003.

—*Terror and Triumph: The Nature of Black Religion*. Minneapolis: Fortress Press, 2003.

Pinn, Anthony B., ed. *Noise and Spirit: The Religious Sensibilities of Rap Music*. New York and London: New York University Press, 2003.

Pryce, Ken. *Endless Pressure: A Study of West Indian Life Styles in Bristol*. Bristol: Bristol Classical Press, 1986.

Raboteau, Albert J. *Slave Religion*. New York: Oxford University Press, 1978.

Raj, Dhadeka Sashedi. "Shifting Culture in the Global Terrain: Culture Identity Construction among Hindu Punjabis in London." Unpublished PhD thesis, University of Cambridge, 1997.

Ramdin, *Reimaging Britain: 500 Hundred Years of Black and Asian History*. London: Pluto Press, 1999.

Reddie, Anthony G. *Growing into Hope: Christian Education for Multi-ethnic Churches*. 2 vols. Peterborough: Methodist Publishing House, 1998.

—"Unbroken Thread of Experience." In *Family and All That Stuff*, ed. Joan King. Birmingham: National Christian Education Council [NCEC], 1998.

—"A Theology of Good Intentions." In *Coming of Age: Challenges and Opportunities in the 21st Century*, ed. Stuart J. Burgess. York: Stuart Burgess, 1999.

—"The Christian Education of African Caribbean Children in Birmingham: Creating a New Paradigm through Developing Better Praxis." Unpublished PhD thesis, University of Birmingham, 2000.

—"Inter-Generational Conversations and Prayer." In *Praying with Power*, ed. Joe Aldred. London: Continuum, 2000.

—"Introduction: In Memory of One Who Was Truly Unique." In *Legacy: Anthology in Memory of Jillian Brown*, ed. Anthony G. Reddie. Peterborough: Methodist Publishing House, 2000.

—*Faith, Stories and the Experience of Black Elders: Singing the Lord's Song in a Strange World*. London: Jessica Kingsley, 2001.

—" 'Pentecost'—Dreams and Visions [A Black Theological Reading of Pentecost]." In *Discovering Christ: Ascension and Pentecost*, ed. Maureen Edwards. International Bible Reading Association, March 2001.

—"Forming Wisdom Through Cross-generational Connectedness." In *In Search of Wisdom: Faith Formation in the Black Church*, ed. Anne E. Streaty Wimberly and Evelyn L. Parker. Nashville, TN: Abingdon Press, 2002.

—"Open to Learning and Nurturing." In *Open All Hours?!* London: Thames North Synod, The United Reformed Church, 2002.

—"Bearing Witness to the Light." *Roots Worship: Worship and Learning for the Whole Church* 5 (May/June 2003).

—"God-Talk and Black Empowerment." *The Epworth Review* 30.4 (October 2003): 53–62.

—*Nobodies to Somebodies: A Practical Theology for Education and Liberation*. Peterborough: Epworth Press, 2003.

—"Editorial." *Black Theology: An International Journal* 2.2 (July 2004): 135–38.

—"Jazz Musicians of the Word." *The College of Preachers—The Journal* (January 2004): 21–28.

—*Acting in Solidarity: Reflections in Critical Christianity*. London: Darton, Longman & Todd, 2005.

Reddie, Anthony G., ed. *Legacy: Anthology in Memory of Jillian Brown*. Peterborough: Methodist Publishing House, 2000.

Richardson, Alan and John Bowden, eds. *A New Dictionary of Christian Theology*. London: SCM Press, 1999.

Richter, Philip, and Leslie Francis. *Gone But Not Forgotten*. London: Darton, Longman & Todd, 1998.

Roberts, J. Deotis. "Common Themes: Black Theology and Minjung Theology." In *Black Theology: A Documentary History. II. 1980–1992*, ed. James H. Cone and Gayraud S. Wilmore. Maryknoll, NY: Orbis Books, 1993.

—*Africentric Christianity: A Theological Appraisal for Ministry*. Valley Forge, PA: Judson Press, 2000.

—*Black Religion, Black Theology: The Collected Essays of J. Deotis Roberts*, ed. David E. Goatley. Harrisburg, PA: Trinity Press International, 2003.

Robins, Carina. *Drama for God: A Handbook of Christian Drama.* Ibadan, Nigeria: Daystar Press, 1977.

Ross, Rosetta E. *Witnessing and Testifying: Black Women, Religion, and Civil Rights.* Minneapolis: Fortress Press, 2003.

Russell, Horace O. "Understandings and Interpretations of Scripture in Eighteenth and Nineteenth Century Jamaica." In *Religion, Culture and Tradition in the Caribbean*, ed. Hemchand Gossai and Nathaniel Samuel Murrell. London: Macmillan Press, 2000.

Sackey, Brigid M. "Spiritual Deliverance as a Form of Health Delivery: A Case Study of the Solid Rock Chapel International." *Black Theology in Britain: A Journal of Contextual Praxis* 4.2 (May 2002): 150–71.

Sanders, E. P. *Jesus and Judaism.* London: SCM Press, 1985.

Saward, J. *Perfect Fools.* Oxford: Oxford University Press, 1990.

Schipani, Daniel S. *Religious Education Encounters Liberation Theology.* Birmingham, AL: Religious Education Press, 1988.

Schlossman, David A. *Actors and Activists: Politics, Performance, and Exchange Among Social Worlds.* New York and London: Routledge, 2002.

Segundo, Juan Luis. *The Liberation of Theology.* Maryknoll, NY: Orbis Books, 1976.

Sewell, Tony. *Black Masculinities and Schooling.* Stoke on Trent: Trentham Books, 1997.

Seymour, Jack L. "The Clue to Christian Religious Education: Uniting Theology and Education, 1950 to the Present." *Religious Education* 99.3 (Summer 2004): 272–86.

Shockley, Grant. "From Emancipation to Transformation to Cosummation: A Black Perspective." In *Does The Church Really Want Religious Education?*, ed. Marlene Mayr. Birmingham, AL: Religious Education Press, 1988.

Silverman, D. *Qualitative Methodology and Sociology.* Aldershot: Gower, 1985.

Singleton, III, Harry H. *Black Theology and Ideology: Deideoligical Dimensions in the Theology of James H. Cone.* Collegeville, MN: The Liturgical Press, 2002.

Sistren (with Honor Ford Smith). *Lionheart Gal: Life Stories of Jamaican Women.* London: The Women's Press, 1986.

Slee, Nicola M. *Women's Faith Development: Patterns and Processes.* Aldershot: Ashgate, 2004.

Sloyan, Gerard S. "Symbols of God's Presence to the Church—Verbal and Nonverbal." *Theology Today* 58.3 (October 2001).

Smith, Fred. "A Prophetic Christian Education for Black Boys: Overcoming Violence." *Black Theology: An International Journal* 1.2 (May 2003): 175–87.

Smith, Honor Ford. *Ring Ding in a Tight Corner: A Case Study of Funding and Organizational Democracy in Sistren, 1977–1988.* Toronto: The Women's Program, 1989.

Smith, Theophus H. *Conjuring Culture: Biblical Formations of Black America.* New York: Oxford University Press, 1994.

Smith, Yolanda Y. *Reclaiming the Spirituals: New Possibilities for Africa American Christian Education.* Cleveland, OH: The Pilgrim Press, 2004.

Sobrino, Jon. *Jesus the Liberator: A Historical-theological Reading of Jesus of Nazareth.* Tunbridge Wells: Burns and Oates, 1993.

Sponsler, Claire. *Drama and Resistance: Bodies, Goods, and Theatricality in Late Medieval England*. Minneapolis: University of Minneapolis Press, 1997.

Stanley, L., and S. Wise. *Breaking Out Again: Feminist Ontology and Epistemology*. London: Routledge and Kegan Paul, 1993.

Stenhouse, Lawrence. "The Teacher as Researcher." In *An Introduction to Curriculum Research and Development*, ed. Lawrence Stenhouse. London: Heinemann, 1975.

Stewart, III, Carlyle Fielding. *Black Spirituality and Black Consciousness*. Trenton, NJ: Africa World Press, 1999.

Sugirtharajah, R. S., *Postcolonial Criticism and Biblical Interpretation*. Oxford: Oxford University Press, 2002.

Sugirtharajah, R. S., ed. *Voices from the Margins*. London: SPCK, 1995.

Sutcliffe, John, ed. *Tuesday's Child: A Reader for Christian Educators*. Birmingham: Christian Education Publications, 2001.

Tafari-Ama, Imani. "Rastawoman as Rebel: Case Studies in Jamaica." In *Chanting Down Babylon: The Rastafari Reader*, ed. N. S. Murrell, W. D. Spencer and A. A. McFarlane. Philadelphia: Temple University Press, 1998.

Tanner, Kathryn. *Theories of Culture: A New Agenda for Theology*. Minneapolis: Fortress Press, 1997.

Terrell, JoAnne Marie. *Power in the Blood?: The Cross in the African American Experience*. Maryknoll, NY: Orbis Books, 1998.

Thomas, Linda E. "Womanist Theology, Epistemology, and a New Anthropological Paradigm." In *Living Stones in the Household of God: The Legacy and Future of Black Theology*, ed. Linda E. Thomas. Minneapolis: Fortress Press, 2003.

Thomas, Linda E., ed. *Living Stones in the Household of God: The Legacy and Future of Black Theology*. Minneapolis: Fortress Press, 2003.

Tomlin, Carol. *Black Language Style in Sacred and Secular Contexts*. Brooklyn, NY: Caribbean Diaspora Press, 1999.

Townes, Emile. *Womanist Justice, Womanist Hope*. Atlanta, GA: Scholars Press, 1993.

—*In a Blaze of Glory*. Nashville, TN: Abingdon Press, 1995.

Trulear, Harold Dean. "African American Religious Education." In *Multicultural Religious Education*, ed. Barbara Wilkerson. Birmingham, AL: Religious Education Press, 1997.

Van Koningsbruggen, Peter. *Trinidad Carnival: A Quest for National Identity*. London: Macmillan Education, 1997.

Vermes, Geza. *Jesus in his Jewish Context*. Minneapolis: Fortress Press, 2003.

Vincent, John, *Hope from the City*. Peterborough: Epworth Press, 2000.

Walker, Alice. *The Color Purple*. London: Women's Press, 1983.

—*In Search of our Mothers' Gardens: Womanist Prose*. London: Women's Press, 1984.

Wallis, Jim. "The Call to Conversion." In *Urban Theology: A Reader*, ed. Michael Northcott. London: Cassell, 1998.

Walton, Heather. *A Tree God Planted: Black People in British Methodism*. London: Ethnic Minorities in Methodism Working Group, The Methodist Church, 1984.

Ware, Frederick L. *Methodologies of Black Theology*. Cleveland, OH: Pilgrim Press, 2002.

Washington, Joseph. *Black Religion*. Boston: Beacon Press, 1964.

Watt, Diane. "Traditional Religious Practices Amongst African Caribbean Mothers and Community OtherMothers." *Black Theology: An International Journal* 2.2 (July 2004): 195–212.

Weems, Renita J. *Just a Sister Away: A Womanist Vision of Women's Relationships in the Bible.* Philadelphia: Innisfree Press, 1988.

Weller, Peter, ed. *Religions in the UK: A Multi-Faith Directory.* Derby: University of Derby in association with the Inter Faith Network for the United Kingdom, 1997.

West, Cornel. *Race Matters.* Boston: Beacon Press, 1993.

—"Black Theology and Human Identity." In *Black Faith and Public Talk: Critical Essays on James Cone's Black Theology and Black Power,* ed. Dwight N. Hopkins. Maryknoll, NY: Orbis Books, 1999.

—*Democracy Matters: Winning the Fight Against Imperialism.* New York: The Penguin Press, 2004.

Westerhoff III, John. *Living the Faith Community.* San Francisco: HarperCollins, 1985.

—"Formation, Education, Instruction." *Religious Education* 82.4 (Fall, 1987): 578–91.

Westerhoff III, John, and William Willimon. *Liturgy and Learning Through the Life Cycle.* New York: Seabury Press, 1980.

Westfield, N. Lynne. *Dear Sisters: A Womanist Practice of Hospitality.* Cleveland, OH: The Pilgrim Press, 2001.

—"Kitchen Table Banter." *Religious Education* 96.3 (Summer 2001): 423–29.

—"Towards a Womanist Approach to Pedagogy." *Religious Education* 98.4 (Fall 2003): 521–32.

—"Teaching for Globalized Consciousness: Black Professor, White Student and Shame." *Black Theology: An International Journal* 2.1 (January 2004): 73–83.

White, Vernon. *Identity.* London: SCM Press, 2002.

Whyte, W. F. *Learning from the Field: A Guide from Experience.* With the collaboration of Kathleen Whyte. London: SAGE, 1984.

Wilkerson, Barbara, ed. *Multicultural Religious Education.* Birmingham, AL: Religious Education Press, 1997.

Wilkinson, John. *Church in Black and White: The Black Tradition in Mainstream Churches in England.* Edinburgh: Saint Andrew Press, 1993.

Williams, Delores S. *Sisters in the Wilderness: The Challenge of Womanist God Talk.* Maryknoll, NY: Orbis Books, 1983.

Williams, Demetrius K. "The Bible and Models of Liberation in the African American Experience." In *Yet With a Steady Beat: Contemporary U.S. Afrocentric Biblical Interpretation,* ed. Randall C. Bailey. Atlanta: Society for Biblical Literature, 2003.

Williams, Eric. *Capitalism and Slavery.* London: Andre Deutsch, 1983.

Willis, Lerleen. "All Things to All Men? Or What has Language to Do with Gender and Resistance in the Black Majority Church in Britain." *Black Theology in Britain* 4.2 (May 2002): 195–213.

Willows, David, and John Swinton, eds. *Spiritual Dimensions of Pastoral Care: Practical Theology in a Multidisciplinary Context.* London: Jessica Kingsley, 2000.

—*Divine Knowledge: A Kierkegaardian Perspective on Christian Education.* Aldershot: Ashgate, 2001.

Willshaw, Mervin. "Apologetics—a Discipline whose Time has Come." In *Coming of Age: Challenges and Opportunities in the 21st Century*, ed. Stuart J. Burgess. York: Stuart J. Burgess, 1999.

Wilmore, Gayraud S., and James H. Cone, eds. *Black Theology: A Documentary History*. I. *1966–1979*. Maryknoll, NY: Orbis Books, 1979.

Wimberly, Anne E. Streaty. *Soul Stories: African American Christian Education*. Nashville, TN: Abingdon Press, 1996.

Wimberly, Anne E. Streaty, and Evelyn L. Parker, eds. *In Search of Wisdom: Faith Formation in the Black Church*. Nashville: Abingdon Press, 2002.

Wimberly, Edward P. *Relational Refugees: Alienation and Reincorporation in African American Churches and Communities*. Nashville, TN: Abingdon Press, 2000.

—*Claiming God, Reclaiming Dignity: African American Pastoral Care*. Nashville, TN: Abingdon Press, 2003.

Wimbush, Vincent L. *African Americans and the Bible: Sacred Texts and Social Contexts*. New York: Continuum, 2000.

—*The Bible and African Americans*. Minneapolis: Fortress Press, 2003.

Woodward, James, and Stephen Pattison, eds. *The Blackwell Reader in Pastoral and Practical Theology*. Oxford: Blackwell, 2000.

Woolf, Rosemary. *The English Mystery Plays*. London: Routledge and Kegan Paul, 1972.

Wright, Cecile, Debbie Weekes and Alex McGlaughan, eds. *"Race," Class and Gender in Exclusion from School*. London: Falmer Press, 2000.

Wright Jr., Jeremiah. "Doing Black Theology in the Black Church." In *Living Stones in the Household of God*, ed. Linda E. Thomas. Minneapolis: Fortress Press, 2003.

Yeboah, Samuel K. *The Ideology of Racism*. London: Hansib, 1988.

Young III, Josiah U. *Dogged Strength Within the Veil: Africana Spirituality and the Mysterious Love of God*. Harrisburg, PA: Trinity Press International, 2003.

Young, Virginia. "Family and Childhood in a Southern Georgia Community." *American Anthropologist* 72 (1970): 269–88.

Index

JY   '07

Printed in the United States
80559LV00002B/718-729